International Prosecution
of Human Rights Crimes

Wolfgang Kaleck · Michael Ratner
Tobias Singelnstein · Peter Weiss
(Editors)

International
Prosecution
of Human Rights
Crimes

Springer

Wolfgang Kaleck
Immanuelkirchstr. 3–4
10405 Berlin
Germany
wka@diefirma.net

Michael Ratner
Center for Constitutional Rights
666 Broadway
10012 New York, NY
USA
www.ccr-ny.org

Tobias Singelnstein
Freie Universität Berlin
Van't-Hoff-Str. 8
14195 Berlin
Germany
singelnstein@rewiss.fu-berlin.de

Peter Weiss
Center for Constitutional Rights
666 Broadway
10012 New York, NY
USA
www.ccr-ny.org

Cataloging-in-Publication Data
Library of Congress Control Number: 2006933086

ISBN-10 3-540-36648-2 Springer Berlin Heidelberg New York
ISBN-13 978-3-540-36648-5 Springer Berlin Heidelberg New York

Springer is a part of Springer Science+Business Media

springer.com

© Springer-Verlag Berlin Heidelberg 2007

Production: LE-TEX Jelonek, Schmidt & Vöckler GbR, Leipzig
Cover: Erich Kirchner, Heidelberg

SPIN 11800958   64/3100YL - 5 4 3 2 1 0   Printed on acid-free paper

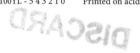

Preface

In his separate opinion in the *Nuclear Weapons* case,[1] Judge Mohammed Bedja-oui, then the President of the International Court of Justice, called nuclear weapons "the absolute evil." There are a few other things which merit being called absolutely evil. They are the predicates of the International Criminal Court and of various domestic laws patterned on the Rome Statute: war crimes, crimes against humanity, genocide, and aggression. A conference organized by the Berlin-based Republikanischer Anwältinnen- und Anwälteverein (Republican Lawyers Association) and the New York-based Center for Constitutional Rights was held in Berlin in June 2005 under the title *Globalverfassung versus Realpolitik* (*Global Constitution versus Realpolitik*). It dealt with the tension between these universally accepted norms and the actual practice of governments in an age characterized by the ill-defined concept of the "war on terror."

This book is the outcome of that conference. It is intended for a wide variety of readers: academics, all kinds of jurists, as well as human rights activists, who sometimes know more about the applicable law than the legal experts. It owes its existence to a paradox: On the one hand, new structures for dealing with the most serious international crimes are being put into place. In addition to the International Criminal Court (ICC), there are the international tribunals for Rwanda (ICTR) and the former Yugoslavia (ICTY); the mixed national and international (hybrid) courts for Bosnia-Herzegovina, Cambodia, and Sierra Leone; and various domestic universal jurisdiction laws, such as those enacted by Belgium, Spain, and Germany. On the other hand, norms of substantive and procedural justice, which have been centuries in the making, are at risk of falling victim to "the war on terror" and the sacred cow of national security. Questions which appeared to have been definitely answered a few short years ago, are being debated anew: Is torture permitted under certain circumstances? What constitutes torture? Is preventive war a violation of the UN Charter? Are the Geneva Conventions inapplicable to certain combatants? How high up does command responsibility go? Are we back to the days of *inter armas silent leges*, with a new and very broad definition of "armas"?

Some of these questions, as well as others, are examined in the articles that follow. There are historical contributions, accounts of current practice under extraterritorial jurisdiction laws and principles, speculations about the future of universal

---

[1] *Legality of the Threat or Use of Nuclear Weapons*, ICJ Advisory Opinion of July 8, 1996, *ICJ Reports* 1996, p. 226.

jurisdiction, and discussions of the German Rumsfeld case as a prime example of justice defeated by realpolitik.

This is not a plea for one method of enforcing international human rights over others. Any experienced practitioner will choose among a plethora of tools and venues: international courts versus municipal courts; at the local level, state, or provincial courts versus national courts; criminal versus civil proceedings; old-fashioned tort actions versus new-fangled universal jurisdiction actions; complaints to domestic or international human rights bodies versus court cases—all of the above subject to the caveat "where applicable."

In addition to the choice of venue and procedure, lawyers and human rights activists, to the extent that they have freedom of choice, will have to prioritize among various plaintiffs. Some advocate a careful selection of plaintiffs calculated to advance the cause of extraterritorial or universal jurisdiction rather than setting it back. They argue that bringing prosecutions at or near the top of the pyramid of command responsibility is likely to lead to bad judicial precedents and retrogression in legislation, as in the case of the Belgian universal jurisdiction law; they would prefer a step-by-step approach beginning with establishing the accountability of foot soldiers and leading eventually to that of generals, to use a military analogy. As against this respectable view, one can propound the opposite: Prosecution of the foot soldier who applies the thumbscrew to a prisoner while letting the defense minister or commanding general who gives the green light for torture off the hook does nothing to counter a system-wide culture of illegality and paints an inaccurate picture of a few "rotten apples" in an otherwise law-abiding structure.

It is self-evident that in the world of realpolitik a case against a minister or president, particularly one still holding office, is more difficult to win than one against a corporal or sergeant. But this overlooks the benefits to be derived from the presentation of a carefully researched, detailed presentation of the case, which is likely to have ramifications in the court of public opinion—not in a narrow party-political sense, but in the crucially important sense of the triumph of justice over criminality. One should never bring a prosecution or lawsuit without being convinced of the rightness of one's cause, but not necessarily of the chances of victory in the real world.[2]

It is hoped that this book will contribute not only to the academic debate about law versus politics, but also to the elevation of law over politics.

New York, August 2006   Peter Weiss

---

[2] For a book-length exposition of this approach, see J. Lobel, *Success Without Victory* (2003).

Table of Contents

Part III: The "War on Terror" in Particular

Part I

Fundamental Questions

Protection of Human Rights by Means of Criminal Law: On the Relationship between Criminal Law and Politics

*Jörg Arnold**

This essay explores the theme *"Globalverfassung* versus *realpolitik,"* where Globalverfassung is understood as the universal claim of human rights and realpolitik is criticized as a means that limits human rights or prevents their realization.[1]

Globalverfassung refers not only to the universality of human rights and their implementation, but it also bears on the concept of globalization. Universal jurisdiction is frequently mentioned as a positive, desirable effect of globalization. A detailed discussion of the issues surrounding international legal globalization is not possible here, especially because the treatment of these issues would require addressing the political, cultural, and economic context of globalization, a complex subject that—it appears—has not yet attracted the necessary attention from criminal law scholars and one that requires an interdisciplinary approach.[2] To begin with, one must question the real world application of universal jurisdiction and whether it endangers human rights themselves via a global criminal law policy.[3] When freedoms originally created as defense against the *state's* monopoly of force

---

[*] I am grateful to Emily Silverman, Max Planck Institute for Foreign and International Criminal Law, for her valuable assistance. The German version of this essay was published in *Ad Legendum* No. 4/2005, pp. 183–187.

[1] Otto von Bismarck justifies realpolitik thus: "We are not presiding over a judgeship, but making German policy." (See http://de.wikipedia.org/wiki/Realpolitik).

[2] But see O. Höffe, *Gibt es ein interkulturelles Strafrecht? Ein philosophischer Versuch* (1999). See also H. Däubler-Gmelin and I. Mohr (eds.), *Recht schafft Zukunft, Perspektiven der Rechtspolitik in einer globalisierten Welt* (2003); H. Brunkhorst and M. Kettner (eds.), *Globalisierung und Demokratie* (2000); R. Voigt (ed.), *Globalisierung des Rechts* (1999–2000); O. Höffe, *Wirtschaftsbürger, Staatsbürger, Weltbürger. Politische Ethik im Zeitalter der Globalisierung* (2004); H. D. Assmann and R. Sethe (eds.), *Recht und Ethos im Zeitalter der Globalisierung* (2004); Adolf-Arndt-Kreis (ed.), *Sicherheit durch Recht in Zeiten der Globalisierung* (2003); A. L. Paulus, *Die internationale Gemeinschaft im Völkerrecht. Eine Untersuchung zur Entwicklung des Völkerrechts im Zeitalter der Globalisierung* (2001).

[3] See J. Arnold, in R. Gröschner (ed.), *Die Bedeutung P. J. A. Feuerbachs (1775-1833) für die Gegenwart, ARSP-Beiheft No. 87* (2003), p. 107 at p. 122.

are translated into a catalog of opportunities for a *global* monopoly of force, often the resulting interventions violate the democratic and human rights values that they seek to protect.[4]

First of all, however, the practice of human rights protections by means of national criminal law deserves attention, though with specific reference to its international bases. Four postulates may provide impetus for an examination.

I. Factors Influencing Protection of Human Rights through Criminal Law

The first postulate is as follows: In addition to its dependence on politics, protection of human rights by means of criminal law is influenced by a multitude of other factors. Criminal law and human rights are connected to different legal cultures and different social, economic, political, cultural, and historical interests and conditions.[5] This becomes particularly apparent in national processes of democratic transformation—that is, when serious violations of human rights by former political systems are addressed by means of criminal law. In countries where the political will to prosecute was particularly strong, as in Germany after 1989 with regard to human rights violations committed in East Germany, the judicial system undertook comprehensive criminal investigations and punishment of state-sponsored crime.[6]

The post-1989 political changes in Eastern and Central European countries such as Poland and Hungary similarly demonstrated these processes, though to a lesser extent.[7] In contrast, the prevailing Russian political mentality is one of closing the book, expressed in legal practice through a complete absence of criminal prosecution.[8] Freedom from prosecution (*impunidad*) can also be observed in Latin American countries such as Argentina, Brazil, Chile, and Uruguay following the end of the military dictatorships in the 1970s and 1980s.[9] In South Africa in 1989–90, lack of criminal prosecution was connected with a peaceful system change and was even considered a prerequisite for such change. It is just now becoming apparent, however, years after the transition, that refraining from prosecu-

---

[4] See J. Hirsch, *Freitag* No. 4/2001.
[5] See H. J. Sandkühler, *Warum brauchen Menschen Menschenrechte? Address on UNESCO Philosophy Day*, University of Bremen, December 2004, http://www.unesco-phil.-uni-bremen.de/texte/unesco-tag_2004_Menschenrechte.pdf.
[6] See K. Marxen and G. Werle, *Die strafrechtliche Aufarbeitung von DDR-Unrecht. Eine Bilanz* (1999); A. Eser and J. Arnold (eds.), *Strafrecht in Reaktion auf Systemunrecht, Vol. 2, Landesbericht Deutschland* (2000); J. Arnold, *Freitag* No. 17/2001; No. 18/2001.
[7] See A. Eser and J. Arnold (eds.), *Strafrecht in Reaktion auf Systemunrecht, Vol. 5, Landesberichte Polen und Ungarn* (2002).
[8] See A. Eser and J. Arnold (eds.), *Strafrecht in Reaktion auf Systemunrecht, Vol. 7, Landesberichte Russland, Weißrußland, Georgien, Estland, Litauen* (2003).
[9] See A. Eser and J. Arnold (eds.), *Strafrecht in Reaktion auf Systemunrecht, Vol. 3, Landesbericht Argentinien* (2002).

tion asked a great deal—sometimes too much—of many victims of serious human rights violations. In Spain, for example, this is only now leading to the development of a "culture of memory,"[10] but one in which criminal law plays no role.

Uniform concepts are apparent in a discussion of the political goals of the criminal-law response to the past, however loosely composed they may be. While for one country, the goal of non-prosecution is reconciliation (for example, South Africa, 1990), for another, prosecution is a means to achieve reconciliation (for example, Germany after 1989). If for one country stabilizing the system is the goal of criminal-law responses to the past (Germany after 1989), for another, it is the act of refraining from punishment that creates conditions conducive to a peaceful transition.

Despite the fact that criminal law responses to serious human rights violations depend on political will, studies conducted by the Max Planck Institute on the role of criminal law in dealing with the past after a political system change also indicate the significance of numerous other factors. Political will, for its part, correlates with a number of different variables: the concrete historical, religious, and transnational conditions of each individual system change. Parameters that play a role include the replacement of the political elite and the country's economic capacity—that is, its resources. The latter also crucially influences the implementation of policies for dealing with the past (*Vergangenheitspolitik*) in the areas of rehabilitation, compensation, and restitution.

Socio-cultural and socio-psychological factors are also influential in the relationship between perpetrators and victims. For example, one speaks typically of a Russian culture of forgiveness, but in Germany after 1989 a variety of victims' organizations, in addition to demanding greater compensation for injustices suffered, called vigorously for punishment of the perpetrators. Conciliation and reconciliation were rarely mentioned. Here, the significance of differing religious views should not be underestimated, such as evidenced, for example, by the willingness to seek reconciliation in South Africa.

II. Differing Concepts of Human Rights

Not surprisingly, states' views on punishment, retribution, and reconciliation vary just as fundamentally as do their understandings of human rights. This is the subject of the second postulate, which looks at these fundamental differences without detailing the concrete effects of differing human rights concepts on criminal law in each case.

During the Cold War, characterized by intense rivalry between the two great power blocs, state socialism's understanding of human rights—where individuality and freedom were accepted only within narrow state, political, and collective bounds—collided with the concept of human rights in constitutional democratic

---

[10] See reports on conference on "Culture of Memory" in *Frankfurter Rundschau*, May 31, 2005; *Die Welt*, May 26, 2005; *die tageszeitung*, May 31, 2005.

societies, which called for the human being's freedom from the state as well as for freedoms guaranteed by the state. Indeed, the understanding of human rights under state socialism had become so ingrained in the Soviet Union over the course of seventy years, and in the other Eastern and Central European countries over the course of forty years, that democratic concepts still find limited traction there. Such concepts prove difficult because economic, social, and cultural rights, which were the starting point for the understanding of human rights in state socialism (while political rights and freedoms were largely negated), are found at the bottom of the human rights spectrum in societies undergoing transformation.

Yet, an understanding of human rights that defines political rights only within the narrow confines of the state and the collective and makes civic duties absolute is not purely the invention of now defunct European state socialism. Such views prevail, for example, in China, where they cannot be ascribed directly to a wrongly understood, dogmatic, and inhumane Marxism, such as was practiced in the socialist countries of Europe. Crucial to the understanding of human rights in China, instead, are the philosophical and religious teachings of Confucianism, which see the human being from the outset not primarily as an individual but as a social being, though various old school, state-socialist influences cannot be ignored.[11]

In contrast, in Africa a human rights concept based on two archetypical arguments prevails. First, the concept adopts pre-colonial traditions "in order to weaken the cultural alienation of colonial rule and protect Africa's autochthonous cultural identity. Second, it views the continent as persisting in a state of underdevelopment and dependence."[12] Human rights in this form thus apply not to all people, but only to members of a particular culture. This African concept of human rights is interpreted as something beyond individualist and collectivist ideas.[13] Islam offers yet another interpretation of human rights.[14] "Classic" Islamic law, or Sharia, which is still applied to some extent today, and modern human rights contradict one another in part because the former stems from the first century of Islamic history. Based on the Koran, Sharia law functions not only as a standard for the faithful, but as a source of legislation. Cruel punishments are justified by God's right of punishment (*Strafanspruch*).[15]

Whereas during the Cold War era, two different human rights concepts dominated the discourse, the post-Cold War era fostered recognition of differences among the understanding of human rights in Western democracies—at first gradually, then ever more clearly. In reality, they had long existed. The Swiss human rights activist and writer Gret Haller has described these differences, especially as they exist between Europe and the United States.[16]

---

[11] See also H.-P. Schneider, in N. Paech et al. (eds.), *Völkerrecht statt Machtpolitik* (2004), pp. 339 et seq.
[12] U. Tonndorf, *Menschenrechte in Afrika* (1997), p. 100.
[13] Id., p. 122.
[14] See H. Bielefeldt, *Europäische Grundrechte-Zeitschrift* 1990, pp. 489 et seq.
[15] See H. Bielefeldt, *Philosophie der Menschenrechte* (1998), p. 132; H. Bielefeldt, *supra* note 14, p. 492.
[16] G. Haller, *Die Grenzen der Solidarität* (2004); G. Haller, *Deregulierung der Menschenrechte*, http://www.linksnet.de/drucksicht.php?id=579.

According to Haller, one conceptual difference consists in the fact that Europe has pursued a clear, internationally defined concept of human rights since World War II, in which each country is supervised by the community of nations in carrying out its duty to guarantee rights. In contrast, the United States has a more national concept of human rights. This leads to the United States' largely rejecting international legal obligations in the area of human rights and, in particular, refusing to submit to international supervisory mechanisms. Haller sees a second conceptual difference in the fact that, for the United States, international human rights are not primarily a legal matter, but rather a matter of political strength. For the United States, international treaties are of less significance than the combination of the rights anchored in the US Constitution and the country's understanding of constitutionality, democracy, and (American) nationhood. Therefore, the understanding of human rights in the United States is mainly determined by the religious and moral elements upon which the nation was founded. In Haller's view, both conceptual differences can be ascribed to the fact that in Europe the state itself guarantees human rights to the individual, while for the individual in the United States, human rights consist exclusively in the guarantee of freedom from the state.[17]

III. Erosion of Human Rights Protections

The fundamental transatlantic differences over human rights stem from the United States' historical view of itself, reaching far into the past, which strongly rejects the separation of law and morality that has taken place in Europe. But while those in power in the United States are unwilling to give up their understanding of human rights in favor of European-style rule-of-law principles, the state in many European countries is today no longer the guarantor of freedom and social rights, and has thus imperiled its own understanding of human rights. Discussions of criminal law development clearly demonstrate this.

In this context, the third postulate is as follows: Over the past several decades, the classic, liberal, rule-of-law concept of criminal law has transformed into a tool for regulating globalization, risk, and information societies. This type of criminal law parades legislatively in the guise of security law, intervention law, and, most recently, in the development of a special criminal law solely applicable to the "enemy" (*Feindstrafrecht*). It goes hand in hand with a dismantling of human rights—first gradually, but now with increasing rapidity—which frequently occurs in the name of human rights.

At first, proponents of this transformation of criminal law attempted to legitimate their goals by referring to the dangers posed by organized crime, which recognizes no national borders. Today the struggle against terrorism is the Trojan horse used to legitimate the departure from the idea of liberal criminal law based on the rule of law. German Constitutional Court judges Jaeger and Hohmann-

---

[17] G. Haller, *supra* note 16, pp. 10 et seq.

Dennhardt expressed this in another way in their dissent to a decision of the Court's First Panel on the admissibility of state wiretapping of private homes (*Großen Lauschangriff*). In their view, the issue today is no longer just one of preventing the beginnings of the dismantling of constitutional positions on basic rights, but of preventing a bitter end in which the concept of the human being created by such a development no longer resembles that of a liberal democracy governed by rule of law.[18]

Security has yet again trumped freedom as evidenced by recent challenges to formerly unshakeable legal guarantees such as human dignity. According to a new commentary on Article 1 of the Basic Law by the Bonn constitutional law scholar Matthias Herdegen in the respected Maunz-Dürig textbook, human dignity may be subject to balancing tests.[19] For example, questioning the absolute prohibition of torture is no longer taboo in German criminal law scholarship,[20] and the killing of bystanders is justifiable under the air security law.[21] Bonn constitutional theorist Günther Jakobs even goes a step further. Jakobs distinguishes between criminal law for citizens and criminal law for enemies. If we wish criminal law for citizens to retain its rule-of-law characteristics, says Jakobs, we must give another name to what we must do in order to combat terrorists if we wish to survive—that is, enemy criminal law and restrained war.[22] According to Jakobs,

> He who deviates on principle offers no guarantee of personal behavior; thus he cannot be treated as a citizen, but must be combated as an enemy. This combat occurs based on a legitimate right of citizens, namely, their right to security.[23]

Although Chief Federal Prosecutor Kai Nehm verbally rejected enemy criminal law, in the same breath he sharply criticized German courts for distancing themselves from the findings of intelligence agencies and from unreachable witnesses in terrorist trials. Nehm declared that, if the judicial system refuses to act, the political branch will "jump into the breach" and "create a diffuse crime of conspiracy." He said there was no desire for "enemy criminal law," but also none for "friend criminal law," in which Islamists are "protected only because Guantánamo—rightly—weighs heavily upon us."[24]

The conceptual distinction between citizen criminal law and enemy criminal law fails to express the political ideas behind these views. Hans-Jörg Albrecht, director of the Max Planck Institute, in an address to the Republican Lawyers Association, suggested the new legislation intervenes in civil society in such a way that

---

[18] *Neue Juristische Wochenschrift* 2004, pp. 1020, 1022.

[19] See *Frankfurter Allgemeine Zeitung*, April 29, 2005, pp. 1 et seq.

[20] See K. Lackner and K. Kühl, *StGB, Kommentar*, 25th ed. (2004), § 32, margin note 17a; V. Erb, in *Münchner Kommentar zum Strafgesetzbuch, Vol. 1* (2003), § 32, margin notes 174 et seq.; V. Erb, *Die Zeit* No. 51/2004, p. 15; V. Erb, *Jura* 2005, p. 24.

[21] See K. Lackner and K. Kühl, *supra* note 20; Erb, *supra* note 20.

[22] G. Jakobs, in *Wen schützt das Strafrecht? Materialheft zum 29. Strafverteidigertag in Aachen* (2005), p. 15; G. Jakobs, *Höchstrichterliche Rechtsprechung Strafrecht* 2004, pp. 88 et seq.

[23] G. Jakobs 2005, *supra* note 22, p. 16.

[24] *Frankfurter Allgemeine Zeitung*, May 21, 2005, p. 4.

it "views its free spaces, and thus the substance of civil society, as potential dangers and places them under general suspicion. Immigration and asylum, religious organizations and political movements, ethnic minorities, foreign citizens and transnational communities, workplaces and fields of activity relevant to security and, finally, entire religions or countries become links for surveillance and in some cases for social and economic exclusion."[25]

Although the judicial branch clearly limits the idea of enemy criminal law—as seen, in the Hanseatic Court of Appeal's in Hamburg and the Federal Supreme Court's acquittal of Abdelghani Mzoudi of Morocco on charges of participation in the terrorist attacks of September 11, 2001—the following assessment can be made of the aforementioned developments in constitutional law: It is not only in authoritarian or totalitarian societies and not only in transitional societies that criminal law finds itself in the stranglehold of politics and power. Criminal law in democratically constituted Europe is increasingly subject to erosion. The factors that influence criminal law in transitional societies are not determinative. Criminal law in the constitutional democratic state is being robbed of its liberal character. Thus, in regard to democracy, we can now only speak of "defective" democracy, to borrow a term from democracy researchers.[26] The end of liberal democracy has already been affirmed, and is on its way to "gentle totalitarianism."[27]

IV. Consequences

The reality described in postulates I to III demands appropriate response. One solution could lie in international law, specifically international criminal law. The newly created International Criminal Court as well as the ad hoc tribunals for the prosecution of serious human rights violations in Yugoslavia and Rwanda serves this purpose. There are, in addition, so-called hybrid courts, which combine national judicial authority with international courts, such as those to investigate and punish serious human rights violations in Sierra Leone, East Timor, and most recently Cambodia. Furthermore, many national legal systems, prodded by the Rome Statute, have adopted provisions for criminal law protection of human rights. The German Code of International Crimes is a model in this area.[28]

These developments can be viewed with optimism. Despite the varying concepts of human rights and the differences in regional implementation, the universality of fundamental political rights is given consensual expression through supranational or internationally-oriented criminal law provisions for the prosecution of crimes under international law. Human rights are spottily and dissentingly practiced. Therefore, legal principles must gain force, serving as the lowest common

---

[25] H.-J. Albrecht, *Informationsbrief des RAV* No. 91/2003, pp. 6–9.

[26] A. Croissant, *Von der Transition zur defekten Demokratie* (2002), pp. 31 et seq.

[27] J. Hirsch, *Das Ende der liberalen Demokratie*, http://www.links-netz.de/K_texte/K_-hirsch_postdemokratie.html.

[28] A. Eser and H. Kreicker (eds.), *Nationale Strafverfolgung völkerrechtlicher Verbrechen, Vol. 1: Deutschland* (2003).

denominator in the creation of crimes under international law. Human rights in national criminal law can expect a positive outcome from such implementation.

Basic human existence[29] and human dignity are central to internationalization of human rights protection through criminal law. Human dignity is the normative reference point for intercultural and interreligious understanding.[30]

Starting with the United Nations Charter and the Universal Declaration of Human Rights, the principle of "human dignity as the elementary basis of the human rights system"[31] entered regional human rights documents, such as the American Convention on Human Rights, the African Charter of Human Rights, and the Universal Islamic Declaration of Human Rights. Because the Statute of the International Criminal Court followed the Geneva Conventions, which first protected human dignity via international criminal law, it also could adopt as a mission the protection of human dignity and state as positive law that every serious violation of international law is based on a violation of human dignity.[32]

Of course, significant international disagreements stemming from different concepts of human rights as well as from various other sources impede the protection of human dignity. The United States can once again serve as an example. The US administration's refusal to accede to the International Criminal Court occurs not least because of its particular understanding of state sovereignty and human dignity as an expression of national interest, which represents a "value in itself."

In regard to power politics and realpolitik, this means that open avowals of the universality of human rights and efforts to implement them globally are as ubiquitous as the *worldwide* practice of serious human rights violations. Ironically, the same policies that originally helped make it possible for human rights to become part of positive law later prevented the assertion of human rights via international criminal law (while often employing two different standards, as in the refusal to investigate NATO war crimes during the war in Yugoslavia)[33] and dismantled human rights on the national level, while creating enemy criminal law.[34]

Not surprisingly, protection of human rights by means of criminal law is extremely limited. Such awareness prevents many errors, misunderstandings, and illusions about the possibility of implementing human rights globally, at least by means of national or international criminal law. It would also be a misunderstanding to recognize the "balancing test"—now considered permissible—involving the absolute prohibition on the use of force, on the one side, and so-called humanitarian military interventions, on the other. Its recognition legitimizes such international punitive interventions and unconscionably erodes human dignity.

Stating this here signifies neither resignation nor a rejection of the "battle for justice." Protection of human rights by means of criminal law is indispensable, de-

---

[29] See H.-P. Schneider, *supra* note 11, p. 344.
[30] H. Bielefeldt, *supra* note 14, p. 491.
[31] R. J. Schweizer and F. Sprecher, in K. Seelmann (ed.), *Menschenwürde als Rechtsbegriff, ARSP-Beiheft No. 101* (2004), pp. 127 et seq., 133.
[32] R. J. Schweizer and F. Sprecher, *supra* note 31, pp. 138 et seq., 157 et seq.
[33] G. Hankel, *Mittelweg 36* No. 3/2003, pp. 77 et seq., 87.
[34] See, e.g., J. Hirsch, *Freitag* No. 4/2001; N. Paech, *Freitag* No. 22/2001.

spite its limitations. How the "battle for justice" might look is impressively illustrated by the attempt undertaken in Germany to begin an investigation of US Secretary of Defense Donald Rumsfeld as well as other military and civilian leaders for torture perpetrated at the Abu Ghraib prison.[35] This attempt has failed for now, and its failure may have been "preprogrammed" by the relationship between law and politics. Germany's Chief Federal Prosecutor made the realpolitik decision that non-intervention in US affairs prevails over human rights. Yet "battles for justice" such as the aforementioned suit have an enormous effect on political discourse and may, by way of the criminal law, help call attention to the subject of human rights. Here, in particular, is a symbolic effect that should not be underestimated.

A similar symbolic effect was evident already in a 2003 suit brought against the German government for its support of the illegal Iraq war, namely, participating in AWACS reconnaissance flights, deploying tanks in Kuwait, and granting overflight rights. The Federal Prosecutor refused to investigate members of government suspected of planning an aggressive war under Section 80 of the German criminal code. Nevertheless, only through the discussion of the suit and the Federal Prosecutor's decision to reject it did it become clear that the relevant provision of the German criminal code is in reality a haven of unaccountability for those conducting and abetting aggressive war. This criminal law failure is diametrically opposed to the German Basic Law, which in Article 26 requires the punishment of any conduct disruptive to peace, and therefore illustrates the compelling need to work to bring national criminal law into conformity with the requirements of the Basic Law.[36]

This leads to the final postulate: The subject "Globalverfassung versus realpolitik" posits an idea of law (*Rechtsidee*) with an ideal. The "idea of law," based on universal human rights and inviolable human dignity, is linked with the ideal of human beings free from fear and want. This ideal, as stated in the International Covenant on Civil and Political Rights of December 19, 1966, can only be achieved under conditions "whereby everyone may enjoy his civil and political rights, as well as his economic, social and cultural rights."[37] However, as Immanuel Kant pointed out, "Out of timber so crooked as that from which man is made nothing entirely straight can be carved."[38]

The freedoms and rights of the "crooked timber" of humanity cannot exist without a policy that enshrines human rights in positive law and that also creates the normative instruments necessary to guarantee these rights. Achieving such a

---

[35] See Republikanischer Anwältinnen- und Anwälteverein and Holtfort-Stiftung (eds.), *Strafanzeige ./. Rumsfeld u. a.* (2005). See also the contributions of W. Kaleck and F. Jessberger in this volume.

[36] See J. Arnold, in K. Ambos and J. Arnold (eds.), *Der Irak-Krieg und das Völkerrecht* (2004), pp. 182 et seq. See also the decision of the Federal Administrative Court of June 21, 2005, according to which the Federal Republic of Germany is not obligated to support the illegal war against Iraq, http://bverwg.de/files/385bac46c40e252408e800418c-5b19c4/3060/2wd12-u-04.pdf.

[37] Quoted in H. J. Sandkühler, *supra* note 5, p. 3.

[38] Quoted in H. Bielefeldt, *supra* note 15, p. 79.

humane policy is primarily possible only through an active political debate—including the application of legal means—that recognizes the various concepts of human rights and their political, historical, religious, and cultural contexts. This requires active legal resistance to realpolitik. Such legal resistance is intrinsic to an international human rights movement that aims both for an open, unprejudiced dialogue on human rights and for concrete change in economic and social conditions as the basis for the progressive implementation of human rights.[39]

---

[39] See J. Hirsch, *Freitag* No. 4/2001; see also the contribution of P. Stolle and T. Singeln-stein in this volume.

Global Constitutional Struggles: Human Rights between colère publique and colère politique

Andreas Fischer-Lescano

I. Introduction

"The problem of international constitutionalism," as Philip Allott writes, "is the central challenge faced by international philosophers in the 21ˢᵗ century. It involves a fundamental re-conceiving of international society."[1] Not only philosophers, but lawyers as well, have reflected upon this central challenge: the United Nations Charter, the constitution of the WTO, the European Union's Constitution, a global political constitution not centered in the UN, global civil constitutions are all such non-state concepts of constitutionalism that draw global society's attention.[2] Clearly, we are dealing with "constitutional pluralism,"[3] in which the "self-fulfilling prophecy"[4] of the globalized semantics of constitution must be taken seriously. As long as its social substratum believes in its validity, a constitution provides society with a social surplus value.[5] This surplus value arises from the fact that the structural coupling of politics and law is achieved through an autological operation, which facilitates the mutual stimulation between politics and law in an era of globalization.[6]

---

[1] P. Allott, *International Law Forum du droit international* 2001, p. 12 at p. 16.
[2] For references to different transnational constitutional concepts, see A. Fischer-Lescano, *Globalverfassung. Die Geltungsbegründung der Menschenrechte* (2005), pp. 195 et seq.
[3] B. de Sousa Santos, *Towards a New Legal Common Sense: Law, Globalization, and Emancipation*, 2nd ed. (2002); see also A. Fischer-Lescano and G. Teubner, *Michigan Journal of International Law* 2004, p. 999.
[4] N. Walker, *Modern Law Review* 2002, p. 317 at p. 333.
[5] G. Teubner, in D. Nelken and J. Pribán (eds.), *Law's New Boundaries: Consequences of Legal Autopoiesis* (2001), p. 21.
[6] For the paradoxes of this coupling, J. Derrida, *New Political Science* 1986, p. 7.

II. The Sovereignty Paradox

Globalization is a challenge that rouses the legal system to emancipate itself from a fixation on the institution of the state. This is why Jacques Derrida has suggested a dual emancipatory strategy: a systemic emancipation of global law, by redefining both its proximity to and its distance from transnational politics, as a means to facilitate the classical emancipatory ideal. According to Derrida,

> Politicization, for example, is interminable even if it cannot and should not ever be total. To keep this from being a truism or a triviality, we must recognize in it the following consequence: each advance in politicization obliges one to reconsider, and so to reinterpret the very foundations of law such as they had previously been calculated or delimited. This was true for example in the Declaration of the Rights of Man, in the abolition of slavery, in all the emancipatory battles that remain and will have to remain in progress, everywhere in the world, for men and for women. Nothing seems to me less outdated than the classical emancipatory ideal.[7]

But how can this be achieved? The Enlightenment philosopher Immanuel Kant tried to solve the difficult relationship between politics and law using the concept of a social contract. But this philosophical model contained a fundamental tautology: the creation of a legally binding social contract assumes the legal validity of contracts.[8] It seems that there is no solution to this fundamental paradox, which consists in the fact that law defines law and that the legal foundation cannot be externalized in a convincing way, either in national legal systems or in international public law. Whereas both Kelsen's "basic norm" and H.L.A. Hart's ultimate rule of recognition oscillate between facts and norms, natural law is only law for those who believe in natural law. The plurality of possible observer positions leads to the conclusion that there is no legal theoretical consensus regarding the foundations of those legal systems.

Also, the fundamental paradox of the political system cannot be eliminated. As in the concept of "natural rights" described by Jeremy Taylor (1613–1667) – "The right of nature is a perfect and universal liberty to do whatsoever can secure or please me" – "equal sovereignty" as a "natural state's right" is a paradox. Consequently, Georges Scelle, Gustav Radbruch, and Hans Kelsen stressed the ambiguities of a world of sovereigns, as exposed, for example, in the Kantian draft of a perpetual peace. Under the conditions of Kant's proposal, states would not be bound by international legal obligations, and not even *pacta sunt servanda* could have any legally binding effect. Yet, Kant failed to explain how it would be possible for free and sovereign nation-states to enter into a situation dominated by legal procedures. His concept of a "perpetual peace" therefore oscillates strangely between absolute sovereignty (later developed by Hegel) and a legal status that is neither *status civilis* nor *status naturalis*. It is not only international public law that must live with these fundamental paradoxes. National subsystems, too, deal with

---

[7] J. Derrida, in D. Cornell et al. (eds.), *Deconstruction and the Possibility of Justice* (1992), p. 3 at p. 28.

[8] N. Luhmann, *Law as a Social System* (2004), pp. 464 et seq.

autological operations, connect operation with operation, and make invisible the "mystical foundations" (Jacques Derrida) of their authority.

III. Global Constitutional Law

Neither legal theory nor philosophy, but rather the practice of law itself has detected the ultimate paralysis of these paradoxes. Since the US Declaration of Independence and the French revolution, it has been *en vogue* to render invisible the paradoxes of the political and legal systems in nation-states' constitutions. For this reason, Niklas Luhmann has explained on several occasions that a constitution— as a special form of structural coupling between political and legal systems—is an evolutionary achievement. It interrupts the fundamental circularity of the political system's paradox of limited sovereignty and the fundamental paradox of law, which consists in the fact that law defines law. On the inside of this coupling, the mutual irritation of politics and law is facilitated, and constitutionally legalized; on the outside, such mutual stimulation is, if possible, excluded, and in all cases made illegal. Thus politics and the administration of justice are supposed to interact "only constitutionally". On condition that other possibilities are excluded, their mutual influence can be increased enormously.

But even ceremonial effects and claims to transcendental powers in *constitutional moments* cannot conceal the element of force when the unorganized crowd metamorphoses into the organized *demos*. There is no universally accepted theoretical explanation for this creation of a "collective singular" and for the distinction between *pouvoir constituant* and *pouvoir constitués*, "a classical piece of jurido-doctrinal work";[9] none of the theoretical conceptions can encapsulate its paradoxes. And whichever assumptions of homogeneity of an ethnic, linguistic, or cultural nature were formulated for the political demos (meaning the crowd that "reflects itself as a political entity and enters as such into history"[10]), the *constitutional* moment is a *mystical* moment, in which the function and force of the structural coupling of two autopoietic systems is rendered invisible. By structurally coupling politics and law, the constitution opens a new symbolic horizon.

Depending on the reflection theory and the position of each observer, a constitution can have various meanings, legal foundations and regulations. We find the same observations in the public law discourse of the twentieth century as in the *international public law approach*: "textualization of the basic norm" (*Kelsen/Verdross*),[11] "constitution of a community" (*Mosler/Tomuschat*),[12] and "highest prin-

---

[9] E.-W. Böckenförde, *Staat, Verfassung, Demokratie* (1991), p. 101.

[10] Id., p. 95.

[11] A. Verdross, *Die Verfassung der Völkergemeinschaft* (1926); H. Kelsen, *Das Problem der Souveränität und die Theorie des Völkerrechts*, 2nd ed. (1928); H. Kelsen, *Heidelberg Journal of International Law* 1958, p. 234.

[12] H. Mosler, *International Society as a Legal Community* (1980); C. Tomuschat, *Recueil des Cours* 1999, p. 1; C. Tomuschat, in UN (ed.), *International Law on the Eve of the Twenty-first Century* (1997), p. 37.

ciple of a political law" (*New Haven approach*)[13]—antinomies everywhere. The basic norm oscillates between facts and norms. The communitarianism of the "international community" is a tautology;[14] its basis of *core values* may be only *Utopia*,[15] and the excluded lurks in each *persistent objection*.[16] The *New Heaven* of the *New Haven school* lies in the netherworld of values that must be achieved by a process in which law is nothing more than an excuse for illegal politics.[17] Nevertheless, the constitution is an "evolutionary achievement"[18] that—if the autological operation is successful—can interrupt the fundamental circularity of the political system and the legal system.

So, legal practice, not legal theory, answers this key question of global law: how is it possible that, on the one hand, international public law is constituted by states and, on the other hand, states are constituted by international public law? The self-transformation of law and law creation and the limitation of sovereigns are not facilitated by an ultimate philosophical basic norm, but by national, supranational, organizational, and global law that possesses the quality, or its functional equivalent, of constitutional law.

Since the decision in *Marbury v. Madison*, the legal system has found its ultimate reflection paralysis in constitutional law:

> The constitution is either a superior, paramount law, unchangeable by ordinary means, or it is on a level with ordinary legislative acts, and, like other acts, is alterable when the legislature shall please to alter it. If the former part of the alternative be true, then a legislative act contrary to the constitution is not law: if the latter part be true, then written constitutions are absurd attempts, on the part of the people, to limit a power in its own nature illimitable [...] If, then, the court are to regard the constitution, and the constitution is superior to any ordinary act of the legislature, the constitution, and not such ordinary act, must govern the case to which they both apply.[19]

This statement was the autopoietic manifesto of a function system and the paradigm for all subsequent concepts of constitutional law. Even nation-states that lack a constitutional text to which courts could refer have constitutional law at their disposal. For example, in Great Britain there is no constitutional document,

---

[13] M. McDougal and F. Feliciano, *Law and Minimum World Public Order: The Legal Regulation of International Coercion* (1961); M. McDougal, H. Lasswell and L.-C. Chen, *Human Rights and World Public Order: The Basic Policies of an International Law of Human Dignity* (1980); see A.-M. Slaughter and W. Burke-White, *Harvard International Law Journal* 2003, p. 1; those constitutional conceptions are euphemist semantics for legally unbound political power politics. For an elaboration of this criticism, see A. Fischer-Lescano, in M. Bothe et al. (eds.), *Redefining Sovereignty* (2005), p. 335.

[14] For a pointed critique of community conceptions, G. Arangio-Ruiz, *European Journal of International Law* 1997, p. 1.

[15] See M. Koskenniemi, *From Apology to Utopia. The Structure of International Argument* (1989), p. 6.

[16] For the doctrine of persistent objection, see D. Charney, *British Yearbook of International Law 1985* (1986), p. 1.

[17] M. Koskenniemi, *supra* note 15, p. 6.

[18] N. Luhmann, *Rechtshistorisches Journal* 1990, p. 176.

[19] *Marbury v. Madison*, 1 Cranch (5 U.S.), 2 L.Ed. 60 (1803), 137.

but there is a constitution. So the thesis seems justified: a constitution is not a text, but a form of structural coupling. A constitution emerges from the processes of law and politics, in the hypercircles of their operation.

In global law, we can observe the generalization of legal rules and the emergence of secondary rules, e.g., the law of lawmaking and networking global legal remedies. The constitutional character of these rules arises from their very nature in legally constituting and limiting collective political bodies. In this sense, we will find a political global constitution if we find norms that regulate the relationship between politics and law in global society. Traditionally, these norms (leaving aside the organizational differentiations in the political system) are classified as (1) constitutional rules of jurisdiction, or "global remedies rules," (2) formal constitutional law, and (3) constitutional norms regarding the legal formation of norms.

1. Global Remedies Rules

At the center of global law, we find a heterachical organization of courts. We observe judicial networks and communicative interferences. Hierarchical and segmented centralizations of global remedies can be localized in supra-national organs such as the ECJ, ICTY, ICTR, ICC, truth commissions established by the UN, regional human rights courts, the WTO appellate body, the ICJ, and special treaty bodies.

Aside from their function in the special institutional context, all of these contribute to the generalization of expectation in the field of global human rights. All of them have their legal basis in international public law treaties, whether between states and states, or between states and international organizations, or in decisions by international organizations. But the trials of Augusto Pinochet and the Argentine military dictators, for example, demonstrate[20] what George Scelle called a *dédoublement fonctionnel* of these courts;[21] decentralized national courts, too, play a particularly important role in the generalization of expectations on a global level. Their jurisdiction is founded upon global remedies rules of civil and criminal law, whereas the most controversial principle is that of universal jurisdiction.[22]

2. Ius Cogens

These global remedies make legally binding decisions. They apply the binary code legal/illegal. Also, only these centers of the legal system can make binding decisions on the international community's core values, collisions between human and

---

[20] For details, see A. Fischer-Lescano, *supra* note 2, pp. 129 et seq.

[21] G. Scelle, *Précis de droit des gens, Vol. 1 and 2* (1932 and 1934).

[22] B. Stephens, *German Yearbook of International Law 1997* (1998), p. 117; J. D. van der Vyver, *South African Yearbook of International Law* (1999), p. 107; for further references and an explanation of the center/periphery divide, A. Fischer-Lescano and G. Teubner, *supra* note 3, pp. 999 et seq.

states rights, and the important questions: which fundamental norms of the International Bill of Rights are included in the *ius cogens* principle, where the border between inside/outside of ius cogens is situated, what is ius cogens, and what is *ius dispositivum*. So far, the catalogues of human rights and the ius cogens norm of Art. 53 of the Vienna Convention on the Law of Treaties presuppose an autopoietic legal system. This assumption is also true for the legal consequences of the application of ius cogens. So the ICTY decision in the Furundzija case, which has been criticized for doctrinal reasons,[23] is necessarily noteworthy, because the tribunal determined that global constitutional law is superior to national law:

> The fact that torture is prohibited by a peremptory norm of international law has other effects at the inter-state and individual levels. At the inter-state level, it serves to internationally delegitimize any legislative, administrative or judicial act authorizing torture. It would be senseless to argue, on the one hand, that on account of the jus cogens value of the prohibition against torture, treaties or customary rules providing for torture would be null and void *ab initio*, and then be unmindful of a State say, taking national measures authorizing or condoning torture or absolving its perpetrators through an amnesty law. If such a situation were to arise, the national measures, violating the general principle and any relevant treaty provision, would produce the legal effects discussed above and in addition would not be accorded international legal recognition.[24]

And it seems to be true: If a society achieves an operatively self-contained legal system only its center—that is, only its courts, can decide the undecidable. Therefore, judicial decisions can also reflect the relationship between law and politics, that it is obviously law that defines law, and that therefore the constitutional debate in international public law is not a theoretical rapturous enthusiasm, but that global law is constitutionalized to such an extent that Art. 53 of the Vienna Convention of the Law of Treaties can be described as "formal constitutional law."[25] The post-Westphalia global legal system has created hierarchies of norms. Its hierarchization model of legal programs copies one of the most important strategies of limitations of interdependencies.[26]

The global constitutional basic norms validated in this process are the principles of sovereign equality,[27] prohibition of force,[28] peaceful settlement of disputes, and prohibition of intervention.[29] Regarding the field of human rights, we must also mention the prohibition of torture, genocide, disappearances, the general prohibition of crimes against humanity, and those norms of humanitarian law that contain direct prohibitions for states and individual perpetrators.[30] These achieved

---

[23] For example, A. Paulus, *Die internationale Gemeinschaft im Völkerrecht* (2001), p. 352.

[24] *Prosecutor v. Furundzija*, ICTY Case No. IT-95-17/1-T, *International Legal Materials* 1999, p. 349, cif. 153.

[25] R. Uerpmann, *Juristen-Zeitung* 2001, p. 565.

[26] N. Luhmann, *Ausdifferenzierung des Rechts* (1981), p. 253.

[27] R. Anand, *Recueil des Cours* 1986 II, p. 9.

[28] See J. A. Carillo Salcedo, *European Journal of International Law* 1997, p. 583.

[29] *Military and Paramilitary Activities in and Against Nicaragua (Nicaragua v. US)*, ICJ *Reports* 1986, p. 98 (use of force), p. 106 (intervention); L. Hannikainen, *Peremptory Norms (Jus Cogens) in International Law* (1988), p. 315.

[30] See T. Meron, *American Journal of International Law* 1986, p. 1.

the special status of ius cogens.[31] Even if not every state in the world signed and ratified the general and special conventions, these legal norms are universally valid.

3. Norms of Legislation

This leads to norms of legislation, the last important component of the political global constitution. All basic norms become norms via attribution to the legal sources indicated in Art. 38 ICJ Statute—above all, international treaties, customary international law, and general principles. The legal paradox becomes visible because this norm has a constitutional quality, presupposing its own validity: a treaty norm states legally that treaties are legally binding. Norms regulate how norms are formed.

In sum, the self-organized communicative process of law has created the normatively valid fundamental norms of a global constitution. They can be classified as (1) rule of law (global remedies rules; independent judicative power) and (2) formal global constitutional law of ius cogens and *erga omnes* rules; that is, fundamental human rights and fundamental state rights.[32]

IV. Global Constitutional Struggles

Today's international public law still takes states as its point of reference. It ignores that states are themselves constructs of international law. This global legal order and its trinity of legal sources in Art. 38 of the ICJ Statute therefore suffer from a fundamental problem far beyond the questions of the relationship between rules of customary international law, treaty rules, and general principles. It is the problem of legitimacy. The threat and the greatest challenge for global constitutionalism is to react in evolutionary fashion to the constitutional struggles we observe in world society. Otherwise, global law will lose its social substratum.

1. Lex Humana

The fundamental challenge law must confront is that of its adequacy to its social environment. The "self-incurred dependence" of law results from a legal depen-

---

[31] C. Tomuschat: "Equality of human beings, protection of human life and physical integrity, freedom from torture and slavery are without any doubt propositions that need no additional confirmation." (*Recueil des Cours* 1993 IV, p. 195 at p. 303); see also L. Hannikainen, *supra* note 29, p. 425.

[32] See A. Fischer-Lescano, *supra* note 2, p. 216 et seq.; for fundamental principles, S. Kadelbach, *Zwingendes Völkerrecht* (1992), p. 210; M. Bothe, in M. Lutz-Bachmann and J. Bohmann (eds.), *Frieden durch Recht: Kants Friedensidee und das Problem einer neuen Weltordnung* (1996), p. 187; L. Hannikainen, *supra* note 29, p. 315.

dence on the states. But states no longer have a monopoly on global legal communication. The globalization catastrophe has made world society much more complex. Civil actors formulate not only their own legal regimes, for example in *lex mercatoria*; they are also present in many other legal fields. World society's normative expectations are no longer formed exclusively within the world of states by political instauration, but also in other function systems. In the field of human rights law, the system of mass media and NGOs must be mentioned, validating human rights by evoking them in response to atrocities. This is what Niklas Luhmann and Gunther Teubner call "law-creation via scandalization,"[33] a post-modern reminder of Emile Durkheim's concept of *colère publique*.[34]

This *lex humana*[35] of post-modern *ius gentium*, formulated by actors in organized and spontaneous civil society, could be reformulated in international public law as "world society's customary law" (and not "international customary law"!).[36] In fact, in her dissenting opinion in the arrest warrant case, decided by the ICJ in February 2002, the Belgian ad hoc judge van den Wyngaert referred to legal instauration processes in civil society. Although in her reformulation, the fixation on NGOs may be called too narrow, her statement is a welcome step towards a reformulation of lex humana: "Advocacy organizations, such as Amnesty International, Avocats sans Frontières, Human Rights Watch, the International Federation of Human Rights Leagues (FIDH), and the International Commission of Jurists have taken clear positions on the subject of international accountability. This may be seen as the opinion of *civil society*, an opinion that cannot be completely discounted in the formation of customary international law today. ... The Court fails to acknowledge this development and does not discuss the relevant sources."[37]

---

[33] See N. Luhmann, in id., *Soziologische Aufklärung, Vol. 6: Die Soziologie und der Mensch* (1995), p. 229; G. Teubner, in id. (ed.), *Global Law without a State* (1996), p. 3.

[34] E. Durkheim, *The Division of Labor in Society* (1893, 1997), pp. 31 et seq.

[35] This wording does not refer to scholastic concepts of lex aeterna/lex naturalis/lex humana, but points to "global law without a state," and to legal pluralistic sources of law in civil society. Not only lex mercatoria, lex informatica, lex construcionis etc., but also human rights law depend on civil society's support. On legal pluralism, see A. Fischer-Lescano and G. Teubner, *supra* note 3, pp. 999 et seq.

[36] For G. Secelle's concept of *droit des gens*, see: "La norme juridique prohibitive, permissive, ne s'adresse donc qu'à des volontés humaines et conscientes et comme il n'y a de compétences qu'individuelles, il n'y a de sujets de droit que les individus." (G. Scelle, *Droit constitutionnel international* 1934, p. 3). Philip Jessup and Roberto Ago, too, remain within a statist paradigm; see P. C. Jessup, *Transnational Law* (1956), and R. Ago, *Archiv des Völkerrechts* 1956/1957, p. 257; for a discussion of "transnational law" concepts, see F. Hanschmann, in S. Buckel et al. (eds.), *Neue Theorien des Rechts* (2006), p. 349.

[37] Dissenting opinion of Judge van den Wyngaert in the case concerning the *Arrest Warrant of 11 April 2000* (*Democratic Republic of the Congo v. Belgium*), Judgement of February 14, 2002, *ICJ Reports* 2002, p. 121 and *International Legal Materials* 2002, p. 536, cif. 27.

2. Universal Jurisdiction

Consequently, the struggle of NGOs like Amnesty International and Human Rights Watch for the recognition of universal jurisdiction turns out to be a constitutional battle par excellence; that is, a battle in which law is struggling for its independence between colère publique[38] and colère politique, between the legal instauration processes of civil society and state society. The question, in the dispute between Amnesty International and Henry Kissinger, whether global law is going to decide in favor of universal jurisdiction should not be marginalized as a technical legal problem.[39] If global law is going to decide the undecidable in world society, this is part of a much larger project, one that challenges law itself to limit its code, to recognize its own limitations, and to take on social responsibility.

Recent (non)applications of the German Code of Crimes against International Law (*Völkerstrafgesetzbuch*, or VStGB) reveal the political pressure on law.[40] It is no accident that since the VStGB came into force in July 2002, none of the 26 lodged complaints have led to court proceedings. The Chief Prosecutor's Office has in no case found occasion to initiate a formal investigative procedure.[41] And yet the project of the VStGB and the principle of universal jurisdiction seemed so promising at first. German politicians of all stripes praised it as an international model. The errors made by the Belgians in the introduction and the application of the principle of universal jurisdiction had apparently been avoided, because more care was taken with regard to restrictions in international law with respect to the temporary immunity of incumbent heads of state and foreign ministers. The German VStGB not only regulates the application of the subsidiarity principle, but also carefully reflects the framework of immunity norms. This means that, even where the legality principle is adopted and the German Federal Prosecutor is obliged to investigate a case, customary international law on immunity is incorporated into German law and prohibits arrest warrants or criminal court proceedings in cases where there is no exception to immunity. Belgium had a much more inflexible provision. After an arrest warrant against the sitting Congolese foreign

---

[38] For the creation of legal norms via colère publique, see N. Luhmann, in E.-J. Lampe (ed.), *Meinungsfreiheit als Menschenrecht* (1998), p. 99; A. Fischer-Lescano, *supra* note 2, pp. 67-128.

[39] For the discussion on universal jurisdiction, see the contributions of L. Reydams, *Universal Jurisdiction: International and Municipal Legal Perspectives* (2003); A. Sammons, *Berkeley Journal of International Law* 2003, p. 111; S. R. Ratner and J. S. Abrams, *Accountability for Human Rights Atrocities in International Law: Beyond The Nuremberg Legacy*, 2nd ed. (2001), p. 151; B. Broomhall, *International Justice and the International Criminal Court: Between Sovereignty and the Rule of Law* (2003), pp. 105 et seq.; C. Maierhöfer, *Europäische Grundrechte-Zeitschrift* 2003, p. 545.

[40] An English translation of the VStGB and the German government's explanatory statement upon introducing the VStGB can be found on the homepage of the Max Planck Institute for Foreign and International Criminal Law available at http://www.iuscrim.mpg.de/forsch/legaltext/VStGBengl.pdf. See also *Annual of German & European Law 2003* (2004), p. 667.

[41] See *International Legal Materials* 2006, p. 115.

minister, more were threatened with arrest, among others Colin Powell, George W. Bush, and Ariel Sharon. The diplomatic entanglements sparked by this went so far that the US administration finally announced it would evacuate NATO Headquarters in Brussels, because it was no longer possible to travel there safely.[42] Finally, in the summer of 2003, Belgium gave in to US political pressure and changed the relevant law so that acts can only be prosecuted under the principle of universal jurisdiction if the victim has lived at least three years in Belgium.[43] This decision provoked obituaries from universal jurisdiction skeptics who have sought to discredit civil society and academic efforts to strengthen the principle.[44]

While Amnesty International, Human Rights Watch and the epistemic community of international lawyers have taken a clear position in favor of the principle of

---

[42] See, e.g., Donald Rumsfeld's statement: "Finally, I discussed the US concern about the lawsuit that's recently been filed in a Belgian court against General Tom Franks and against Colonel Brian McCoy alleging that they were responsible for war crimes in Iraq, as well as suits that have been filed here in Belgium against former President Bush— George Herbert Walker Bush as opposed to George W. Bush—General Norman Schwarzkopf, Vice President Cheney and Secretary Powell. The suits are absurd. Indeed, I would submit that there is no general in history who has gone to greater lengths than General Franks and his superb team to avoid civilian casualties. I am told that the suit against General Franks was effectively invited by a Belgian law that claims to give Belgian courts powers to try the citizens of any nation for war crimes. The United States rejects the presumed authority of Belgian courts to try General Franks, Colonel McCoy, Vice President Cheney, Secretary Powell and General Schwarzkopf, as well as former President Bush. I will leave it to the lawyers to debate the legalities. I am not a lawyer. But the point is this: By passing this law, Belgium has turned its legal system into a platform for divisive, politicized lawsuits against her NATO Allies. Now, it's obviously not for outsiders, non-Belgians, to tell the Belgian government what laws it should pass and what it should not pass. With respect to Belgium's sovereignty, we respect it even though Belgium appears not to respect the sovereignty of other countries. But Belgium needs to realize that there are consequences to its actions. This law calls into serious question whether NATO can continue to hold meetings in Belgium and whether senior U.S. officials, military and civilian, will be able to continue to visit international organizations in Belgium. I would submit that that could be the case for other NATO Allies, as well. If the civilian and military leaders of member states can not come to Belgium without fear of harassment by Belgian courts entertaining spurious charges by politicized prosecutors, then it calls into question Belgium's attitude about its responsibilities as a host nation for NATO and Allied forces." (News Transcript: Secretary of Defense Rumsfeld at NATO Headquarters, *Defenselink* (June 12, 2003), available at http://www.defenselink.mil/ transcripts/2003/tr20030612-secdef0271.html).

[43] See *Loi relative aux Violations graves du Droit Humanitaire*, August 5, 2003, available at http://www.coe.int/T/E/Legal_Affairs/Legal_cooperation/Transnational_criminal_justice/International_Criminal_Court/Documents/ConsultICC(2003)11F.pdf; on this, L. Reydams, *Journal of International Criminal Justice* 2003, p. 679.

[44] See the summary in S. Ratner, *American Journal of International Law* 2003, p. 888; see also M. Kirby, in S. Macedo (ed.), *Universal Jurisdiction: National Courts and the Prosecution of Serious Crimes under International Law* (2004), p. 240.

universal jurisdiction in the Princeton Principles on Universal Jurisdiction,[45] the phalanx of opponents of the principle is led by Henry Kissinger, who himself is endangered by numerous investigative procedures (in Chile, France, Spain, etc.), among other things for the so-called *Operación Condor*.[46] In an angry article in *Foreign Affairs*, which some commentators think Kissinger wrote in view of the impending restriction of his freedom to travel,[47] he states,

> The advocates of universal jurisdiction argue that the state is the basic cause of war and cannot be trusted to deliver justice. If law replaced politics, peace and justice would prevail. But even a cursory examination of history shows that there is no evidence to support such a theory. The role of the statesman is to choose the best option when seeking to advance peace and justice, realizing that there is frequently a tension between the two and that any reconciliation is likely to be partial. The choice, however, is not simply between universal and national jurisdictions.[48]

In fact, Kissinger's dramatic presentation does outline the problem. What is at stake in the principle of universal jurisdiction is not merely a technical juridical question about jurisdictional boundaries; it is the fundamental organizing principle of the constitutional idea. Will international law, driven by the development of international criminal law and by the founding of numerous special regimes ranging from the WTO, to the United Nations, to human rights pacts,[49] succeed in reacting to its increasing politicization by generating a movement capable of guaranteeing legal autonomy? Can global law be more than an apologetic accessory of realpolitik? These questions are as yet unanswered, and the complaint over the occurrences at Abu Ghraib is a part of the world social struggle for the rule of law on a global scale.

The lines of conflict in this struggle do not run between Europe and the U.S. Ironically, it is US courts—for example, from the German perspective, in regard to decisions in forced labor cases—that have in numerous proceedings adjudicated

---

[45] *The Princeton Principles on Universal Jurisdiction: Joint Declaration of the Princeton University's Program in Law and Public Affairs, Woodrow Wilson School of Public and International Affairs et al. on Universal Jurisdiction*, available at http://www.law.uc.edu /morgan/newsdir/univjuris.html; see also Human Rights Watch documentation of texts on transitional justice at http://www.hrw.org/doc/?t=justice; Amnesty International, *Universal Jurisdiction: The duty of states to enact and enforce legislation* (AI Index 53/002/2001), at http://web.amnesty.org/pages/uj-memorandum-eng.

[46] A. Fischer-Lescano, *supra* note 2, pp. 157-175.

[47] See, e.g., Jonathan Powers' presumption: "After Pinochet and Milosevic does Kissinger see the writing on the wall for himself? Could some lone magistrate somewhere— another Baltasar Garzon—set the ball rolling towards him? Could he be picked up while attending some academic conference in France, or giving political advice on behalf of Kissinger Associates to the government of Taiwan or to multinational companies in Malaysia or taking a holiday in India?" (J. Powers, *Henry Kissinger Has Become a Very Nervous Person*, available at http://www.globalpolicy.org).

[48] H. Kissinger, *Foreign Affairs* 4/2001, p. 86; for an opposing view, see, e.g., the reply to Kissinger by the Chair of Human Rights Watch, K. Roth, *Foreign Affairs* 5/2001, p. 150 and the references at note 45.

[49] On this see A. Fischer-Lescano and G. Teubner, *supra* note 3, pp. 999 et seq.

infractions of international law's core human rights content.[50] It is precisely these rules that threaten to strike back at powerful practitioners of realpolitik. Postnational fronts, therefore, do not line up geographically, but functionally, between politics and law. *Hamdi v. Bush, CCR v. Rumsfeld, Käsemann v. The Argentine military junta, Belgium v. Congo*—all of these are only ciphers for a worldwide social conflict of constitutional proportions. Are there legal norms in global society that limit the political system and protect the most elementary human rights? Before which courts can these fundamental laws be asserted, such that they become more than symbolic texts that are taken into account on ceremonious holidays and as excuses when there is a wish to legitimize force?

3. Law between colère publique and colère politique

Global law finds itself caught between civil society's colère publique and a colère politique of the states' world. This is a description we find in George Scelle's work. It is widely assumed that Scelle's objective law is a model of natural law.[51] Scelle adopts from Duguit[52] a reinterpretation of Durkheim's concept of solidarity, understanding the legal order as a biological fact, based on the two modi of solidarity conceptualized by Durkheim. Its natural law connotation results from Scelle's idea of objective/natural law—that is, a counterpoint to positive law,[53] although Scelle himself always rejected classification as a neo-natural lawyer. His reference to Durkheim's concept of solidarity reveals that his *droit objectif ou naturel* should not be misunderstood in a transcendental way, because the contradiction between *droit naturel* and *droit positif* is a question of adequate reformulation of social solidarity in law.[54] So, for global law it is advisable to observe the droit naturel, reformulated here as lex humana; otherwise, it operates outside of its social environment and will lose, along with its legitimacy, the attention of its social and individual substrata.[55]

Like Durkheim's traditional way, Scelle formulates the problem that law cannot avoid to this day, and that can be defused by internally reformulating the lex humana: how to decide on the heterogeneous legal instauration processes at the periphery of society's law. International public law could reformulate the linguistic

---

[50] A summary of these trials should start with *Filártiga v. Peña-Irala*, 630 F.2d 876 (2nd Cir. 1980); see the inventory in B. Stephens, *Yale Journal of International Law* 2002, p. 1; concerning the legal actions arising from forced labor cases, the establishment of the Foundation for Memory, Responsibility and the Future and the German-US governmental agreement, see L. Adler and P. Zumbansen, in P. Zumbansen (ed.), *Zwangsarbeit im Dritten Reich: Erinnerung und Verantwortung* (2002), p. 333.

[51] H. Thierry, *European Journal of International Law* 1990, p. 193.

[52] L. Duguit, *Traité de Droit constitutionnel, Vol. 5*, 3rd ed. (1927).

[53] G. Scelle, *supra* note 21, p. 5.

[54] Id., p. 4.

[55] N. Luhmann, *supra* note 8, p. 464; see also G. Teubner, in M. Escamilla and M. Saavedra (eds.), *Law and Justice in a global society, International Association for Philosophy of Law and Social Sociology* (2005), p. 547.

turn if it recognized that a legal system and a hierarchy of law is not an apriority of legal certainty, but the result of the operation of an autopoietic legal system that must deal with a plurality of communicative processes, that observes social action via its legal/illegal binary code, and in which norm projections and norms can only be differentiated if the system is operatively self-contained. This would be the form, and international public law could take an important step towards a reformulation of social legal instauration processes. In Antonio Cassese's description of Scelle's concept, global law does not have its source in apriority, but creates its own myriad sources passing through world society: "The world community swarms with myriad legal orders (in today's parlance we would call them 'subsystems'); they do not live by themselves, each in its own area, but intersect and overlap with each other."[56]

The political global constitution—and especially those rights that enjoy the status of ius cogens—is the structural coupling of two different global systems into one decision making unit: the international community. As such, it is the functional equivalent of national constitutions, but it is not a complete constitution. It cannot be attributed to an act of a global *demos*. There was no assembly that could be called *pouvoir constituant*, there was no assembly that called itself thus, and there is to this day no recognition of lex humana in the legal system of *ius gentium*. Therefore, from the point of view of democratic theory, there is no immediate legitimation of governance by the governed on the level of the political system of world society.[57] Thus no democratic global constitution exists, even if world society has achieved a structural coupling of its legal and political systems, i.e., a functional global constitution.

Besides its democratic deficiencies, the political global constitution suffers from the restricted jurisdiction of global remedies, whereby the restraints on legal control of Security Council resolutions and the lack of mandatory ICJ jurisdiction must be mentioned in particular. This partial failure of global constitutional separation of powers leads to the problem of symbolic constitutionalism.[58] At the periphery of law, doctrinal justifications of humanitarian interventions and of an unspecified war on terror, rogue states, etc. claim the core values of the international community.[59] But because of the restricted jurisdiction of global remedies, these norm projections cannot be repudiated by an entirely self-contained legal system.

As long as global law does not achieve institutionalized universal jurisdiction on all issues of use of force in world society, e.g., by expanding the principle of universal jurisdiction or by re-strengthening the *erga omnes* principle, there is no right of humanitarian intervention, and especially no global constitutional right of humanitarian intervention. Thus, the primary challenge is to strengthen and extend

---

[56] A. Cassese, *European Journal of International Law* 1990, p. 210.

[57] H. Brunkhorst, *Solidarity: From Civic Friendship to a Global Legal Community* (2005).

[58] For the problem of symbolic constitutionalism, see M. Neves, *Journal of Law and Society* 2001, p. 242.

[59] Against actual strategies of modifying the *ius contra bellum* and of sacrificing legal autonomy on the altar of political logics, see A. Fischer-Lescano and P. Liste, *Zeitschrift für internationale Beziehungen* 2005, p. 209.

the jurisdiction of global remedies and to prevent the global political system from symbolically abusing global constitutional law. But this is a legal pacifist project that is against the spirit of a time that—to use Niklas Luhmann's formulation—"repeats to be blue-eyed in political issues and that substitutes structural achievements by good purposes," and that therefore believes itself unable to refrain from much more drastic forms of conflict repression.[60]

V. Conclusion

If we are serious about constitutionalizing international relations,[61] if we want to see the rule of law not as an abortive episode in human history, which perished with nation-states, then we must be prepared for a sharpening of the conflicts between law and politics. We must come to terms with the fact that law cannot always guarantee observance of legal norms. If, however, we enable the law to decide legality and illegality in concrete questions, we can expect it to structure expectations of each other under global law in the future and to make available to us its symbolic apparatus, so that we can react to disappointed expectations. This would include penal mechanisms, but also civil law damage claims. The latter have, until now, been only insufficiently acknowledged for transnational cases in Germany.[62] Redressing this is urgently necessary.

One need not be an abolitionist[63] to see that it is precisely the penal sanction apparatus that has constantly caused the legal system to flinch from initiating judicial proceedings[64]—for example, against members of the federal government for German participation in various military interventions from Kosovo to Iraq—or to conclude these proceedings with a decision on legality and illegality.

Instead of hastily retreating before political pressure, global remedies must be based on a variety of *causae*. In particular, the principle of universal jurisdiction

[60] N. Luhmann, *Legitimation durch Verfahren*, 2nd ed. (1975), pp. 2 et seq. (author's translation).

[61] On global constitutionalism, see J. Habermas, in J. Habermas, *Der Gespaltene Westen. Kleinere Politische Schriften X* (2004), p. 113; J. A. Frowein, *Berichte der deutschen Gesellschaft für Völkerrecht* 2000, p. 427; A. Fischer-Lescano, *supra* note 13, p. 335.

[62] See the instructive analysis by A. Halfmeier, *Rabels Zeitschrift für ausländisches und internationales Privatrecht* 2004, p. 653; B. Heß, *Berichte der Deutschen Gesellschaft für Völkerrecht* 2003, p. 107; on what is possible in terms of international law, see T. van Boven, *Revised set of basic principles and guidelines on the right to reparation for victims of gross violations of human rights and humanitarian law*, UN Doc E/CN4/Sub 2/1996/17, 5/24/1996.

[63] Even if there are good reasons for this position, see K. Lüderssen, *Abschaffen des Strafens?* (1995), p. 22.

[64] See, e.g., the decision of the Federal Prosecutor of March 21, 2003, which ended the proceedings regarding the complaints in respect to the Iraq War, i.e., the accusation (due to rights granted to use German air space and the German AWACS deployments in Turkey) of a war of aggression punishable under Sec. 80 Criminal Code, *Juristen-Zeitung* 2003, p. 908; on this, see C. Kress, *Journal of International Criminal Justice* 2004, p. 245.

should be codified for private law restitution disputes as well.[65] Instead of restricting the legal possibilities of access for the victims of serious human rights crimes, expanded possibilities for complaints are needed. In these proceedings, one need not always use as a threat the strongest weapons of democratic constitutional states, i.e., penal sanctions, but should make it possible, as a minimal goal, to open a legal avenue of communication for the victims. Most importantly, procedures in democratic constitutional states must be strengthened; thus legal responsibility can be attributed, and the lines between global legality and illegality can be drawn.[66] The alternative would not be an alternative: Abandoning the structural achievements of the rule of law and leaving decisions on war and peace and the form of war to politics alone, as practitioners of realpolitik like Henry Kissinger advocate, would only lead to the further domination of conflicts by fundamentalism and to much more drastic means of conflict repression.

Hans Kelsen once said, "Each conflict that is described as a conflict of interests, power or politics ... can be decided as a legal dispute."[67] Indeed, that which distinguishes totalitarian from constitutional orders is their openness to an independent legal system and pass conflicts to the judiciary to decide and protect each procedure from political influence.[68] Last but not least, this normative desire is expressed in numerous UN documents.[69] This and the implementation of democratic procedures is also the core of modern constitutionalism. To dampen the destructive tendencies of political and other function systems, world society will have to be prepared for an enduring fight for an autonomous, global legal system.

---

[65] Regarding the decentralized processes of precedent establishment in the realm of civil law, Axel Halfmeier correctly states, "The future of judicial decisions in private law under conditions of globalization does not lie in a centralized system of world courts but in a decentralized patchwork of decisions of national civil courts on transnational issues. Out of these decentralized decisions a transnational civil law regarding human-rights violations is currently developing." (A. Halfmeier, *supra* note 62, p. 685).

[66] See the stocktaking by P. Zumbansen, *German Law Journal* 2004, p. 1499.

[67] H. Kelsen, *Wer soll der Hüter der Verfassung sein?* (1931), reprinted in H. Klecatsky et al. (eds.), *Die Wiener Rechtstheoretische Schule: Ausgewählte Schriften von Hans Kelsen, Adolf Julius Merkl und Alfred Verdross* (1968), p. 1883 (author's translation).

[68] On the political nature of these processes, see A. Fischer-Lescano and R. Christensen, *Der Staat* 2005, p. 213.

[69] See the endorsement of the concluding statement of the Seventh UN Congress on Prevention of Crimes Through the UN General Assembly (GA Resolutions 40/32 of November 29, 1985 and 40/146 of December 13, 1985), the Basic Principles on the Independence of the Judiciary, UN Doc. GA/40/146 and GA/41/149; see also Human Rights Committee, *General Comment 13*, Article 14 (Twenty-first session, 1984), Compilation of General Comments and General Recommendations Adopted by Human Rights Treaty Bodies, UN Doc. HRI\GEN\1\Rev.1, no. 14 (1994).

The Future of Universal Jurisdiction

Peter Weiss

Universal Jurisdiction: What a novel, revolutionary idea! No wonder it is meeting with so many difficulties. That is one way of looking at it. Another way is just the opposite: It is one of the oldest ideas around, and, while its translation into enforceable legal norms will take some time, its underlying principles are too firmly established ever to be dislodged again. Let me illustrate with a few quotes:

> Particular law is that which each community lays down and applies to its own members: this is partly written and partly unwritten. Universal law is the law of Nature. For there really is, as every one to some extent divines, a natural justice and injustice that is binding on all men, even on those who have no association or covenant with each other.

This is Aristotle speaking in Book I of his *Rhetoric*[1] ca. 350 BCE. About five centuries later, Cicero puts it this way:

> There will not be different laws at Rome and Athens, or different laws now and in the future but one eternal and unchangeable law will be valid for all nations and for all times.[2]

And Marcus Aurelius, shortly after Cicero, explains the principle of universality in the following syllogism:

> If our intellectual part is common, the reason also, by virtue of which we are rational beings, is common; if so, common also is the reason which commands us what to do and what not to do; if so, there is a common law; if so, we are fellow citizens; if so, we are members of some political community; if so, the world is in a manner a state.[3]

None of these statements is a prescription for world government, which, in any case, would be a bad idea, given the enormous disparity of wealth and power prevailing in the world today. But all, allowing for a certain amount of evolution, are formulations of the fundamental norms defining common decency in human behavior, in war as well as peace. In war, they have come to be articulated in the major instruments of humanitarian law of the last century and a half, led by the products of Hague and Geneva; in peace, by the Universal Declaration of Human Rights and its many offspring in treaties and conventions.

---

[1] Aristotle, *Rhetoric, Book I*, Ch. 13.
[2] M. T. Cicero, *De Legibus*.
[3] M. Aurelius, *Meditations, Book IV*, Sec. 4.

In this sense, the world is indeed a state. "No man is an island, entire of itself," rings truer in this age of globalization than when John Donne penned these famous words. And he would agree, I think, that not only any man's death diminishes him because he is "involved in mankind," but every act of torture, every violation of what we have come to call a basic human right, diminishes each one of us, no matter by whom or where committed. Universal jurisdiction is the expression of this yearning for Aristotle's natural justice, derived from the nature of human beings in society. It is the attire draped over the naked body of universal norms.

But, I can hear you say, didn't Aristotle defend slavery and wasn't he also something of a male chauvinist? Precisely. Some of the loftiest principles are enunciated by those least able or willing to put them into practice. We must always be careful to separate the enunciator from the practitioner. How else to explain US Secretary of State Condoleezza Rice's fondness for saying that no country—I repeat, no country—has done more for human rights than the United States of America? Or that, every time new atrocious details about the treatment of detainees in Abu Ghraib or Afghanistan or Guantánamo are disclosed, some general or other assures the world that the United States is fully committed to humane treatment in accord with the Geneva Conventions? Or that President Bush rarely misses an opportunity to say, "We don't do torture." Well, of course not, we just call it by a different name. Try "aggressive interrogation."

How then are we to deal with this dysfunction between the law and practice of universal jurisdiction? The same way, I suppose, that progress is made in any other area of domestic or international law: through a combination of creative litigation; civil society pressure on executive, legislative, and international bodies; and, in terms of Article 38 (d) of the Statute of the International Court of Justice, "the teachings of the most highly qualified publicists of the various nations" (including some of those attending this conference). If, as I believe, Aristotle was right in saying that "everyone to some extent divines a natural justice and injustice that is binding on all men," then, sooner or later, the paradox of unpunished genocide, war crimes, or crimes against humanity, will lead to a new willingness on the part of prosecutors to indict and judges to convict the perpetrators of such crimes in universal fora, both domestic and international. It is not foolhardy to predict that this trend will be fueled by the rising anger of civil society at the varieties of false reasoning, which prosecutors and judges have been using to date to escape their moral and legal obligations in this respect.

There is a threshold of unacceptability, which the manipulators of political power cross at their risk. A good example is the decision of the American administration to hold detainees of the Afghan and Iraq wars indefinitely, or until "the war on terror is over," a chronological, limit, which, according to Secretary of Defense Rumsfeld, may require several generations to reach, and to bar them from seeking relief in American courts. This position was so shocking in its disregard for the most fundamental norms of procedural justice that the United States Supreme Court, which normally defers to the administration in matters of national security, decided last year that the detainees could have their day in court,[4] and

---

[4] *Rasul v. Bush*, 542 U.S. 466 (2004).

that 50 law firms, including some of the most establishment firms, are now undertaking a mass, pro bono defense of the Guantánamo detainees coordinated by the Center for Constitutional Rights.[5]

I. Rays of Hope

In speculating about the future of criminal universal jurisdiction, one must pay homage to the pioneering role of Spain, its internationalist legislature, its vigorous human rights lawyers and its courageous judges. Spain has given us not only the Pinochet precedent,[6] but, more recently, the first case in which a non-citizen, the Argentine Adolfo Scilingo, has been found guilty in a fully litigated trial of crimes against humanity committed in Argentina, i.e., outside of the country exercising jurisdiction, and sentenced to serve a prison term of 640 years in the country exercising jurisdiction.[7] Even more important is the October 5, 2005 decision of the highest court of Spain, the Constitutional Court, reversing the decision of the Supreme Court and holding that the principle of universal jurisdiction takes precedence over national interests and ordering the National Court (Audiencia Nacional) to proceed with the case brought by Nobel Peace Prize winner Rigoberta Minchu alleging genocide, torture, murder and illegal imprisonment committed by the government of Guatemala between 1978 and 1986.[8] There are other straws in the wind. To name a few:

- On July 19, 2005, an Afghan warlord was convicted by a British jury of crimes against humanity committed in Afghanistan during the reign of the Taliban, following a seven-week trial under the British Criminal Justice Act and the UN Convention Against Torture.[9]

[5] See *New York Times*, May 30, 2005. On June 29, 2006, the Supreme Court of the United States issued its opinion in *Hamdan v. Rumsfeld* (http://www.supremecourtus.gov/opinions/05pdf-05-184.pdf). While it does not deal with universal jurisdiction as such, it is extremely important as an affirmation of the Geneva Conventions and of international law, including customary international law, contrary to the position of the US administration.

[6] For a history of the groundbreaking Pinochet litigation and some of its progeny see N. Roht-Arriaza, *The Pinochet Effect: Transnational Justice in the Age of Human Rights* (2005).

[7] See report by ASIL (American Society of International Law) at http://www.asil.org/ilib/2005/04/ilib050426.htm#j3, with links to the decision in Spanish and analysis by Prof. Richard Wilson.

[8] See *International Justice Tribune*, October 10, 2005, at http://www.justicetribune.com/index.php?page=v2_article&id=3195. On July 7, 2006, the Spanish court issued an arrest warrant for former President Efrain Montt and seven other defendants and an international order, transmitted through Interpol, freezing their assets. See http://www.cja.org/cases/Guatemala_News/guatemalawarrants.pdf.

[9] http://www.globalpolicy.org/intljustice/universal/2005/0720afghan.htm.

- On November 15, 2005, the former dictator of Chad, Hissène Habré was arrested in Senegal on a Belgian arrest warrant issued.[10] After the Court of Appeal in Dakar declared itself incompetent to rule on Chad's extradition request, Senegal requested the African Union to determine "the competent jurisdiction." The AU set up a committee of eminent African jurists to report back to its summit in July 2006.[11]

- The (not entirely up-to-date) website of the British human rights organization REDRESS contains an extremely informative list of universal jurisdiction laws and cases from ten European countries: Austria, Belgium, Denmark, France, Germany, Italy, Netherlands, Spain, Switzerland, United Kingdom.[12]

- On October 14, 2005, a Dutch court convicted two Afghan generals who had sought asylum in the Netherlands of war crimes committed under Afghanistan's communist regime.[13]

- On June 28, 2003, Ricardo Miguel Cavallo, a former Argentine navy officer known as "the angel of death," was extradited from Mexico to Spain, where he is currently awaiting trial for kidnapping and torture. This is believed to have been the first instance of universal jurisdiction extradition under the age-old principle of *aut dedere aut judicare.*[14]

- On November 26, 2005, a federal district court judge in Washington, DC, found Michael Townley, an American citizen formerly in the service of Augusto Pinochet's DINA, guilty by default of the murder of a Spanish diplomat in Chile and sentenced him to pay $ 7,259,700 to the victim's widow.[15]

II. Is Universal Jurisdiction Applicable to Perpetrators in Office or Only to Disgraced Perpetrators out of Office?

As the foregoing recital shows, to date universal jurisdiction as a working tool of international justice functions mostly as a kind of victors' justice. Thus, the *Rums-*

---

[10] As is well known, many cases were filed under Belgium's pioneering universal jurisdiction law before it was repealed under pressure from the US in 2002. The Habré case was filed before the repeal took effect.

[11] Cf. *The Case Against Hissène Habré, an "African Pinochet,"* http://www.hrw.org/english/docs/2005/09/30/chad11786.htm. On July 2, 2006, the African Union, opting for an "African solution", declared that Hissène Habré should be tried in Senegal despite the ruling of its Supreme Court and Senegalese President Abdoulaye Wade said: "We will not shirk our responsibilities." (http://www.justicetribune.com/v2_print.php?page=v2_article&mode=print).

[12] See http://www.redress.org/documents/inpract.html#b. Many of these cases arose from war crimes and crimes against humanity committed during the recent Balkan wars.

[13] See http://www.rferl.org/featuresarticle/2005/10/d3185711-2419-4fb5-b5f3-f4c613773c-70.html.

[14] See http://www.crimesofwar.org/onnews/news-argentina.html.

[15] *Gonzalez Vera et al. v. Henry Kissinger et al.*, D.C.D.C. 2005, Civil Action 02-02240 (HKK).

feld case[16] was dismissed in Germany on extremely weak grounds; the Belgian universal jurisdiction law, under which a number of high officials were indicted, had to be repealed under political pressure; the *Gonzalez Vera* case (see text at footnote 14) was dismissed against Henry Kissinger but was successful against an actual perpetrator farther down the chain of command.[17] There are, of course, a variety of legal doctrines which are frequently invoked in an attempt to shield sitting presidents, generals, cabinet members, etc. from the long arm of the law, including sovereign immunity, political question, act of state and action within the scope of employment. However, the Rome Statute of the International Criminal Court, which serves as a model for various national universal jurisdiction laws, makes it perfectly clear that these defenses are not available to persons—any persons—charged with "supercrimes," i.e., war crimes, crimes against humanity, genocide, and aggression. Thus, Article 27 provides: "This Statute shall apply equally to all persons without any distinction based on official capacity"; Article 28 deals with the responsibility of commanders and superiors, including crimes of omission; and Article 33 negates the defense of superior orders. At this point realpolitik rears its head, not as a legal defense, but as an element illegitimately overriding legal principles in the interest of diplomacy or "national security."

Even the ICC, the tribunal best placed to initiate action against perpetrators in office is so far proceeding very cautiously. Of the three situations currently on the Chief Prosecutor's docket—Uganda, Democratic Republic of the Congo, and Darfur—the only arrest warrants issued to date are addressed to five commanders of the Liberation Resistance Army in Uganda, i.e., non-official persons.[18] It is possible, however, that once the prosecution completes its investigation of the situation in Darfur, arrest warrants will be issued against members or officials of the Sudanese government.

III. Complementarity: Respect for Sovereignty or Escape Hatch?

Certain words in legal texts are "killer words." Article 2 (4) of the United Nations Charter, the prohibition of aggression, was intended to put an end to war. But the reference to "individual and collective self-defense" in Article 51 has been so tweaked and stretched beyond its original meaning that the core purpose of the United Nations, "to save succeeding generations from the scourge of war," has been all but lost. It is to be hoped that universal jurisdiction will not suffer the same fate because of the words "unwilling or unable" in Article 17 of the Rome

---

[16] See text at note 21 *infra.*

[17] Henry Kissinger was no longer in office when the case was brought, but he was still under the protection of the government of the United States, which appeared in his defense. Michael Townley, a co-defendant of Kissinger, was an agent of the Pinochet government, which was no longer in office at the time of institution of the suit.

[18] See statement by Chief Prosecutor Luis Moreno-Ocampo, October 14, 2005, at http://www.icc-cpi.int/press/pressreleases/113.html.

Statute or interpretations of national universal jurisdiction laws based on Article 17, as happened in the *Rumsfeld* case.

Fortunately, given the relative newness of the Rome Statute and other universal jurisdiction laws, the words "unwilling or unable" still represent nebulous concepts lacking authoritative interpretations. However, certain elements of interpretation can already be derived from the language of Article 17 itself.

In the first place, under Art. 17 (1) (a), unwillingness or inability come into play only once "the case is being investigated or prosecuted by a State, which has jurisdiction over it, unless the State is unwilling or unable genuinely to carry out the investigation or prosecution," or, under Art. 17 (1) (b), once an investigation has been completed but no prosecution has followed. Leaving aside the somewhat puzzling question how a State, which is investigating or has investigated can be said to be unwilling or unable to investigate, it is clear that there is no such thing as unwillingness or inability *ab initio,* as General Prosecutor Kay Nehm seems to have assumed in his *Rumsfeld* decision.

In the second place, Art. 17 (2) lists certain criteria for determining unwillingness, including a purpose to shield "the person concerned" from criminal responsibility, unjustified delay, and lack of independence or impartiality in the procedure. Art. 17 (3) furthermore deals with inability to investigate or prosecute due to the "collapse or unavailability" of the judicial system in the State concerned.

It will be interesting to see how, as the jurisprudence on unwillingness and inability develops, tribunals will determine the criteria enunciated in Art. 17 (2) and (3), including such terms as "genuinely," "unjustified delay," and "independence or impartiality." Presumably the well-developed law of *forum non conveniens* will have something to contribute to the exercise.[19]

IV. What Is To Be Done?

As stated above, a multifaceted approach is required in order to bring the practice of universal jurisdiction in line with its theory. "The 14 Principles on the Effective Exercise of Universal Jurisdiction," proposed by Amnesty International, are a good beginning.[20] Let me here concentrate on Step No. 7: *No political interference.* In the days of the Soviet Union, the reliance of judges on orders from the government or the party was known as "telephone justice." Something similar may be at work in certain dismissals of universal jurisdiction complaints by prosecutors, particularly in high profile cases. A perfect example of this is the dismissal by the German Federal Prosecutor on February 10, 2005, of the complaint filed on November 29, 2004, against Donald Rumsfeld, Secretary of Defense of the United States, and ten other defendants, alleging torture and other war crimes committed

---

[19] For a comment on complementarity with bibliographic footnotes, see http://www.welt-politik.net/print/171.html (in English).

[20] http://web.amnesty.org/library/index/engior530011999?OpenDocument).

by US personnel at Abu Ghraib and elsewhere.[21] The dismissal was based primarily on the prosecutor's finding that the principle of subsidiarity—another word for complementarity—applied because there was no reason to believe that these defendants would not be prosecuted in the United States. This finding, it must be pointed out, was made without referring in any way to a twelve-page affidavit submitted by Professor Scott Horton, who teaches a war crimes course at Columbia University in New York, which explained in great detail why there was not the slightest possibility of seeing these defendants prosecuted in the United States.

This is not, however, a general condition. It is well known, for instance, that the Aznar government in Spain did not look with favor on the Pinochet case initiated by Judge Garzon. Nevertheless, that case went forward and became an inspiration to prosecutors and judges in other countries. But where the political branches do not hesitate to interfere with the judicial ones, civil society should not hesitate to make its views known to the politicians. That, after all, is how democracy is supposed to work. As of this writing, thousands of Cubans and Venezuelans are demanding the extradition to Venezuela from the United States of Luis Posada Carriles, the notorious plane bomber, yet the American public is strangely silent about the apparent division by the American government of terrorists into good terrorists and bad terrorists.[22]

One way to take politics out of the quest for justice is for the victims to become prosecutors in civil cases. The Alien Tort Claims Act,[23] which the Center for Constitutional Rights resuscitated from its 200-year slumber in 1978,[24] has become one of the most successful instruments for exposing torture, disappearance and other grave human rights violations committed outside the United States, through civil suits brought in American courts. There are many advantages for victims or their survivors to proceeding in this way: (1) they can initiate the litigation instead of having to persuade a public prosecutor to do so; (2) once commenced, they can control the litigation through lawyers of their choice; (3) they can introduce all the admissible evidence at their disposal, including that which public prosecutors might be reluctant to use for political reasons; and (4) last, but not least, they can receive compensation for the injury done to them or their murdered relatives. It is somewhat paradoxical that the United States, enemy number one of the International Criminal Court, is also the country whose judiciary—including, as of last year, the Supreme Court[25]—has been most hospitable to the exercise of this kind of self-help universal jurisdiction. It would, in my view, advance the cause of jus-

---

[21] See several relevant documents at http://www.ccr-ny.org/v2/search/results.asp. See also, inter alia, the contributions of W. Kaleck and F. Jessberger in this volume.

[22] In an "Open Letter to the Families of the Victims of 9/11," run as a full page advertisement in the *New York Times* on November 18, 2005, the Committee of Families of the Victims of the Cuban Airliner Bombing in Barbados pointed out that both Orlando Bosch and Luis Posada Carilles, generally believed to be responsible for the airliner bombing, which killed 73 Cuban citizens on October 6, 1976, were currently residing as free men in the United States.

[23] 28 U.S.C. 1350.

[24] In the landmark case *Filartiga v. Pena-Irala*, 630 F.2d 876 (1980).

[25] *Sosa v. Alvarez-Machain*, 542 U.S. 692 (2004).

tice if other countries adopted legislation similar to the Alien Tort Claims Act and its more recent offshoot, the Alien Torture Victims Protection Act.[26]

Another advantage of civil cross-border litigation is that it is frequently the only way to prosecute corporations, which are among the most serious violators of human rights through their activities in developing countries with less-than-democratic regimes. Criminal universal jurisdiction laws do not readily lend themselves to prosecutions against corporations, or, at least, have not done so until now. In the United States, the Center for Constitutional Rights[27], Earthrights International[28] and the International Labor Rights Fund[29] have pioneered this kind of litigation, bringing cases in US courts against multinational corporations engaging in or abetting such crimes as slave labor, torture and execution of labor organizers, and environmental crimes in various countries, including Burma, Nigeria, Colombia, Ecuador, and Turkey. As a result, business organizations have waged a campaign for the repeal of the Alien Tort Claims Act, but without success so far.

V. Conclusion

Even without 9/11, Bali, London, Madrid, and Amman, there was a need for effective mechanisms to enforce international human rights. The "war against terror" and its use to roll back long-standing human rights protections have merely reinforced this need. Universal jurisdiction, which may be viewed as the globalization of human rights, has a crucial role to play in this process. And civil society has a major role to play in protecting and nurturing the principle of universal jurisdiction and its application, or, in a worst case scenario, in saving it from extinction.

---

[26] 28 U.S.C. 1350.
[27] http://www.ccr-ny.org.
[28] http://www.earthrights.org.
[29] http://www.laborrights.org.

On the Aims and Actual Consequences of International Prosecution of Human Rights Crimes

Peer Stolle and Tobias Singelnstein

Three decades ago, scholars in the disciplines of criminology and critical jurisprudence began to look more intensively at how the preventive function of an expanding criminal law remains ineffective, how far it takes one-sided action against only certain forms of deviance and certain strata of the population, and thereby serves the interests of specific social groups. Crimes that failed to be targeted or prosecuted, they pointed out, included in particular so-called macrocriminality, for example, state and war crimes, crimes against humanity, and genocide, as well as forms of "organized crime," white-collar, and environmental crime ("criminality of the powerful").[1] What was seen at the time as proof of criminal law's latent functionality and capacity to serve power, and consequently as an argument for eliminating it, now serves the opposite purpose. On the basis of this critique, statutes and institutions were created on the national and international levels for the

---

[1] This critique was based on the assumption that penology does not predominantly serve to settle societal conflicts, but pursues other aims, in that it repressively enforces the interests of certain powerful societal groups and suppresses the interests of less powerful groups. It was thus regarded as an instrument in the conflict between various social groups and strata. For example, it was pointed out that the criminal code penalizes typical underclass and youth delinquency, whose social ill-effects falls far short of those of the so-called criminality of the powerful, which for a long time has in great part not been prosecutable. Moreover, the criminal code was also said to be discriminatory in its practical application, since it is predominantly youth and members of (ethnic) minorities who are targeted by monitoring agencies, while the prosecution of presumed perpetrators belonging to higher social strata is relatively rare. This critique was the basis of a demand for extensive decriminalization of petty crime, the abolition of the death penalty and prison sentences, and even the abolition of criminal law altogether. See U. Eisenberg, *Kriminologie*, 6th ed. (2005), pp. 71 et seq., 77 et seq., 618; D. Garland, *The Culture of Control* (2001), pp. 55 et seq.; F. Sack, in: F. Sack and R. König (eds.), *Kriminalsoziologie* (1968), pp. 431 et seq.; T. Singelnstein and P. Stolle, *Die Sicherheitsgesellschaft. Soziale Kontrolle im 21. Jahrhundert* (2006), pp. 100 et seq., 104 et seq.; G. B. Vold, T. J. Bernard and J. B. Snipes, *Theoretical Criminology*, 4th ed. (1998), pp. 219 et seq., 260 et seq.

prosecution of macrocriminality respective of international crimes in particular.[2] This expansion of the concept of criminal law was welcomed almost unanimously and possesses a systematic logic. If society in general resorts to criminal law to regulate behavior, there is no justification for limiting intervention to petty and middle-range criminality while exempting especially grave infringements. NGOs, human rights organizations and defense attorneys—precisely the groups that previously tended to doubt the efficacy of criminal law and stressed its negative consequences—now see this kind of criminal prosecution as an opportunity and point to its positive uses.

However, from the perspective of critical jurisprudence, skepticism is warranted, even if we take seriously the problem of so-called impunity in many countries. It is true, on the one hand, that the establishment of constitutional standards as a constraint on power and domination—standards fought for in social struggles—is an important step towards the idea of international enforcement of human rights and is fundamentally to be welcomed. On the other hand, it is obvious that such developments always take place in a context of politics and power.[3] Moreover, criminal law is a highly problematic instrument of state social control. This is true in regard both to its actual effectiveness (see I below) and to the danger of its selective deployment and political use (see II). Finally, one should consider the possible implications on the national level of such an increase in the importance and legitimacy of criminal law and its use in the context of repressive state control (III). This article represents an attempt to apply insights from critical jurisprudence and criminology—predominantly taken from the German debate—to the discussion of international criminal prosecution.

I. Aims and Effects of Punishment

On the theoretical or conceptual level, the questions posed for criminal law include what goals to pursue and whether they are achievable. Although these are fundamental to criminal law, neither the scholarly literature nor case law has conclusively resolved these questions for nascent international criminal law. This is also because there exist extensive differences between the varying national criminal justice systems. However, in some cases international criminal courts came to these questions during sentencing, where retribution, deterrence, reprobation, and rehabilitation were cited as the function of punishment.[4] Various authors have also addressed issues including reconciliation, restoration of peace, victim redress and satisfaction.[5] In the following sections we discuss these goals of punishment from

---

[2]   On the various concepts and their ordering, see U. Eisenberg, *supra* note 1, pp. 194–201.

[3]   On the relation between law and power, including in the context of international criminal law, see M. Maiwald, *Juristen-Zeitung* 2003, pp. 1073 et seq. See also the contribution of J. Arnold in this volume.

[4]   See A. Cassese, *International Criminal Law* (2003), pp. 427 et seq.

[5]   See M. C. Bassiouni, *Introduction to International Criminal Law* (2003), pp. 680 et seq.; K. Ambos, *Internationales Strafrecht* (2006), p. 254.

the German criminal justice system's point of view. While retribution is accorded a very low priority here, punishment is mainly and can only be justified by aims to prevent crimes in the future. In respect thereof the aforementioned aims of international criminal prosecution can in section 1 be divided into general prevention (the effect on the general public) and specific prevention (the effect on the perpetrator). Section 2 then considers the victim's point of view (redress and satisfaction) and criminal law's function in providing reconciliation and restoration of peace.[6]

1. General and Specific Prevention

If we consider first the legitimacy of criminal prosecution of human rights violations with respect to criminal law's aim of general prevention (deterrence, reprobation to boost public confidence in the legal system) and with respect to specific prevention (rehabilitation, incapacitation), we can look to criminological findings. In so doing, we should bear in mind that, as a rule, human rights violations are based on quite different circumstances than "normal" criminality; therefore one must examine the extent to which findings regarding national criminal law practice are applicable. The object of criminal prosecution under consideration here is so-called macrocriminality in the form of international crimes—that are, particularly severe violations of human rights, specifically genocide, war crimes, and crimes against humanity, which have emerged as elements of substantive international criminal law.[7] Thus we are talking about a particular group of offenses generally characterized by a particular context and committed by persons or groups of persons of a particular social status. Especially significant in this regard are national or supranational crises or wars, in which specific societal groups attempt to assert their interests. These groups are frequently located within state leaderships, the military, the police, and other state institutions.[8]

a) Specific Prevention

Against this background, specific prevention has been accorded a relatively subordinate role in international criminal law relative to its position in German criminal law.[9] The significance of incapacitation as *negative* specific prevention lays not so much in imprisoning the perpetrator, as in depriving him of the special social position that permitted the criminal behavior in the first place.

The rehabilitation or correction of the convicted perpetrator (*positive* specific prevention) is considered secondary, since the person concerned is in general held

---

[6] See F. Neubacher, *Kriminologische Grundlagen einer internationalen Strafgerichtsbarkeit* (2005), pp. 422 et seq.; G. Werle, *Völkerstrafrecht* (2003), pp. 35 et seq.

[7] See G. Werle, *supra* note 6, pp. 28 et seq.

[8] On state leaderships as communities of perpetrators, see, for example, U. Eisenberg, *supra* note 1, pp. 941 et seq.; C. Kress, *Neue Zeitschrift für Strafrecht* 2000, p. 617 at pp. 620 et seq.

[9] See C. Möller, *Völkerstrafrecht und Internationaler Strafgerichtshof: kriminologische, straftheoretische und rechtspolitische Aspekte* (2003), pp. 485 et seq.

to be socially integrated, his deeds committed in extraordinary situations that cannot be repeated in this form.[10] These findings are accurate, first of all, in so far as the perpetrators are often (high-ranking) representatives of state institutions who essentially codetermine the norms and values of a society, and consequently the standard for social integration. Moreover, it is in fact a hallmark of various forms of macrocriminality that the perpetrators generally recognize and respect the national legal system, yet nevertheless commit serious breaches of human rights. Thus, if one takes human rights and related international legal agreements as the standard for social integration, we cannot consider protagonists of macrocriminality to be socially integrated. Nevertheless the question arises whether rehabilitation is actually necessary in such cases, since there is often no danger of repetition, as the deeds were part of a conflict that no longer exists. Furthermore, empirical studies have cast grave doubt on the possibility of preventative, effective reeducation through criminal law;[11] so it is doubtful whether criminal law is in any position at all to effect relevant changes in attitude and behavior.[12]

b) Public Confidence in the Legal System

In view of this finding, general prevention takes on a central role in the rationale for criminal law intervention in human rights violations. This is the case, both in relation to its negative variant in the form of deterrence and to its positive variant, defined as public confidence in the legal system.

Positive general prevention proves to be problematic even at the national level, since it is based on a disproportionate and instrumental concept of punishment.[13] It is hardly possible to empirically substantiate the belief that punishment symbolically restores the violated norm and consequently confirms its standing.[14] In addition, the penal objective of positive general prevention cannot simply be translated into terms of international criminal law, since its norms are not as established as other rules of law and are not generally recognized as binding.[15] In fact, it is only recently that the human rights protected by international criminal law have become tentatively established as part of the international legal system and the corresponding understanding of law. They are therefore of little use as a *basis* for criminal law intervention in the context of positive general prevention.

Positive general prevention could indeed also be understood in this context as education through global stigmatization of human rights violations. International

---

[10] See K. Ambos, *Kritische Vierteljahresschrift für Gesetzgebung und Rechtswissenschaft* 1996, p. 355 at p. 366; H. Jäger, *Kritische Vierteljahresschrift für Gesetzgebung und Rechtswissenschaft* 1993, p. 259 at p. 271; F. Neubacher, *supra* note 6, pp. 423 et seq.

[11] For a useful summary, see P.-A. Albrecht, *Kriminologie*, 3rd ed. (2005), pp. 48 et seq.; P. Stolle, *Studentische Zeitschrift für Rechtswissenschaft* 2006, pp. 27 et seq.

[12] Doubting, C. Möller, *supra* note 9, pp. 467 et seq.

[13] See the overview and criticism in H. Koriath, in H. Radtke et al. (eds.), *Muss Strafe sein?* (2004), pp. 49 et seq.

[14] Thus also F. Neubacher, *supra* note 6, p. 425, who, in accord with some others, nevertheless sees positive general prevention as playing a central role.

[15] Thus K. Ambos, *supra* note 10, p. 366.

criminal law would then have the task of demonstratively enhancing human rights through criminal law enforcement, in order to confer on the international legal order the same binding character that obtains in national legal systems.[16] But for this purpose, it would not inevitably be necessary to *punish* the perpetrator, and it is precisely here that the above-mentioned instrumental understanding of punishment emerges. Criminal law would not, then, be a means of guaranteeing an established legal order but would be used to enforce human rights as they are currently being established. But other measures are more significant for this process of establishment.[17] Human rights will not be considered a binding aspect of a legal system as long as states that invoke human rights as a motive for their actions do not themselves consistently observe them.[18] International criminal prosecution cannot substitute for lack of political will. In this light, it seems urgent that, in relation to criminal prosecution of *individuals*, human rights actually be realized on a *political* level. Criminalization of human rights violations could actually work against this, if states hesitate to recognize human rights agreements because they do not want their representatives exposed to the danger of criminal liability for disregarding these rights.[19]

c) General Deterrence

Deterrence as negative general prevention also encounters objections. Even in national criminal law, the concrete threat of punishment has little deterrent effect, and the probability of discovery and punishment hardly more so.[20] In the area of macrocriminality, the latter will increase through enforcement of appropriate criminal prosecution.[21] But it remains to be seen whether this enforcement will in practice lead to an increased risk of punishment and develop a deterrent effect for *all* perpetrators, or to what extent various states and groups of people will be affected to differing degrees, as a result of selective criminalization (see II below). Such doubt appears reasonable, considering that the establishment of the International Criminal Tribunal for the former Yugoslavia (ICTY) in 1993 prevented neither the massacre at Srebrenica and further war crimes in the context of the war in Bosnia, nor the expulsion of the Krajina Serbs and the war in Kosovo.[22]

Furthermore, we should bear in mind that the probability of discovery and punishment as a factor for deterrence is especially significant for crimes that follow a rational cost-benefit analysis on the part of the perpetrator. This is problematic for several reasons regarding forms of macrocriminality, in contrast, e.g., to property

---

[16] Thus K. Ambos and C. Steiner, *Juristische Schulung* 2001, pp. 9, 13; C. Möller, *supra* note 9, pp. 522 et seq.

[17] On the meaning of this process, see K. Ambos and C. Steiner, *supra* note 16, p. 11.

[18] This is not only a question of breaches committed by representatives of such states, but is increasingly also seen as a political strategy in the "war on terror."

[19] Cf. P. Roberts and N. McMillan, *Journal of International Criminal Justice* 2003, p. 315 at p. 324.

[20] P. Stolle, *supra* note 11, pp. 33 et seq.

[21] F. Neubacher, *supra* note 6, p. 424.

[22] G. Werle, *supra* note 6, p. 36, is also skeptical.

crimes.[23] Macrocriminality is largely interpreted as the result of conflicts of values and interests, especially in the form of political conflict. Thus it seems doubtful that the anticipation of possible criminal prosecution weighs more heavily in a cost-benefit-calculation than the achievement of central political interests that are often constitutive of identity.[24] In this context one has also to keep in mind that in such crimes *states and other organizations* follow their interests. That is why most of the motivational elements arise within these organizations themselves but not in their agents. Merely focusing on deterrence of *individuals* has therefore limited effect in avoiding or stopping core crimes.[25]

Additionally, in anticipating a risk of punishment, the development of a corresponding awareness of wrongdoing is important since only someone who believes he is doing wrong expects criminal prosecution. This, however, is exactly what is normally missing in macrocriminality because those involved are convinced of the rightness of their goals and develop corresponding neutralization techniques like denying responsibility, blaming the victim, and rejecting the reality of victimization.[26] This is reinforced by the tendency of protagonist groups in such cases to proceed by means of a division of labor in which no person is alone in undertaking the different steps of a criminal behavior. What is more, these organizations are often pervaded by a rigid system of internal norms, which can take priority in guiding behavior compared to legal norms.[27]

Finally, representatives of state institutions tend toward imitation—a tendency that likewise affects their awareness of wrongdoing.[28] This can be further reinforced if these institutions receive support from other states. Recall, for example the School of the Americas in Fort Benning (USA), which trained numerous future dictators and torturers, especially from Latin America.[29] Another example is the claim of the German Minister of the Interior, Wolfgang Schäuble, that secret service information can be utilized even if it is unclear whether it was obtained through torture in other states.[30] In this context, possible criminal prosecution could become a factor that plays a role in the decision whether to participate in or initiate a human rights violation and could thus narrow the scope of action for potential perpetrators. Whether this factor will in fact be decisive, and thus function as a deterrent, depends essentially on how great the probability of prosecution is estimated to be. If the likelihood of criminal prosecution is based on political con-

---

[23] See P. Roberts and N. McMillan, *supra* note 19, pp. 331 et seq.
[24] See C. F. Stuckenberg, in J. Menzel, T. Pierlings and J. Hoffmann (eds.), *Völkerrechtsprechung* (2005), p. 772; K. Ambos, *supra* note 10, p. 355 at p. 366.
[25] See C. W. Mullins, D. Kauzlarich and D. Rothe, *Critical Criminology* 2004, p. 285 at pp. 286, 300 et seq.
[26] P. Roberts and N. McMillan, *supra* note 19, p. 327. On techniques of neutralization in organizational contexts, see H. Jäger, *Makrokriminalität* (1989), pp. 200 et seq.; R. Hefendehl, *Monatsschrift für Kriminologie und Strafrechtsreform* 2003, pp. 31 et seq.
[27] See also N. Roth-Arriaza, in N. Roth-Arriaza (ed.), *Impunity and Human Rights in International Law and Practice* (1995), pp. 14 et seq.
[28] U. Eisenberg, *supra* note 1, pp. 944 et seq.
[29] On this, see the homepage of "School of the Americas Watch," at http://www.soaw.org.
[30] See *Frankfurter Rundschau*, December 17, 2005.

siderations rather than on neutral, legally established criteria, it will probably fail to function as a deterrent; observance of human rights will then be overshadowed by political factors.

2. Further Aims of Punishment

For the legitimization of criminal prosecution of international crimes, two further aims are mentioned: the settlement of existing conflicts (reconciliation and restoration of peace) and the establishment of justice or of solidarity with the victims (redress and satisfaction). Both are clearly related to positive general prevention.[31] Criminal prosecution, so goes the argument, is necessary in order to restore the destroyed moral order and to deprive the perpetrators of any possibility of justification and neutralization. It is claimed that the question of power can only be definitively settled through criminal prosecution of the (formerly) powerful.

a) Settlement of Conflicts

To settle conflicts, investigation of the events and conditions underlying human rights violations is of central importance.[32] Here it seems questionable whether criminal law is capable of restoring peace and actually preventing subsequent conflicts. It is true that criminal prosecution of serious infractions of human rights can make possible societal acknowledgement of the pain suffered by victims and their families, stigmatize the acts as injustice, and limit the perpetrators' scope of action. Furthermore, naming individual guilt and wrongdoing is important in order to prevent responsibility from disappearing behind social structures and collective contexts.[33] However, this is only possible if a complex web of events is reduced to individually attributable consequences. This procedure is problematic even in general criminal law, since reducing complexity in this way is only an apparent solution to the social conflicts of interests and values that underlie criminal behavior. This is especially reflected in macrocriminality, where a great number of persons, institutions, and actions are normally involved within an extended time period and a complex history of conflict. Because of this, an effective investigation that can serve as the basis for societal debate aimed at long-term restoration of peace can rarely be achieved in the context of criminal prosecution.[34]

Additionally, one-sided criminal prosecution in situations of macrocriminality can worsen the conflicts or may only temporarily suppress them. In this respect, a peace-restoring function is more likely if criminal prosecution is the result of an intrasocietal process than an international or "foreign" act, which in some instances can be perceived as interference and disempowerment, at times even as a

---

[31] F. Neubacher, *supra* note 6, pp. 425 et seq.; G. Werle, *supra* note 6, pp. 28 et seq.

[32] See K. Ambos, *supra* note 10, p. 355 at p. 366.

[33] See C. Möller, *supra* note 9, pp. 521 et seq., 529 et seq.

[34] On this, see H. Jäger, *supra* note 10, pp. 262 et seq. See also M. Kaiafa-Gbandi, in K. Amelung et al. (eds.), *Strafrecht, Biorecht, Rechtsphilosophie* (2003), pp. 199, 215.

new form of colonization. It can thus bring about the opposite of what was intended: solidarity with the alleged perpetrators.[35] This negative effect could in part be seen in the case of the criminal prosecution of human rights violations and war crimes in former Yugoslavia by the ICTY.

b) Protection of the Rights of Victims and Justice

For victims of human rights violations, coping with the consequences, especially traumata, is of central importance. Ignoring their injuries and suffering can worsen these consequences. That is why a transparent, institutionalized, and guaranteed process is necessary whose framework gives victims the possibility of a hearing, and where the deeds are admitted, judged, and condemned as injustice, enabling the victims to work through injuries according to their dignity and personality. A criminal proceeding is one way of carrying out this function.[36] But this aims primarily at fixing individual responsibility and punishment through a strictly formalized procedure. It does not necessarily have to accord with the views of the victims, who are often more interested, at least within the context of general criminal law, in the reparation of damages than in the punishment of the perpetrator.[37] Even in normal criminal proceedings, conflicts among goals often appear, for example, if victims have little input into the judgment or if the strict conditions for conviction are not met and the defendant is acquitted, to the consternation of the victim. This occurs because criminal law reasonably focuses on the perpetrator and the public interest but only in a limited way on the satisfaction of the victim's needs.[38] Experience with the prosecution of East German state criminality, for example, shows that prosecution satisfies the interests of victims in only a limited way.

However, no generalizations can be made in this area. Thus, scholars, human rights organizations, and victim associations often stress that criminal convictions are also at issue—that is, guilty verdicts with tangible consequences and not just publicity or the attribution of responsibility. This position is understandable insofar as criminal law is the strongest legal means available to a state or society in dealing with conflicts, making it reasonable to deploy in massive breaches of the law. Thus, the work of the Truth and Reconciliation Commission of South Africa[39] was indeed very much praised internationally, and its victim orientation widely admired. But especially in South Africa, the resulting exemptions from punishment met with incomprehension.[40] The situation is different in Latin America.

---

[35] Cf. R. Keller, *Golddammer's Archiv für Strafrecht* 2006, p. 25 at p. 32.

[36] Thus F. Neubacher, *supra* note 6, pp. 425 et seq.

[37] See the references in P. Stolle, *supra* note 11, pp. 27 and 41.

[38] D. Frehsee, in B. Schünemann and M. Dubber (eds.), *Die Stellung des Opfers im Strafrechtssystem* (2000), pp. 126 et seq., maintains that meeting the needs of victims is not a function of criminal law.

[39] The Truth and Reconciliation Commission of South Africa enabled the victims to tell their stories publicly for the first time and have them acknowledged by society. Even perpetrators were subpoenaed by the Truth Commission. Admission of guilt was rewarded with exemption from punishment.

[40] See C. Möller, *supra* note 9, pp. 164 et seq.

There the lack of criminal prosecution of human rights violations committed during the military dictatorships created a culture of *impunidad*,[41] which lives on in today's Latin American countries. In this case, criminal prosecution not only has the task of providing justice and restoring the rights of victims, but also of binding the contemporary state security institutions to justice and the law. In this sense, criminal prosecution would be a precondition for building constitutional structures.

With regard to concrete crimes, it is nevertheless doubtful victims would consider formal sanctioning of macrocriminality as just. Actual punishment proportionate to guilt is hardly imaginable in these cases, as long as international criminal law does not apply actual retributive justice. But this would nullify central tenets of at least Germany's criminal law and constitutional state. Thus, the motivation of protecting human rights would itself be extended ad absurdum. A purely repressive procedure for establishing justice carries with it the danger that, under the cloak of justice and in relation to positive general prevention, the absolute penal aims of retribution and atonement would again take pride of place.[42] Therefore, one may ask whether criminal prosecution is fundamentally an appropriate and necessary means of guaranteeing a solution or the settlement of conflicts and protecting the rights of victims. Given the comprehensive and complex character of macrocriminality, both goals presuppose a broad national debate in which the events and their social background are examined. Criminal proceedings can indeed provide impetus for this, and in a culture of *impunidad* it can also be of short- and long-term significance to achieve social stability through criminal convictions. But it remains questionable whether conviction and *punishment* is necessary, or if the public debate and education stimulated by criminal *trials*, along with the delegitimization and loss of power of the defendants, are more significant,[43] as the Pinochet case suggests. On the other hand, criminal prosecution can also hinder societal debate. This effect is possible because criminal law can block possibilities for conflict resolution by putting those involved on the defensive. Furthermore, criminal law is customarily employed by political actors to demonstrate activity and a willingness to act. The goal of its employment, however, is not the initiation and intensification of a social debate, but its termination.[44]

3. Summary

After pure retribution—at least from the German criminal justice system's point of view—can never be reason enough to justify punishment further aims with preventive goals are necessary. However, to recapitulate, it is also appropriate to doubt whether criminal prosecution of international crimes can actually achieve this desired aims and thus contribute to the international enforcement of human

---

[41] On this, it is sufficient to consult K. Ambos, *supra* note 10, pp. 355 et seq.

[42] On this, see T. Singelnstein and P. Stolle, *supra* note 1, pp. 29 et seq.

[43] See also K. Ambos and C. Steiner, *supra* note 16, p. 12.

[44] See P. Roberts and N. McMillan, *supra* note 19, p. 331.

rights. In regard to its deterrence and rehabilitation functions, there is a fundamental question of the efficacy of punishment. For the aims of negative specific prevention, maintaining public confidence in the legal system, the settlement of conflicts, and demonstrating solidarity with the victims, it is possible to imagine international criminal prosecution achieving partial effectiveness. The question therefore arises whether the expectations associated with international criminal law are too high, such that there is danger that they will necessarily be disappointed and thus discredit international criminal prosecution.[45] Concentrating on a criminal law response to serious human rights infractions can also distract from alternatives that possibly may more effectively achieve the intended goals.

II. Selectivity

Nevertheless, if one sees the aims of punishment discussed above as a sufficient conceptual legitimation of the international prosecution of human rights violations, the question arises whether these goals can be reached *in practice*, i.e., whether, going beyond individual cases, conflicts can be settled, justice and support for the victims done, and destroyed social orders restored. It is the character of criminal prosecution as a process of social construction, attribution and selection,[46] in particular, which could prove problematic here. This process of criminalization, which is especially pronounced in international criminal prosecution, could lead, for example, to such prosecution being seen as unjust or as the instrument of powerful (groups of) states.

1. Attribution and Selectivity in the Process of Criminalization

It is a fundamental element of criminological insight that the extent and composition of recorded criminality depends essentially on the effect of criminal prosecution institutions.[47] Empirical investigations have shown that their work is selective; in other words, they do not recognize and/or sanction every breach of norms. Although delinquent behavior is a widespread social reality, only a fraction of it is discovered and very few people are convicted for it. Deviance is accordingly not a specific characteristic of a person, on the basis of which a distinction between criminal and noncriminal can be made, but the result of a process of attribution and criminalization.[48] To be criminal is thus a characteristic attributed to a person externally by the institutions of social control. The choice of who is criminalized and who is not does not occur by accident, but on the basis of criteria that are influenced by power. In general criminal law, this choice is, for example, oriented

---

[45] Thus C. Möller, *supra* note 9, pp. 491 et seq., regarding the deterrence function.
[46] Thereto G. B. Vold, T. J. Bernard and J. B. Snipes, *supra* note 1, pp. 227 et seq.
[47] See, for example, K.-L. Kunz, *Kriminologie*, 3rd ed. (2001), pp. 178 et seq., 243 et seq.
[48] On this, F. Sack, *supra* note 1, pp. 431, 433 and 470; H. Peters, *Kriminologisches Journal* 2000, pp. 256 and 262.

around criteria such as class or family environment and depends on the ability of those involved to define facts and law.[49] Thus one is, for example, more likely to be sanctioned for an infraction of a norm if one is considered to be of a lower class, is young, or is viewed as deviating from the dominant culture. The result of this selective process is the unequal distribution of the label "criminal."

2. Selectivity and International Criminal Prosecution

These insights can also be applied in assessing international criminal prosecution.[50] Selective attribution in the process of criminalization on the nation-state level is dependent on the power of social groups to define, and their resultant hegemony over the processes of law making and prosecution. This power divergence is reflected, on the level of international criminal prosecution, in the relationship between states and their varying levels of influence on the process of criminal prosecution. Thus international criminal prosecution can be seen as an instrument for the exercise of power and the achievement of interests between (groups of) states or, within a state, among the groups contesting state power.[51] The problem becomes clear if one bears in mind that political conflicts generally underlie the relevant forms of macrocriminality. The tool of international criminal law can be deployed in this context to stigmatize one's opponent and achieve one's own interests. Thus, for example, criminal prosecution by the ICTY of Serbian politicians and members of the military also represented an attempt legally to justify the later NATO intervention. By contrast, the refusal of the German Federal Prosecutor to open investigations into the involvement of US Secretary of Defense Donald Rumsfeld and the US military in torture at Abu Ghraib aimed at avoiding such stigmatization. Both decisions are therefore (also) an expression of constellations of political interests. The same goes for attempts to include "terrorism" in the catalogue of crimes subject to international criminal prosecution.

The effect of this power to define situations and the meaning of rules of law is, on the one hand, reinforced by the relevant act's often extreme complexity and by the fluid character of the boundaries between criminal acts and activities that are (still) legal, for example, in wartime.[52] On the other hand, the legal, constitutional and institutional limits to criminal prosecution are far less pronounced on the international level than on the national level and thus more open for influence. Of course, institutions like the ICC are currently emerging that are committed not to the interests of individual states, but to the independence and neutrality of criminal prosecution; and that also represent a distinct improvement over the so-called ad hoc tribunals for Rwanda and former Yugoslavia. Nevertheless, even here it must be assumed that individual states are able, to varying degrees, to influence the

---

[49] F. Sack, *supra* note 1, pp. 469 et seq.

[50] On selectivity in the context of international criminal prosecution, see also H. Jäger, *supra* note 10, pp. 264 et seq.

[51] See P. Roberts and N. McMillan, *supra* note 19, pp. 322 et seq.

[52] U. Eisenberg, *supra* note 1, p. 655.

practice of criminal prosecution in regard to who is prosecuted and for what crimes. This is due, in the case of the ICC, to its dependence on the financing and—because it does not have its own executive—on the cooperation and therefore the good will of member states and other involved countries. Such dependence limits the court's room to maneuver.[53] So is doing, for example, the political and economic pressure the US administration puts on a lot of states and the UN.

In this sense, international criminal prosecution can also be seen as a tool of political power struggles among states.[54] While these states have up to now used political and military means to realize their interests, they now have at their disposal an instrument of international criminal justice. The latter's formal independence and impartiality make it an especially effective means for stigmatizing specific states and opposition groups, all the while giving the impression of neutrality. This effect could be observed in the ICTY, which in its initial phase was clearly constituted so as to attribute sole responsibility for the Yugoslav civil war to the Bosnian Serbs and the Serbian army and state leadership. Selective criminal prosecution oriented according to political criteria is also evident in the practical implementation of the German Code of Crimes against International Law (*Völkerstrafgesetzbuch*): all attempts to bring a case against Donald Rumsfeld et al., Uzbeki Ministers, and the former Chinese party and state leadership have so far foundered due to termination by the Federal Prosecutor.[55]

3. Summary

Just as in the case of national criminal prosecution, international criminal prosecution of human rights violations is selective and determined by considerations of power. Because of this, there is danger that international prosecution will be used principally against less powerful, or *no longer* powerful, states and state actors. The criminal prosecution of international crimes can thus be seen as a domain in which the selectivity and power-related aspect of penal intervention is especially evident. It is true that legal institutions are not subject to external influence to the same degree as political and other state structures. Thus the possibility of criminal prosecution even of representatives of influential states cannot be completely ruled out. However, in practice this will be distinctly more difficult, and the room to maneuver for criminal prosecution institutions is more limited here. Thus there is reason to fear that, due to selective attribution through criminal prosecution, the same types of political interests will prevail as in the past, with the danger that the

---

[53] Cf. C. W. Mullins, D. Kauzlarich and D. Rothe, *supra* note 25, pp. 303 et seq.

[54] See R. Keller, *supra* note 35, pp. 30 et seq.; M. Kaiafa-Gbandi, *supra* note 34, pp. 202 et seq.

[55] See Generalbundesanwalt, decision February 10, 2005, *Juristen-Zeitung* 2005, pp. 311 et seq.; OLG Stuttgart, decision September 13, 2005, *Zeitschrift für internationale Strafrechtsdogmatik* 2006, pp. 143 et seq. as well as the review of this in T. Singelnstein and P. Stolle, *Zeitschrift für internationale Strafrechtsdogmatik* 2006, pp. 118 et seq., available at http://www.zis-online.com.

international criminal justice system will help achieve these interests of the more powerful states.[56]

III. Actual Consequences

Aside from the question whether criminal prosecution of macrocriminality is actually in a position to achieve the goals associated with it, it produces consequences of significance far beyond the realm of human rights crimes—consequences that are relevant to criminal justice as a whole.[57] Criminal law has gained overall legitimacy as an instrument of intervention. At the same time, criminal law is becoming more distant from its constitutional foundations, as it is continually strengthened and broadened. These two consequences play a role principally in Western European and in North American societies. In Latin America, which is dominated by a culture of *impunidad*, criminal law must first be granted a regulatory function.

The prosecution of serious infractions of human rights confers a legitimacy on criminal law that it could never achieve in prosecuting ordinary crime. It is therefore regaining significance as an instrument of social regulation, which has been justifiably contested by social movements and critical scholars. In the wake of this, the notion of victimhood—which no longer functions to protect victims and is now being used as a vehicle for the implementation of repressive criminal law—and the absolute penal aims of retribution and atonement have gained in significance.

At the same time, specific forms of criminality, especially macrocriminality, are used to intensify and broaden repressive social control. This effect, for example, could be observed in the discussion occurring principally in the 1990s, not only in Germany, on white-collar crime and sexual offenses. In the context of a broad social consensus, it was possible to tighten criminal law and criminal procedure, which had effect far beyond this realm and which would not have been possible in the case of other forms of crime that do not provoke such powerful outrage. On the supranational level, this was reinforced by the fact that, following international accords and agreements, criminal law regulations often go beyond national legal systems and not infrequently serve as Trojan horses that erode central legal and constitutional norms: money laundering, international corruption, the "war on drugs," and so-called organized crime are only some examples that illustrate the difficulty of undertaking internationally binding coordination of laws and how easily these accords can be, and are, used to justify a national discussion.[58] Thus "organized crime" and "international terrorism" served as vehicles to justify more intensive punishments and very problematic and highly invasive investiga-

---

[56] Cf. C. W. Mullins, D. Kauzlarich and D. Rothe, *supra* note 25, p. 304.

[57] See S. Quensel, in B. Menzel and K. Ratzke (eds.), *Grenzenlose Konstruktivität? Standortbestimmung und Zukunftsperspektiven konstruktivistischer Theorien abweichenden Verhaltens* (2003), pp. 32 et seq.

[58] On this, see T. Singelnstein and P. Stolle, *supra* note 1, pp. 73 et seq.

tive measures, as for example the European arrest warrant and the EU directive on retention of communications data independent of suspicion.

This development has special relevance in the realm of macrocriminality, since the latter provides the already overburdened concept of criminal law with a nearly insoluble task. On the basis of the specifics of such delinquency (complex successions of events, criminal relevance that is hardly apparent and susceptible to investigation, prudent action by alleged perpetrators, etc.) the instruments of criminal law come up against their limits. Examples are—alongside the above-mentioned investigative measures—questions of responsibility of associations, institutions, and organizations[59] (such as corporate hierarchy); the principle of legal certainty,[60] which prevents the creation of general clauses for socially harmful behavior in the realm of politics and the economy (the possibilities of action there are enormously varied); and the constant transfer of criminal intervention to the sphere of risk prevention.[61] Scientific debates about prosecution of human rights crimes already present such attempts, too.[62]

IV. Conclusion and Alternatives

Is international criminal law a further step toward the international implementation of human rights or is it a new way of implementing political power interests? Between these poles lies the discussion on aims and consequences of criminal prosecution of human rights crimes. Also between these two poles the answer must be sought to the question of the adequacy of criminal law intervention as a tool against breaches of human rights. Increasingly, the debate on alternatives breaks down.

1. Conclusion

There is serious doubt as to whether criminal prosecution of international crimes can actually achieve the aims it pursues. It appears, however, capable of aiding greater implementation of human rights on an international level. To what degree this succeeds will essentially depend on the *practice* of international criminal law. The creation and application of laws are the object and result of political and social conflicts. Thus they are, on the one hand, indeed formed by political interests that have prevailed in these conflicts. On the other hand, law can be understood as

---

[59] For criticism of the German Völkerstrafgesetzbuch, see T. Weigend, in O. Triffterer (ed.), *Gedächtnisschrift für Theo Vogler* (2004), p. 197 at pp. 214 et seq.

[60] On lack of certainty in the German Völkerstrafgesetzbuch, see H. Satzger, *Neue Zeitschrift für Strafrecht* 2002, p. 125 at p. 131.

[61] On the lack of consideration for limiting criminal law precepts in the ICC Statute, see M. Kaiafa-Gbandi, *supra* note 34, pp. 214 et seq.

[62] See, e.g., M. Pawlik, *Zeitschrift für internationale Strafrechtsdogmatik* 2006, p. 274 at p. 291, available at http://www.zis-online.com.

a containment of power and domination. This ambivalence in the law appears precisely and especially at the international level and in the realm of macrocriminality, because for the most part this involves circumstances of great economic and political explosiveness, and the groups of perpetrators in most cases consist of powerful and influential actors. The establishment of criminal prosecution of violations of human rights should therefore be interpreted as a political process for the legal regulation of political activity. Such criminal prosecution—as opposed to any *national* form of criminal prosecution—will encounter greater difficulties in eluding political influence and instead establishing its own rules.

Recognizing this means interpreting international criminal law not as the establishment of the rule of law, but as a constant political struggle, which although it can be influenced, cannot automatically be considered positive. The hope for consistent and independent international criminal prosecution of human rights crimes, which should effect a just and peaceable resolution of conflicts, will (at first) not be fulfilled. The extent, however, to which practice approximates this ideal goal and the extent to which prosecution is deployed as a mere instrument of hegemonic interests depends essentially on the degree to which states and other powerful actors prevail in this conflict or whether a democratization of international trial and decision structures is achieved. The proscription of abuse of power and breaches of human rights by juridical process is not automatic. It depends on who is granted access to the instrument of international criminal prosecution and the purpose for which this instrument is used: for confrontations between states and other powerful actors, or to criticize and limit illegitimate state power. Thus the contradictory relationship between power and law reappears here: law must fall back on power in order to make its implementation possible. At the same time, power uses the law to expand its influence; power thus limits and misuses law.[63] In order to use the law to delegitimize criminal state structures, one must be conscious of this contradictory relationship.

Independently of this, the instrument of criminal law can, through its use in the prosecution of human rights crimes, achieve social legitimacy, which is also reflected on the national level. As a result, the scope of criminal law can undergo further expansion and shift, and constitutional standards will in turn be questioned. Just as in the question of political influence, the issue is not one of startup problems, but of fundamental problems inherent in these instruments of intervention that accompany the positive goals of criminal prosecution. A position in support of the use of criminal law to combat macrocriminality must therefore include an awareness that criminal law is suitable only in limited fashion for the achievement of its recognized aims and that it can, in practice, produce unwanted effects or be misused as an instrument for the achievement of political goals. Moreover, this position must take into account that in the process it becomes increasingly difficult to critique the selective use of criminal law, its increasingly repressive and controlling character, and its expansion and intensification. This erosion of the rule of law and civil rights could otherwise unintentionally counteract the goal of implementation of human rights.

---

[63] See also M. Maiwald, *supra* note 3, p. 1073.

2. Alternatives

In light of these findings, the question arises of how to deal with international criminal prosecution of human rights violations. It would be wrong to assume that criminal law will fulfill the expectations placed on it. Instead, it should be used in the sense that the Enlightenment conceived of it: as a check on state power. In this spirit, international criminal law could serve, on the one hand, as a stage for the denunciation of human rights crimes principally committed by powerful states and influential international actors. On the other hand, a critique of criminal law can be linked to it, since in this area the deficiencies of repressive social control can be clearly understood.

In addition, efforts should be strengthened to move states themselves, and not primarily individuals, to recognize human rights standards, a path that was smoothed by the European Convention on Human Rights, among others, and which is reflected for example in the European Court of Human Rights. These instruments, which often are more effective and generate more concrete consequences for the victims and for society, should be strengthened and augmented.[64] They are meaningful both for the *working through* of human rights crimes, and for the social conflicts and structures that lie behind them,[65] in order to deal with victim powerlessness and traumatization. At the same time, such procedures could serve as institution to pursue a clarification of the events and thereby form a basis for social dialogue—a forum for discussing the crimes, the context in which they arose, the consequences for the victims and society, and possible counterstrategies, rather than remaining at the level of individual attributions of guilt.

---

[64] See also C. W. Mullins, D. Kauzlarich and D. Rothe, *supra* note 25, pp. 301 et seq.
[65] See P. Roberts and N. McMillan, *supra* note 19, pp. 335 et seq.

Part II

Developments in Law and Practice

Prosecuting International Crimes at the National and International Level: Between Justice and Realpolitik

*Kai Ambos**

I. Introduction

The International Criminal Court (ICC) in The Hague is the first permanent, treaty-based international criminal court in the history of mankind. It was established on July 17, 1998, by more than 120 states adopting the so-called Rome Statute of the ICC at the United Nations Diplomatic Conference of Plenipotentiaries on the Establishment of an International Criminal Court. Till March 1, 2006, 100 states ratified and 139 signed the Statute.[1] The Statute entered into force on July 1, 2002, and by February 1, 2006, 1732 "communications" from 103 different countries reporting alleged crimes in 139 countries have been received.[2]

Only in three cases has a formal investigation according to Article 53 of the Statute been opened.[3] Two of these cases (Uganda and Democratic Republic of Congo) have been referred to the Prosecutor by States Parties on the basis of Article 13 (1) (a), 14 ICC Statute, and one (Darfur, Sudan) has been referred by the Security Council on the basis of Article 13 (1) (b).[4] A third state referral by the

---

[*] I thank my research assistant and doctoral candidate Ignaz Stegmiller for his assistance in preparing this paper.

[1] For an updated list of signatures and ratifications, see the official ICC webpage at http://www.icc-cpi.int/asp/statesparties.html; see also http://www.iccnow.org/countryinfo/worldsigsandratifications.html and http://web.amnesty.org/pages/icc-signatures_ratifications-eng. On the historic event of the 100th ratification, see the statements on http://www.iccnow.org/100th/index.html.

[2] See Office of the Prosecutor (OTP), *Update on Communications*, press release of February 10, 2006, http://www.icc-cpi.int/organs/otp/otp_com.html. According to the *Report on Activities of the Court*, as of September 16, 2005 1497 communications were submitted (ICC-ASP 4/16, Assembly of State Parties Fourth Session, p. 7, http://www.icc-cpi.int/library/asp/ICC-ASP-4-16_English.pdf).

[3] See for this and the following information in the OTP press release, *supra* note 2.

[4] Security Council Resolution 1593 (2005), adopted by a vote of 11-0, 4 abstentions (Algeria, Brazil, China, United States).

Central African Republic remains under analysis as well as a situation brought before the Court by a declaration of acceptance of jurisdiction from a Nonstate Party (Ivory Coast) pursuant to Art. 12 (3) ICC Statute. Thus, none of the three investigations currently under way is a *proprio motu* investigation, i.e., in none of these investigations did the Prosecutor act ex officio on the basis of the powers assigned to him by the states parties by way of Article 15, relying on information submitted as "communications" by crime victims (channeled through the UN or other organizations, see Article 13 (1) (c), 15 ICC Statute). We will come back to this question.

II. Initiating an Investigation proprio motu

This brings us to the role of the Prosecutor in the procedural system of the ICC. From the very beginning of the ICC negotiations, the so-called, like-minded states wanted an independent and strong prosecutor, comparable to the prosecutor in national criminal justice systems who—of course!—possesses the power to initiate investigations ex officio (*von Amts wegen*).[5] Clearly, there was strong resistance against such a *proprio motu* power of the prosecutor on the part of major powers, above all, the US, but also China and India. At that time, the Clinton administration was suffering Independent Counsel Kenneth Starr's investigation into the Lewinsky affair and was, therefore, highly sensitive to any independent prosecutor who could unpredictably press charges at any time.

In the light of these conflicting views, the best compromise that could be reached was to provide for an early judicial control of the prosecutorial investigations and this was the origin of the so-called Pre-Trial Chamber, modeled after the French Chambre d'Accusation and the US Grand Jury. This Chamber intervenes at a very early stage in case of a *proprio motu* investigation, namely, if the Prosecutor concludes, "there is a reasonable basis to proceed with an investigation." (Article 15 (3) ICC Statute). This intervention takes place much earlier than in national criminal proceedings, e.g., in the German *Zwischenverfahren*. While this may prompt criticism from a prosecutorial perspective, the alternative to political control of the Prosecutor, for example, by the Security Council (and thereby by the US), was a worse scenario. In the end, the Security Council won a triggering competence (Article 13 (b)) and the right to suspend an investigation or prosecution for renewable 12-month periods (Article 16). Yet, while the momentousness of the occasion may explain the restrictions imposed on the ICC Prosecutor during the pretrial phase it does not explain why the Prosecutor has not invoked his explicit *proprio motu* powers so far.

Despite the previously mentioned, huge number of communications sent to the ICC, not even one has triggered a formal investigation per Article 53 of the Stat-

---

[5] See, e.g., the *Freiburg Declaration on the Position of the Prosecutor of a Permanent International Criminal Court*, in L. Arbour et al. (eds.), *The Prosecutor of a permanent ICC* (2000), pp. 667 et seq. (printed versions in English, French, Spanish and German).

ute. According to a recent information by the Office of the Prosecutor (OTP),[6] 80% of these communications were found to be manifestly outside the jurisdiction of the Court; in 5% of the communications the Court lacked temporal jurisdiction (Art. 11)[7] for events occurring before July 1, 2002, the date the ICC Statute went into effect; in 24% the allegations did not fall within the subject-matter jurisdiction, i.e., they did not refer to genocide, crimes against humanity, or war crimes (Art. 5–8);[8] 13% concerned alleged crimes outside the personal or territorial jurisdiction (Art. 12);[9] and, last but not least, 38% of the communications were manifestly ill-founded, e.g., involving general conspiracy claims without specific details or expressing concerns about local or national politics.

The remaining 20% of communications (346 communications), which, according to the OTP warrant further analysis, were categorized by situation, yet the OTP does not say how many situations were identified in total. Under the title "Analysis of Situation", it only refers to 23 situations, i.e., including those referred via communications, the (three) State referrals, the (one) Security Council referral, and the one ad hoc declaration of a Nonstate Party mentioned above.[10] Thus, it seems as if the OTP reduced the remaining 346 communications to 18 *situations* (23 minus 5). Of the total 23 situations (18 on the basis of Art. 15-defined communications), six have been dismissed; seven are labeled "basic reporting"; and ten are elevated to "intensive analysis".[11] Of these 10 situations, three have led to the initiation of an investigation (DRC, Uganda and Sudan, as mentioned above); two have been dismissed (Iraq and Venezuela)[12]; and five remain under analysis.

---

[6] See *supra* note 2. For the management of referrals and communications in general see OTP, *Paper on some policy issues before the Office of the Prosecutor*, Annex: Referrals and Communications, http://www.icc-cpi.int/library/organs/otp/policy_annex_final_210-404.pdf.

[7] According to Article 11 ICC Statute the "Court has jurisdiction only with respect to crimes committed after the entry into force of this Statute," i.e., after July 1, 2002, or, for a state which acceded to the Statute afterwards, "on the first day of the month after the 60th day following the deposit by such State of its instrument of ratification, acceptance, approval or accession." (Article 11 (2), 126 (2) ICC Statute).

[8] According to Article 5 of the ICC Statute the Court has jurisdiction over the crime of genocide, crimes against humanity, war crimes, and the crime of aggression (the latter being subject to a definition still to be found, para. 2). Thus, "ordinary" crimes like single murder, theft or rape are outside its subject matter jurisdiction. On the crimes see K. Ambos, *Internationales Strafrecht* (2006), § 7, margin notes (mn.) 122 et seq.; id., in AIDP (ed.), *International Criminal Law: Quo vadis? Nouvelles Études Pénales* (2004), pp. 219–282.

[9] Art. 12 (2) limits the (formal) competence of the ICC to the territory of States Parties (subpara. (a)) or to the accused's (correctly: suspect's) state (subpara. (b)).

[10] See *supra* note 4 and text.

[11] The OTP (see *supra* note 2; text with footnotes 5 and 7) distinguishes between "basic reporting" (Phase II-A) and "more thorough and intensive analysis" (Phase II-B and Phase III).

[12] See the decisions published as an annex to OTP, *supra* note 2.

The OTP does not say which five situations these are but it can be inferred from the other pending situations that Central African Republic and Ivory Coast are included. Of the remaining three, one certainly, to the knowledge of this author, involves Colombia; the others, Afghanistan, Burundi, Iraq, or Nigeria.[13] Regarding the relationship between situations that originate from communications—and thus are legally based on the *proprio motu* power of the Prosecutor—and the ones that are based on the other trigger mechanisms provided for by the ICC Statute (State and Security Council referral or declaration of acceptance of jurisdiction), five of these ten situations originate from communications, two of which have been dismissed (Iraq, Venezuela) and three remain under analysis. In other words, while at least some communications (the ones grouped together in these three situations) have made it to the stage of intensive analysis, *none* has reached the stage of an investigation pursuant to Art. 53 of the ICC Statute.

The Court's disregard of the huge number of communications certainly deserves further attention and gives rise to various legal and factual questions whose analysis, however, would go beyond the scope of this paper. It is clear that some call should be made for judicial control or even for intervention by the Pre-Trial Chamber on behalf of the victims who do not see their interests sufficiently taken into account by the OTP. Be that as it may, it is difficult to understand why not even one communication (as part of a situation) initiated a formal investigation. It would certainly improve the image of the OTP and of the Court as a whole if this would happen.

Take, for example, the case of Colombia where in the decades-long conflict between insurgents, official armed forces and paramilitaries, thousands of civilians have been killed, tortured, disappeared, etc.[14] Although Colombia ratified the Statute as late as August 5, 2002, becoming effective on November 1, 2002 (Article 126 (2)), and, that the government suspended for seven years Article 124's provision, which gives the ICC jurisdiction over war crimes (i.e., until October 1, 2009), it would not be too difficult to find crimes against humanity committed after October 2002 on Colombian territory by Colombian nationals. In other words, if the Chief Prosecutor, the Argentinean Luis Moreno Ocampo, were willing to investigate the Colombian situation *proprio motu*, he could certainly do so. So, why has he up to now not done so? The answer to this question is closely linked to *realpolitik*, which returns us to one of the leading themes of our conference.

III. State Cooperation in the Investigative Stage

It is important while talking about realpolitik in international criminal justice to take a look at the ICC cooperation regime on a more technical level. Let me first

---

[13] These were the situations, which were in Phase II (see *supra* note 11) in September 2005 (Interview with Xabier Aguirre, senior case analyst, ICC-OTP, The Hague, September 30, 2005).

[14] See most recently Human Rights Watch, *World Report 2006*, Events of 2005, Colombia, pp. 179–186, http://hrw.org/wr2k6/wr2006.pdf.

make some general remarks about interstate cooperation versus state cooperation with international criminal tribunals before then coming to some practical problems.

1. Enforcement of International Criminal Law, Vertical Cooperation, and Obligation to Cooperate

International Criminal Law (ICL) can be enforced *directly* (direct enforcement model) by international criminal courts or *indirectly* (indirect enforcement model) by national courts.[15] One can only speak of direct enforcement of ICL in a *genuine* sense if the concerned international tribunals have supranational powers to enforce their own rulings and decisions, such as arresting alleged criminals or carrying out investigative procedures on sovereign territory. This can only be envisaged in the case of occupant tribunals such as the ones in Nuremberg and Tokyo as well as the Special Tribunal for Iraq; however, their powers are nonetheless limited to the occupied territory.[16]

As a rule, international tribunals depend on the cooperation with national states, not only for prosecution of international core crimes, but also for the execution of sentences.[17] International tribunals are, thus, to quote Kern's famous metaphor of the international criminal law judicial system, "a head without arms."[18] From this perspective, there is, in the genuine sense mentioned above, no direct implementation of ICL because the organs in charge of direct implementation established by international law depend on the "indirect enforcement model" in order to function properly.[19]

It is thus evident that there must also be precise rules and principles on cooperation between international tribunals and states. In principle, the same rules governing cooperation (extradition, other legal assistance, and assistance in the execution of sentences) apply as in interstate cooperation concerning criminal matters. However, great attention has to be paid to the major differences, which do exist regarding cooperation terminology, prerequisites, and procedures. Concerning the rules on cooperation, it is worth pointing out that the correct term is *vertical cooperation* to describe the relationship between supranational, international organiza-

---

[15] G. Werle, *Principles of International Criminal Law* (2005), mn. 195 et seq.; M. C. Bassiouni, *Introduction to International Criminal Law* (2003), pp. 18 et seq. and 333 et seq.

[16] Cf. A. Ciampi, in A. Cassese, P. Gaeta and J. R. Jones (eds.), *The Rome Statute of the ICC, A Commentary, Vol. 2* (2000), pp. 1711 et seq.

[17] C. Kreß et al., in O. Triffterer (ed.), *Commentary on the Rome Statute of the International Criminal Court* (1999), part 9, mn. 1 et seq.; A. Ciampi, *supra* note 16, pp. 1607 et seq.; B. Swart, in A. Cassese, P. Gaeta and J. R. Jones (eds.), *supra* note 16, pp. 1589 et seq.

[18] E. Kern, *Gerichtsverfassungsrecht* (1965), p. 227 with regard to the relationship between the prosecutor and the police.

[19] Cf. M. C. Bassiouni, *supra* note 15, pp. 18 et seq. and 388 et seq.

tions, and states.[20] Vertical cooperation differs from the *horizontal cooperation* between equal sovereign states,[21] in that there is no general international law-based obligation to cooperate, but, rather, such cooperation depends on the sovereign decision of the state concerned.[22] Interstate cooperation entails many preconditions, which have to be fulfilled, such as the principle of reciprocity and the consideration of certain other obstacles, which jeopardize its efficiency.[23] The goal of an efficient (regional), horizontal, cooperative system should be the reduction of these obstacles.

In a vertical cooperation regime cooperation does not, at least theoretically, depend on the sovereign decision of the states concerned, but these are, as a general rule, obliged to cooperate. Thus, the Ad hoc Tribunals established by the UN Security Council can direct binding requests and orders to the Member States of the UN. Their *duty to cooperate* is required by the Security Council Resolution (Art. 25 UN Statute) that established the Statutes and provided for a duty to cooperate in Art. 29 of the ICTY Statute and Art. 28 of the ICTR Statute.[24] These Statutes themselves do not contain any grounds for refusal of cooperation; equally, national rules and international conventional obligations, which are opposed to the

---

[20] *Prosecutor v. Blaskic*, ICTY Case No. IT-95-14-AR108*bis.*, App. Judgment of October 29, 1997, paras. 47 and 54. More detailed regarding the vertical character of cooperation G. Sluiter, *International criminal adjudication and the collection of evidence* (2002), pp. 82 et seq.; G. Sluiter, in H. Fischer, C. Kreß and S. R. Lüder (eds.), *The Rules of Procedure and Evidence on Cooperation and Enforcement* (2001), pp. 688 et seq.; B. Swart, *supra* note 17, pp. 1592 et seq.; J. Meißner, *Die Zusammenarbeit mit dem Internationalen Strafgerichtshof nach dem Römischen Statut* (2003), pp. 10 et seq. (about cooperation with interstate organizations Art. 87 (6) ICC Statute).

[21] Cf. B. Swart, *supra* note 17, pp. 1590 et seq.; G. Sluiter 2002, *supra* note 20, pp. 81 et seq.; K. Ambos, *Finnish Yearbook of International Law* 1998, pp. 413 et seq.; W. Schomburg and O. Lagodny, *Internationale Rechtshilfe in Strafsachen*, 3rd ed. (1998), introduction, mn. 45–46; J. A. Vervaele and A. Klip, *European cooperation between Tax, Customs and Judicial Authorities* (2002), pp. 35 et seq.; C. Kreß in H. Grützner and P. G. Pötz (eds.), *Internationaler Rechtshilfeverkehr in Strafsachen*, 63. Ergänzungslieferung (2004), preliminary remarks to III 26, mn. 205 et seq.; C. Kreß et al., *supra* note 17, part 9, mn. 3; P. Wilkitzki, *International Criminal Law Review* 2002, p. 198; J. Meißner, *supra* note 20, pp. 10 et seq. and 275 et seq.

[22] K. F. Nagel, *Beweisaufnahme im Ausland* (1988), p. 72; H. Grützner, in M. C. Bassiouni and V. Nanda (eds.), *A Treatise on International Criminal Law* (1973), pp. 234 et seq.; B. Swart, *supra* note 17, pp. 1590 et seq.

[23] Cf. B. Swart, *supra* note 17, pp. 1590 et seq.; M. C. Bassiouni, *supra* note 15, pp. 333 et seq.; G. Sluiter 2002, *supra* note 20, pp. 81 et seq.; J. Meißner, *supra* note 20, pp. 12 et seq.

[24] Cf. A.-L. Chaumette, *International Criminal Law Review* 2004, pp. 357 et seq. Bilateral agreements on cooperation, like the ones between the USA and the ICTY/ICTR, are therefore superfluous since UN Member States only have to establish the prerequisites for cooperation in their domestic law (cf. G. Sluiter 2002, *supra* note 20, pp. 63 et seq.; J. Godinho, *Journal of International Criminal Justice* 2003, pp. 502 et seq.; contra R. Kushen, *Journal of International Criminal Justice* 2003, pp. 517 et seq.).

Statutes, cannot, in principle, be regarded as grounds for refusal.[25] In case of non-compliance with the duty to cooperate, the UN Security Council can impose sanctions on the violating state.[26]

During the negotiations for the ICC Statute, the states, which adopted a rather critical position towards the ICC, pleaded for a cooperation regime based on the traditional horizontal law of mutual assistance, while the like-minded states proposed a new form of cooperation taking into account the sui generis position of the ICC.[27] As a result, the ICC Statute now contains a mixed regime of cooperation that is, on the one hand, less vertical than the one of the Ad hoc Tribunals, but, on the other hand, goes beyond a merely horizontal cooperation.[28] This is because the ICC cooperation regime is based on an international law treaty, which must reconcile the above-mentioned conflicting interests and, to be sure, was not imposed by the UN Security Council. In principle, the *duty to cooperate* provided for in Art. 86 of the ICC Statute first of all presupposes the states' ratification of this treaty or at least a conclusion of an ad hoc agreement according to Art. 87 (5) of the ICC Statute.[29] Therefore, a distinction has to be made between the general duty to cooperate of the *State Parties* and a limited one of *Nonstate Parties.* Furthermore, the duty to cooperate is linked with the investigations of the Prosecutor (*Anklagebehörde*), because it is a prerequisite for the authorization of an investigation by the Pre-Trial Chamber according to Art. 15 (4) or the decision to investigate according to Art. 53 (1) ICC Statute.[30]

There are also a few *grounds for refusal of cooperation* to be considered. For example, the surrender of a person can be postponed if the ICC has not yet made its admissibility decision (Art. 17 (1) (c), Art. 20 (3) ICC Statute), or if a dispute over the case's admissibility pursuant to Art. 18, 19 is pending (Art. 95 ICC Stat-

---

[25] Cf. *Prosecutor v. Blaskic, supra* note 20, paras. 26, 47, 54 and 63; see also Art. 25, 103 UN Statute; C. Kreß, *supra* note 21, III 27, mn. 57; B. Swart, *supra* note 17, pp. 1592 et seq.; A. Ciampi, *supra* note 16, pp. 1610–11; A. Cassese, *International Criminal Law* (2003), pp. 357 et seq.; G. Sluiter 2002, *supra* note 20, pp. 47 et seq., 139 et seq.

[26] *Prosecutor v. Blaskic, supra* note 20, paras. 26–31, 33–37 and ICTY/ICTR rules 7–11, 59 (b) and 61 (e).

[27] For more details on the negotiations, see P. Mochochoko, in R. S. Lee (ed.), *The International Criminal Court* (1999), pp. 305 et seq.; C. Kreß, *European Journal of Crime, Criminal Law and Criminal Justice* 1998, pp. 449 et seq.; C. Kreß et al., *supra* note 17, part 9, mn. 4.

[28] See C. Kreß, *supra* note 21, preliminary remark to III 26, mn. 206 for examples of horizontal and vertical elements; B. Swart, *supra* note 17, pp. 1594 et seq.; C. Kreß et al., *supra* note 17, part 9, mn. 5; K. Ambos, *supra* note 21, pp. 413 et seq.; J. Meißner, *supra* note 20, pp. 275 et seq.; G. Sluiter 2002, *supra* note 20, pp. 82 et seq.; P. Caeiro, in V. Moreira et al. (eds.), *O Tribunal Penal Internacional e a ordem jurídica portuguesa* (2004), pp. 69–157 at p. 70.

[29] Thereto G. Sluiter 2002, *supra* note 20, pp. 68 et seq.; A. Ciampi, *supra* note 16, pp. 1615 et seq.; C. Kreß and K. Prost, in O. Triffterer, *supra* note 17, Art. 87, mn. 18 et seq.; G. Palmisano, in F. Lattanzi and W. A. Schabas (eds.), *Essays on the Rome Statute* (1999), pp. 402 et seq.

[30] OTP, *supra* note 6, p. 10.

ute).[31] Also, the non-compliance regime regarding the duty to cooperate varies for State Parties and Nonstate Parties. In case of a failure to cooperate, the ICC may make a finding to that effect and refer the matter to the Assembly of State Parties or, where the Security Council referred the matter to the Court, to the Security Council (Art. 87 (7) and Art. 112 (2) (f)).[32] In the case of Nonstate Parties, the ICC can also address the matter to the Assembly of States or if need be, to the Security Council, although without a declaratory judicial finding as mentioned above.

2. Cooperation in Practice

If one moves from this theoretical framework to the practical questions involved, the first thing the Prosecutor must know is with whom to cooperate. This question should, among others, be dealt with in *national cooperation laws* of the States Parties but up to now only few of them have implemented such legislation and, basically, only those where the commission of international crimes is not very likely, e.g., the member States of the European Union and Canada.[33] Thus, the Prosecutor, in practice, will be confronted with the situation in which he wants to investigate a certain State but this State does not provide for a proper legal framework regarding cooperation with the ICC. This is the case in all African states where currently investigations are under way, and for this reason the Prosecutor must seek specific separate agreements with these states to define the cooperation rules.

Various practical problems arise independently of the existence of cooperation legislation. A quite telling example refers to the question of transport and movement within the country concerned. While a team of investigators may more or less easily to get from The Hague to the capital of a state under investigation, internal transport must be organized with the help of local authorities in order, for example, to get the necessary authorization to buy or rent a car and travel all over the country. While bureaucratic problems may be overcome with patience and insistence, lack of security for the investigators may completely hinder an investiga-

---

[31] For more examples and references see K. Ambos, *supra* note 8, § 8, mn. 65, 79.

[32] Cf. C. Kreß, in O. Triffterer, *supra* note 17, Art. 86, mn. 1 et seq.; A. Ciampi, *supra* note 16, pp. 1608 et seq.; C. Kreß and K. Prost, *supra* note 29, Art. 87, mn. 32 et seq.; G. Sluiter 2002, *supra* note 20, pp. 67 et seq. Concerning the special position of the Security Council, see G. Palmisano, *supra* note 29, pp. 416 et seq.; P. Gargiulo, in F. Lattanzi and W. A. Schabas (eds.), *supra* note 29, pp. 100 et seq.

[33] Cf. Amnesty International on implementation at http://web.amnesty.org/pages/icc-imple-mentation-eng. According to the report *International Criminal Court: The failure of States to enact effective implementing legislation* (AI Index: IOR 40/019/2004), September 1, 2004, to August 23, 2004 only 36 out of 94 States Parties have enacted legislation implementing *any* of their obligations under the Rome Statute. According to the *ICC Monitor*, Issue 32, May 2006, p. 5, up to January 2006 40 of the 100 State Parties have enacted some form of legislation implementing the Rome Statute. 30 States enacted (substantive) "complementarity legislation" and 32 cooperation legislation. 37 States have some form of "draft complementarity legislation" and 27 "draft cooperation legislation". 33 have no complementarity legislation whatsoever, and 41 lack any form of cooperation legislation.

tion. The Sudanese government, for example, expressed various times its general unwillingness to cooperate with the ICC in the Darfur investigation,[34] and upon the first ICC mission's arrival at the beginning of March, the Minister of Justice made clear that it would not get to Darfur.[35] At the initial stage of the investigation the Sudanese government even threatened the Prosecutor, "If you send an investigation team you may already prepare a second one because the first one will not survive." Thus, it is clear that any investigation of this sort requires military support either by local or multinational peacekeeping forces to overcome the logistical and security problems. At the end of the day, detaining a suspect is a police or military task as the experience in the former Yugoslavia shows.

Against this background, it is understandable that the Prosecutor hesitates to make use of his *proprio motu* powers under Article 13 (c), 15 ICC Statute. While a state referral under Article 13 (a), 14 implies the willingness of the referring state to cooperate—otherwise, it would not make sense for the state to ask the Prosecutor for an investigation—and a Security Council referral under Article 13 (b) is backed by the authority of the Security Council and its powers under chapter VII of the UN Charter,[36] in the case of a *proprio motu* investigation, the Prosecutor is basically acting on its own and can only rely on the support of those who submitted the information within the meaning of Article 15 (2), i.e., the victims themselves or (their) NGOs.

From the perspective of the state concerned, a *proprio motu* investigation will most certainly be regarded as an intrusion into its internal affairs, as an unfriendly act, and the state will do everything possible to frustrate such an investigation. This scenario is also true for Colombia where, on the one hand, as mentioned above, crimes within the jurisdiction of the ICC have been and are being committed but, on the other hand, the government does everything to avoid a formal ICC investigation. Still, for all these important considerations of realpolitik one must not lose sight of the actual objective of the ICC, viz., "to put an end to impunity for the perpetrators" of international (core) crimes (Preamble ICC Statute, para. 5). This ultimate objective can certainly not forever be postponed for reasons of realpolitik. This leads us to the question of how the ICC can—despite the resistance of certain States or governments—ensure a proper investigation.

---

[34] See, for example, http://www.alertnet.org/thenews/newsdesk/MCD344183.htm.

[35] See "ICC delegation to visit Sudan's Darfur," *Sudan Tribune*, February 27, 2006, http://www.sudantribune.com/article.php3?id_article=14271.

[36] In Resolution 1593, *supra* note 4, the Security Council limits the powers of the ICC: "*6. Decides* that nationals, current or former officials or personnel from a contributing State outside Sudan which is not a party to the Rome Statute of the International Criminal Court shall be subject to the exclusive jurisdiction of that contributing State for all alleged acts or omissions arising out of or related to operations in Sudan established or authorized by the Council or the African Union, unless such exclusive jurisdiction has been expressly waived by that contributing State."

IV. Possible Pressure Exercised on States Not Willing to Cooperate

At this point the most important question is what pressure could be exercised on states that are not willing to cooperate with the ICC. First of all, as stated above, an obligation to cooperate only exists with regard to State Parties (Article 86 ICC Statute). Nonstate Parties can only, in the absence of an ad hoc agreement under Article 87 (5) ICC Statute, be obliged to cooperate by a Security Council resolution because of its binding character on all UN member states pursuant to Article 25 UN Charter. In any case, regarding States under an obligation to cooperate, the only legal way to achieve their compliance is to refer the non-cooperation issue—after a statement to that effect by the Court—to the Assembly of State Parties (Article 87 (5) (b), (7), Article 112 (2) (f)). It is then up to the State Parties to decide what measures are adequate to ensure compliance. In case of a Security Council referral, as for example in the Darfur case, the matter can, as mentioned above (III. 1.), also be referred to the Security Council (Article 87 (5) (b), (7)).

While this is certainly the best possible compliance regime within the framework of a treaty-based international criminal court, it shares the problems of any compliance regime in international law. While various theoretical enforcement mechanisms are available, e.g., the use of economic aid inducements and diplomatic economic sanctions, freezing the assets of indicted war criminals, offering individual cash rewards, and, last but not least, the use of military force to effect apprehension,[37] in practice any of these mechanisms proves highly controversial.

Apart from that, the fact that we are dealing with non-cooperation in investigations in crimes committed on the territory or even by the forces of certain Third World states makes things more complicated. Would it really be feasible, for example, for the EU to exercise economic pressure on "unwilling" African States in times of debt reduction and the fight against global poverty? If the EU were to cut down development aid because a state does not cooperate with the ICC, it would come into conflict with its development policy. One might even induce the current US administration into the comfortable position of arguing against the ICC as an antidevelopment Court with the EU only supporting (financially) cooperative States and the US, in contrast, financially benefiting from non-cooperation. These quite superficial considerations show, on the one hand, that economic pressure can be counterproductive, and, on the other hand, that the issue of non-cooperation requires more sophisticated solutions, which certainly are not easy to find.

V. Complementarity and Criminal Justice Systems

According to the principle of complementarity the ICC "complements" the domestic criminal justice systems with regard to the prosecution of genocide, crimes

---

[37] Cf. A. Wartanian, *Georgetown Journal of International Law* 2005, pp. 1302 et seq.; M. P. Scharf, *DePaul Law Review* 2000, pp. 938 et seq.

against humanity, and war crimes. In fact, the ICC steps back if the state, "which has jurisdiction," investigates the crimes seriously and punishes those responsible. Para. 10 of the Preamble outlines this principle and various provisions for the state, the most important of which is Article 17 (see also Articles 1, 18 and 19). The underlying rationale of the principle is that, on the one hand, it is the primary task of states to prosecute international crimes, especially if committed on their territory; on the other hand, an international criminal court, even if willing, will never be able in terms of prosecutorial capacity to substitute for states in this task. The ICC's role, thus, is in principle limited to monitoring or supervising national systems and eventually supporting them in their national prosecutions. This is clearly expressed in the initiative by some states to establish a "justice rapid response capacity" of the ICC in order to help willing but unable states to carry out their own prosecutions.[38] This is, overall, a convincing approach, not only for reasons of realpolitik—the territorial state is "closer" to the facts and the evidence, for example—but also because the ultimate objective of the prosecution of international crimes is not only the prevention of impunity in the concrete cases (the *human rights aspect*), but also the improvement of the criminal justice systems concerned as a whole (the *judicial reform aspect*). In other words, the question of the prosecution of serious human rights violations by the territorial State itself is linked to the question, for example, of judicial reform, rule of law, and better access to justice.

The ultimate goal is to achieve a system governed by the rule of law that provides access for all citizens, independent of their social status. Clearly, this is the broader perspective of governance and judicial reform that encompasses the human rights aspect. Indeed, human rights proceedings should be a vehicle for better judicial systems; the human rights question cannot be limited to international crimes alone. It affects other "normal" cases in all areas of the legal system.

VI. Problems with Universal Jurisdiction and the German Solution

The above-mentioned phrasing, "which has jurisdiction," in Article 17 ICC Statute is very broad. Indeed, taking the wording seriously, any form of jurisdiction, including all forms of extraterritorial jurisdiction and especially universal jurisdiction, is covered. Thus, even a state, which has no genuine link to the situation,

---

[38] See the *Justice Rapid Response Feasibility Study* (October 2005), produced at the request and the support of the governments of Finland, Germany, Liechtenstein, Sweden, Switzerland, and the United Kingdom; see also K. Ambos, *supra* note 8, § 8, mn. 16. In the fifth meeting on Justice Rapid Response (JRR) group the value of JRR as an international cooperation mechanism was emphasized and the following practical steps were introduced: 1. Focal Points, 2. Rosters, 3. Training, 4. Standard operating procedures, 5. Cooperation among interested parties, 6. Ultimate coordination of JRR, 7. Promoting participation (cf. *Chair's Conclusions of the Venice Conference on Justice Rapid Response*, June 15–17, 2006).

could claim jurisdiction on the basis of universal jurisdiction if the crime was an international core crime.[39] As a consequence, this state would have primacy over the ICC with regard to the crime in question. Concretely speaking, in the Pinochet case, where various states, inter alia Spain and Germany, invoked the principle of universal jurisdiction to prosecute Pinochet before their national courts, these States would have primacy over the ICC. This is indeed the interpretation taken by the OTP[40] and by the International Commission of Inquiry on Darfur.[41]

The latter case makes clear that such a broad interpretation of Article 17 ICC Statute may generate counterproductive results. First, it would increase instead of diminish the tensions between states that claim universal jurisdiction in Pinochet-like cases and those which consider the exercise of extraterritorial jurisdiction in such cases as an intervention in internal affairs. Secondly, it would leave the ICC virtually without cases since all the crimes within the subject matter jurisdiction of the ICC fall, *per definitionem*, under universal jurisdiction and could therefore be prosecuted by states instead of the ICC. For these reasons, the official German view is more restrictive with regard to Article 17 ICC Statute, interpreting "which has jurisdiction over it" as referring to the traditional forms of jurisdiction, i.e., jurisdiction based on the principles of territoriality, (active and passive) personality, and the protective principle.[42] The German law implements this approach with a peculiar substantive-procedural combination of norms. The substantive law, i.e., the German Code of International Criminal Law (*Völkerstrafgesetzbuch*, or VStGB)[43], provides in Section 1 for a broad principle of universal jurisdiction stating that:

This Act shall apply to all criminal offences against international law designated under this Act, to serious criminal offences[44] designated therein even when the offence was committed abroad and bears no relation to Germany.

---

[39] See on the rationale and scope of universal jurisdiction K. Ambos, *supra* note 8, § 3, mn. 93 et seq.

[40] See F. de Gurmendi, Chef de Cabinet and Special Advisor to the Prosecutor, interview with the author, The Hague, September 27, 2005.

[41] *Report of the International Commission of Inquiry on Darfur to the United Nations Secretary-General pursuant to Security Council Resolution 1564 of September 18, 2004* (2005), para. 616: "The ICC should defer to national courts other than those of Sudan which genuinely undertake proceedings on the basis of universal jurisdiction"; see also M. Delmas-Marty, *Journal of International Criminal Justice* 2006, p. 6.

[42] On these principles see K. Ambos, *supra* note 8, § 3, mn. 1 et seq.

[43] For a translation in several languages (English, Arabic, Chinese, Spanish, French, Greek, Russian, Portuguese), see http://www.jura.uni-goettingen.de/k.ambos/Forschung/laufende_Projekte_Translation.html.

[44] In German law the term "serious criminal offence" (*Verbrechen*) is used to denote criminal offences (*Straftaten*) that are punishable with not less than one year of imprisonment. Mitigating (and aggravating) circumstances—as regulated for instance in Section 8 Subsection (5)—are to be disregarded in this respect (Section 12 German Criminal Code). As a result, all criminal offences in the VStGB are "serious criminal offences" with the sole exception of the criminal offences in Sections 13 and 14.

This norm is the broadest possible solution and reflects the German view, also held in Rome, that for core crimes such as crimes against humanity, genocide, and war crimes, the principle of universal jurisdiction must apply. However, for practical reasons or, again, realpolitik (inter alia, pressure by the Federal Prosecutor's Office, or *Generalbundesanwaltschaft*), a restriction of this broad substantive principle had to be found and therefore Section 153f of the German Code of Criminal Procedure (*Strafprozessordnung*, or StPO) was created. This complex norm[45] reads as follows:

(1) In the cases referred to under Section 153c Subsection (1), numbers 1 and 2 [extraterritorial crimes], the public prosecution office may dispense with prosecuting an offence punishable pursuant to Sections 6 to 14 of the Code of Crimes against International Law, if the accused is not present in Germany and such presence is not to be anticipated. If in the cases referred to under Section 153c Subsection (1), number 1, the accused is a German, this shall however apply only where the offence is being prosecuted before an international court or by a state on whose territory the offence was committed or whose national was harmed by the offence.

(2) In the cases referred to under Section 153c Subsection (1), numbers 1 and 2, the public prosecution office can, in particular, dispense with prosecuting an offence punishable pursuant to Sections 6 to 14 of the Code of Crimes against International Law, if

1. there is no suspicion of a German having committed such offence,
2. such offence was not committed against a German,
3. no suspect in respect of such offence is residing in Germany and such residence is not to be anticipated and
4. the offence is being prosecuted before an international court or by a State on whose territory the offence was committed, whose national is suspected of its commission or whose national was harmed by the offence.

The same shall apply if a foreigner accused of an offence committed abroad is residing in Germany but the requirements pursuant to the first sentence, numbers 2 and 4, have been fulfilled and transfer to an international court or extradition to the prosecuting State is permissible and is intended.

(3) If in the cases referred to under Subsection (1) or (2) public charges have already been preferred, the public prosecution office may withdraw the charges at any stage of the proceedings and terminate the proceedings.

This norm provides for an exception from the principle of mandatory prosecution, which governs, in principle, German criminal procedure. While the rule of mandatory prosecution is severely weakened, some may even say undermined, by various exceptions (Sections 153, 153a, 153b, 153c, 153d, 153e, 154, 154a StPO), leaving the Prosecutor wide discretion to close or suspend an ongoing investigation, the main difference between these exceptions and the new Section 153f is that the former ones (the traditional exceptions), generally speaking, refer to less important offences but not to the most serious international crimes. Only Section 153c StPO, referred to in para. 1 of Section 153f, refers to any crime "committed abroad," i.e., also covers, in theory, international crimes. Be that as it may, the conceptual problem of Section 153f is that it is difficult to justify an exception

---

[45] For an analysis see K. Ambos, *supra* note 8, § 3, mn. 100; more detailed, id., in *Münchner Kommentar StGB und Nebenstrafrecht, Vol. VI*, § 1 VStGB, mn. 24 et seq. (to be published 2007).

from the principle of mandatory prosecution in cases of international crimes whose prosecution is mandated by international treaty and customary law.[46] In addition, at least according to the dominant view, there is no remedy against the negative prosecutorial decision to abstain from an investigation or stop the investigation. This view has been confirmed by the Stuttgart Court of Appeals (*Oberlandesgericht*)[47] in the Rumsfeld/Abu Ghraib case analyzed in detail in this volume.[48] This restrictive view is difficult to sustain given the broad legal or normative evaluation to be carried out by the Prosecutor when taking a decision under Section 153f StPO. It should, therefore, be possible to submit this legal evaluation to a judicial review.[49]

VII. Conclusion

The paper tried to demonstrate that the prosecution of international crimes at a supranational as well as at a national level encounters several limitations and problems, which in one way or the other can be traced to realpolitik. The ICC is still an institution in the making and cannot do away overnight with the centuries-old problems of impunity for grave human right violations. Too high expectations may prove counterproductive leading to a Court workload, which, ultimately, may lead to its failure. Thus, caution and a dose of realpolitik from some of the non-governmental friends of the court is required. At this moment, the ICC, at least the Office of the Prosecutor, operates with full capacity in its four cases and it is difficult to see how it can take more.[50] While from a purely legal perspective the Prosecutor might be under an obligation to prosecute, *proprio motu*, cases on the basis of Article 13 (c), 15 ICC Statute, the factual situation apparently does not allow for more cases to be investigated and, in any case, a *proprio motu* investigation encounters more problems than investigations on the basis of a state or Security Council referral. Again, while this is a problem of realpolitik and it is therefore difficult to accept for a lawyer, there is no alternative than to take into account the factual limitations, especially of an institution, which is still in the phase of construction and consolidation.

---

[46] See K. Ambos, *Archiv des Völkerrechts* 1999, pp. 318 et seq.; id., *Impunidad y derecho penal internacional*, 2nd ed. (1999), pp. 66 et seq.

[47] Decision of September 13, 2005, published in *Neue Zeitschrift für Strafrecht* 2006, p. 117. For a critical commentary K. Ambos, *Neue Zeitschrift für Strafrecht* 2006, pp. 434 et seq.

[48] See especially the contributions of W. Kaleck and F. Jessberger in this volume.

[49] For a more detailed discussion see K. Ambos, *supra* note 47; id., *supra* note 45, § 1 VStGB, mn. 31.

[50] Thus, Deputy Prosecutor Serge Brammertz stated that all investigators are working in teams spread worldwide and he cannot relinquish one of them to hold lectures in universities or other interested circles (interview with the author, The Hague, September 26, 2005).

Addressing the Relationship between State Immunity and Jus Cogens Norms: A Comparative Assessment

*Lorna McGregor**

In the context of a publication on universal jurisdiction, the issue of state immunity presents an important corollary, as was noted by Judges Higgins et al. in their Separate Opinion in the International Court of Justice Arrest Warrant case who described immunity and jurisdiction as "inextricably linked."[1] In the context of crimes under international law, the issue of state immunity is of topical importance due to a series of recent and ongoing decisions by national courts and the opening for signature of the United Nations Convention on the Jurisdictional Immunities of States and their Property.[2]

However, because the laws on state immunity and *jus cogens* norms developed separately from each other, even now, very little analysis or commentary exists on

---

[*] This paper was significantly informed and developed by the workshop REDRESS organized in conjunction with the Republican Lawyers' Association within the main conference. REDRESS would like to thank all of the participants at the workshop, including, in particular, the panelists Tamsin Allen, Mark Arnold, Christopher Hall, Dr. Maria Gavouneli, Michael Ratner, Sérgio Saba, Jürgen Schneider, and Peter Weiss for their insightful contributions as well as Wolfgang Kaleck and Hannes Honecker for all their help and support. A fuller discussion of the issues raised in this contribution can be found in the report of REDRESS, *Immunity v. Accountability: Considering the Relationship between State Immunity and Accountability for Torture and Other Serious International Crimes* (2005).

[1] Separate Opinion of Judges Higgins, Kooijmans and Buergenthal in the case concerning the *Arrest Warrant of 11 April 2000* (*Democratic Republic of the Congo v. Belgium*), *ICJ Reports* 2002, at para. 3.

[2] General Assembly, Resolution 59/38 United Nations Convention on Jurisdictional Immunities of States and Their Property, A/RES/59/38 (December 16, 2004). Room does not permit for a detailed discussion of the Convention within this article. Please refer to REDRESS' Report, *supra* first note, for a full examination of the potential impact of the Convention on this developing area of law. For further discussion on the human rights implications of this Convention, see C. Hall, *International and Comparative Law Quarterly* 2006, pp. 411–426 and L. McGregor, *International and Comparative Law Quarterly* 2006, pp. 437–446.

how the two relate and the approach of domestic courts has varied significantly. This article provides a comparative analysis of developments at the national level. In particular, the article contrasts the approach of monist and dualist countries. In countries such as Italy and Greece, the courts have found that immunity does not apply in cases of jus cogens norms, although the reasoning advanced therein has differed. On the other hand, dualist states have tended to adopt a formalistic approach to domestic legislation on immunity without adequate examination of how the statutes comport with the requirements of international law and as a result have upheld pleas of immunity, the underlying violations of jus cogens norms notwithstanding.

I. The Concept of Jus Cogens Norms

The concept of jus cogens norms evolved out of the recognition that certain values or interests are common to and affect the international community as a whole,[3] and that the violation of these values or interests threatens peace, security, and world order. Jus cogens norms command a peremptory status under international law. They are superior to other rules of international law because of their very nature and cannot be changed or derogated from through agreement or custom.[4] The

---

[3] In one of the first cases to look at the notion of jus cogens, Judge Schucking, in his dissenting opinion, discussed the possibility of jus cogens norms under international law as norms closely resembling rules of public morality and international public policy in *Oscar Chinn* case, PCIJ, Ser. A/B, no. 63 (1934); see also *South West Africa* case (Second Phase), *ICJ Reports* 1966 (Judge Tanaka, Dissenting); *Military and Paramilitary Activities in and Against Nicaragua* (*Nicaragua v. US*), *ICJ Reports* 1986. For more recent commentary on jus cogens, see A. Orakhelashvili, *European Journal of International Law* 2005, pp. 59–88.

[4] Specifically they cannot be changed by state practice, agreement, unilateral reservation or customary international law. On agreements, Article 53 of the Vienna Convention on the Law of Treaties provides, "A treaty is void if, at the time of its conclusion, it conflicts with a peremptory norm of general international law. For the purposes of the present Convention, a peremptory norm of general international law is a norm accepted and recognized by the international community of States as a whole as a norm from which no derogation is permitted and which can be modified only by a subsequent norm of general international law having the same character." Article 64 continues, "If a new peremptory norm of general international law emerges, any existing treaty which is in conflict with that norm becomes void and terminates."

On unilateral reservation, see UN Human Rights Committee, *General Comment No. 24: Issues Relating to Reservations Made Upon Ratification or Accession to the Covenant or Optional Protocols Thereto, or in Relation to Declarations under Article 41 of the Covenant*, CCPR/C/21/Rev.1/Add.6 (1994), commenting that, "Reservations that offend peremptory norms would not be compatible with the object and purpose of the [International] Covenant [on Civil and Political Rights]" (at para. 8); and "some non-derogable rights, which in any event cannot be reserved because of their status as peremptory norms, are also of this character—the prohibition of torture and arbitrary deprivation of life are examples" (at para. 10).

binding nature of jus cogens norms renders any attempt to derogate from them void ab initio[5]; jus cogens norms can only be modified by new norms of equal status.[6] In contrast to most areas of international law, jus cogens norms have independent validity and status, separate and untouched by the consent and practice of states.[7]

Although considerable debate persists on which norms can be considered to have reached this status, the prohibition of torture has been recognized to constitute a jus cogens norm.[8] This has been confirmed by the International Criminal Tribunal for the former Yugoslavia in the *Furundzija* case, in which it was held that

> because of the importance of the values it protects, [the prohibition of torture] has evolved into a peremptory norm or jus cogens, that is a norm that enjoys a higher rank in the international hierarchy than treaty law and even 'ordinary' customary rules. ... Clearly the jus cogens nature of the prohibition against torture articulates the notion that the prohibition has now become one of the most fundamental standards of the international community. Furthermore, this prohibition is designed to produce a deterrent effect, in that it signals to all members of the international community and the individuals over whom they wield authority that the prohibition of torture is an absolute value from which nobody must deviate.[9]

In almost all of the cases addressing the relationship of state immunity to torture and other serious international crimes, national courts have acknowledged the nature of the underlying crime as a jus cogens norm under international law. However, because the doctrine of jus cogens developed without specific reference to state immunity and its relationship to state immunity still remains unclear,[10] na-

---

[5] On customary international law, see N. G. Onuf and R. K. Birney, *Denver Journal of International Law and Policy* 1974, pp. 187–198 at p. 192; A. Orakhelashvili, *supra* note 3, p. 60; G. A. Christenson, *Virginia Journal of International Law* 1988, pp. 585–648 at p. 594.

[6] *Reservations to the Convention on the Prevention and Punishment of the Crime of Genocide* (ICJ Advisory Opinion of May 28, 1951) held that "the principles underlying the Convention are principles which are recognised by civilised nations as binding on States, even without any conventional obligation."

[7] Of course, in reality, the enforcement of such norms to a large extent still depends on the will of states. This creates a point of conflict; see G. A. Christenson, *supra* note 5, p. 593, discussing, "It is precisely in the areas most vitally important to the power of States that the jus cogens concept should apply. If wider interests and demands clash with the state system, how can any limits beyond those of general international law effectively stem from the community of States as a whole?"

[8] See *Draft Articles on Responsibility of States for Internationally Wrongful Acts*, in *Report of the International Law Commission on the Work of Its Fifty-Third Session*, UN GAOR 56th Sess., Supp. No. 10, UN Doc A/56/10 (2001), available at http://www.un.org/law/ilc/texts/State_responsibility/responsibilityfra.htm.

[9] *Prosecutor v. Furundzija*, ICTY Case No. IT-95-17/1-T, judgment of December 10, 1998, at paras. 153–154.

[10] A. C. Belsky, M. Merva and N. Roht-Arriaza, *California Law Review* 1989, pp. 365–415 at p. 377.

tional courts have differed in their approaches to the significance of the jus cogens status.

II. Judicial Practice on State Immunity versus Jus Cogens

In monist states, the courts of countries such as Italy and Greece have interpreted state immunity and jus cogens norms as rules of international law directly incorporated into domestic law through provisions in their respective constitutions.[11] As two rules of international law, the courts have denied the availability of state immunity in cases involving jus cogens norms due to their peremptory status under international law.

In one of the most recent cases on immunity, Mr. Ferrini brought a civil claim for reparation for his alleged capture and deportation from Italy to Germany by the German military forces during World War II for the purpose of forced labor. He had first attempted to bring a claim for compensation in Germany, but the courts refused his claim on the basis that it did not fall within the terms of the domestic statute that provided the exclusive basis upon which compensation could be sought.[12] In Italy, both the Court of First Instance and the Court of Appeal acknowledged that the violations amounted to war crimes but held that state immunity applied by characterizing Germany's actions as acts of a sovereign nature. The Corte di Cassazione, however, rejected the lower courts' reasoning, to find that immunity does not extend to violations of jus cogens norms, their sovereign nature notwithstanding.[13]

In defining the prohibition of forced labor as a jus cogens norm, the Corte di Cassazione contrasted the progressive movement away from the principle of absolute immunity, which "has become, and continues to become, gradually limited,"[14] to the absolute nature of a jus cogens norm.[15] Although the court conceded that Germany's actions would normally be characterized as "sovereign acts" committed in a time of war and therefore immune, the nature of the underlying violation

---

[11] Article 10 (1) of the Italian Constitution; Article 28 (1) of the Greek Constitution.
[12] Bundesverfassungsgericht, 2 BvR 1379/01, June 28, 2004 (Chamber of the German Constitutional Court).
[13] *Ferrini v. Federal Republic of Germany* (Cass. Sez. Un. 5044/04), reproduced in the original Italian text in *Rivista di diritto internazionale* 2004, p. 539.
[14] Id. at para. 5 (translated in P. De Sena and F. De Vittor, *European Journal of International Law* 2005, pp. 89–112 at p. 94).
[15] In order to answer this question, the Court had to distinguish the facts of the case from two previous decisions of the Italian courts, *Presidenza Consiglio dei ministri e Stati Uniti d'America v. Federazione italiana lavoratori dei trasporti della provincia di Trento and others*, Italian Court of Cassation, judgement no. 530, August 3, 2000, 530/2000, *Rivista di diritto internazionale private e processuale* 2001, at 1019, and *Presidenza Consiglio ministri v. Markovic and others*, order No. 8157, June 5, 2002, *Rivista di diritto internazionale* 2002, at 800, as well as the judgement of the European Court of Human Rights in *McElhinney v. Ireland*, Application No. 31253/96 (2001).

which reached the status of a peremptory norm under international law rendered immunity unavailable.

Thus, the central question for the court was whether "immunity from jurisdiction can exist even in relation to actions which ... take on the gravest connotations, and which figure in customary international law as international crimes, since they undermine universal values which transcend the interest of single States."[16] Due to the peremptory status of the prohibition of forced labor under international law, the court determined that it ranked higher than state immunity as a customary international law rule.[17] The court found that the grant of immunity "would hinder the protection of values whose safeguard is to be considered ... essential to the whole international community."[18] The court employed what is often referred to as the *hierarchy of norms*, or "trumping" argument to deny the applicability of state immunity.

This argument is based on the premise that jus cogens norms displace "lower" rules in the international law hierarchy, such as state immunity. The hierarchy is justified by focusing on the nature of both sets of norms: jus cogens norms enjoy a peremptory status under international law, from which no derogation is permitted; ordinary customary rules like state immunity[19] are not absolute but can be waived by either the foreign state submitting to the jurisdiction of the forum state or denied by the forum state in certain circumstances.[20]

In 2001, the Areios Pagos (Greek Supreme Court) in Prefecture of *Voiotia v. the Federal Republic of Germany*,[21] also found that the Federal Republic of Germany did not enjoy immunity in another civil claim for reparation arising out of jus cogens violations committed during World War II. The court acknowledged the rationale for state immunity as "a consequence of the sovereignty, independence, and equality of states and purports to avoid any interference with international affairs."[22]

However, the Areios Pagos found that immunity did not apply to Germany's actions on two grounds. First, the court found that immunity was not absolute, but rather, under customary international law, only applied to acts of a sovereign or public nature; because Germany's actions were "in breach of rules of peremptory international law, ... they were not acts jure imperii."[23] Second, in contrast to the

---

[16] Judgment, *supra* note 13, at para. 7 (translated in P. De Sena and F. De Vittor, *supra* note 14, p. 98).

[17] Id., at para. 9 (translated in P. De Sena and F. De Vittor, *supra* note 14, p. 101).

[18] Id., at para. 9.2 (translated in P. De Sena and F. De Vittor, *supra* note 14, p. 102).

[19] Since a state can waive immunity (and therefore derogate from it), state immunity cannot enjoy the status of a peremptory norm under international law. The minority European Court of Human Rights judges addressed this issue in *Al-Adsani v. The United Kingdom* (35763/97) (2001) ECHR 752 and is discussed below.

[20] K. Bartsch and B. Elberling, *German Law Journal* 2003, pp. 477–491 at p. 489.

[21] *Prefecture of Voiotia v. Federal Republic of Germany*, Case No. 11/2000, Decision of May 4, 2000, Areios Pagos, translated by M. Gavouneli, *American Journal of International Law* 2001, pp. 198–201.

[22] Id., p. 198.

[23] Id., p. 200 (translating the decision of the court at 15).

Italian Corte di Cassazione, the Areios Pagos found that a breach of a peremptory rule of international law invoked an implied waiver of immunity. The theory of implied waiver is based on the argument that by violating a peremptory norm under international law, the state is understood to have waived any immunity that might otherwise attach by implication.[24]

However, it should be noted that the concept of implied waiver has lost favor in other courts. In the United States, following a seminal article written by three law students,[25] attempts were made to use the explicit provision for implied waiver to address jus cogens violations in 28 U.S.C. Sec. 1605 of the United States' FSIA, which states that

(a) a foreign state shall not be immune from the jurisdiction of courts of the United States or of the States in any case
(1) in which the foreign state has waived its immunity either explicitly or by implication, notwithstanding any withdrawal of the waiver which the foreign state may purport to effect except in accordance with the terms of the waiver.

In the first case to address the issue, the District Court in Siderman de Blake found that Argentina had waived its immunity by implication. The Court of Appeal for the Ninth Circuit then reversed the District Court's judgment on the basis of the terms of the domestic statute on immunity. However, the Court of Appeal highlighted the inconsistency of the national legislation with international law by stating that under international law, the peremptory status of jus cogens norms would render immunity inapplicable.[26]

In the later case of *Princz v. Federal Republic of Germany*,[27] Mr. Princz, a United States citizen who was sent with his family to a concentration camp in Czechoslovakia during World War II, argued that an exception to state immunity applied for violations of the law of nations by virtue of the implied waiver clause. Mr. Princz argued that the German state had been "on notice" of its obligations under international law and thus indicated its amenability to suit. Again, the District Court denied the availability of state immunity but the Court of Appeal reversed. It found that jus cogens violations alone do not satisfy the implied waiver exception: "An implied waiver depends upon the foreign government's having at

---

[24] R. O'Keefe, *Cambridge Yearbook of European Legal Studies* 1999, pp. 507–520 at p. 512, discusses the implied waiver theory with regard to the immunities of individual officials in cases involving allegations of international crimes: "It is relevant to note that all conventions recognising or creating an international crime of universal jurisdiction make this jurisdiction *mandatory*—that is, they impose on states parties the obligation to try or extradite (*aut dedere aut judicare*) any offender over whom they have custody. In other words, states parties to these conventions clearly foresee the exercise by foreign criminal courts of universal jurisdiction over offenders" (at pp. 517–518).

[25] See A. C. Belsky, M. Merva, and N. Roht-Arriaza, *supra* note 10, proposing a theory of implied waiver for jus cogens violations, which was later cited in *Princz v. Federal Republic of Germany*, 26 F.3d 1166 (DC Cir. 1994), at 58.

[26] *Siderman de Blake v. the Republic of Argentina*, 965 F.2d 688 (9th Cir. 1992) at 718.

[27] *Princz v. Federal Republic of Germany, supra* note 25.

some point indicated its amenability to suit."[28] In Ferrini, the Italian Corte di Cassazione also rejected the doctrine of implied waiver. The court commented that "a waiver cannot … be envisaged in the abstract, but only encountered in the concrete."[29]

The uncertainty over the current status of the implied waiver doctrine and the divergence in reasoning notwithstanding, the approach of the Italian and Greek Supreme Courts undermines the arguments of some commentators that jus cogens norms simply constitute "symbolic principles"[30] or "signify only the existence of a right rather than a binding legal obligation."[31] Rather, the peremptory status of jus cogens norms under international law requires that they be made practical and effective. However, because much of the judicial and academic analysis on jus cogens norms has so far focused on the identification of jus cogens norms, very little attention has been paid to the implications and consequences of the achievement of a peremptory status under international law. The Vienna Convention on the Law of Treaties provides little guidance in this respect because its sole concentration was on the impact of jus cogens norms on treaties and as such, cannot have been expected to address wider aspects of international law.[32] Judicial opinion, such as the minority in *Al-Adsani v. The United Kingdom* before the European Court of Human Rights, also does not assist since the judges simply pronounced upon the peremptory status of the prohibition of torture without, as one commen-

---

[28] Id., at 1174. However, Judge Wald, in her dissent (at 1182), argued that the implied waiver exception applied to jus cogens norms "because the Nuremberg Charter's definition of *crimes against humanity* includes what are now termed jus cogens norms, a state is never entitled to immunity for any act that contravenes a jus cogens norm, regardless of where or against whom the act was perpetrated. The rise of jus cogens norms limits state sovereignty 'in the sense that the *general will* of the international community of states and other actors will take precedence over the individual wills of states to order their relations.'" (quoting M. E. Turpel and P. Sands, *Connecticut Journal of International Law* 1988, p. 365). More recently, the District Court applied the Court of Appeal's reasoning in *Princz* to find that Japan enjoyed immunity in a civil claim for reparation brought for the sexual enslavement of the "Comfort Women" during World War II. The court found that a violation of a jus cogens norm does not constitute an implicit waiver and rejected the argument that the enslavement of women for the purpose of rendering sexual services met the requirements of the commercial activity exception, *Hwang Geum Joo et al. v. Japan* (D.C.C.C., June 27, 2003). The Court of Appeal for the Seventh Circuit reached a similar decision in *Wei Ye v. Jiang Zemin and Falun Gong Control Office*, 383 F. 3d 620 (7th Cir. 2004) at para. 4 (citing *Sampson v. Federal Republic of Germany*, 250 F. 3d 1145 (7th Cir. 2001) at pp. 1149–1150).

[29] *Ferrini v. Germany, supra* note 13, at para. 8.2 (translated in P. De Sena and F. De Vittor, *supra* note 14, pp. 101–102; emphasis in translation and original).

[30] N. G. Onuf and R. K. Birney, *supra* note 5, pp. 190 and 196; see G. A. Christenson, *supra* note 5, pp. 589–591.

[31] M.C. Bassiouni, *Law and Contemporary Problems* 1996, pp. 63–74 at p. 65.

[32] N. G. Onuf and R. K. Birney, *supra* note 5, p. 187, discuss "the inquiring into the relationship between peremptory norms and the sources and functions of international law has been virtually non-existent".

tator puts it, "telling us what else, apart from acts of torture and agreements not to commit torture, the prohibition actually proscribes or demands."[33]

However, the ICTY in Furundzija made clear that the jus cogens norm of the prohibition of torture entails more than simply "delegitimi[zing] any legislative, administrative or judicial act authorizing torture."[34] The Tribunal found that

it would seem that one of the consequences of the jus cogens character bestowed by the international community upon the prohibition of torture is that every State is entitled to investigate, prosecute, and punish or extradite individuals accused of torture who are present in a territory under its jurisdiction. Indeed, it would be inconsistent on the one hand to prohibit torture to such an extent as to restrict the normally unfettered treaty making powers of sovereign States, and on the other hand bar States from prosecuting and punishing those torturers who have engaged in this odious practice abroad. ... It would seem that other consequences include the fact that the torture may not be covered by a statute of limitations and must not be excluded from extradition under any political offence exemption.

Although this case concerned criminal proceedings against an individual, the tribunal's discussion highlights that consequences flow from the peremptory status of a jus cogens norm in order to make it practical and effective. This is supported by a number of commentators, such as Bartsch and Elberling who argue that "every jus cogens rule contains or presupposes a procedural rule, which guarantees its judicial enforcement."[35] Furthermore, Bassiouni goes so far as to suggest that

[legal] obligations which arise from the higher status of such crimes include the duty to prosecute or extradite, the non-applicability of statutes of limitations for such crimes, the non-applicability of any immunities up to and including Heads of State, the non-applicability of the defense of ‚obedience to superior orders' ... the universal application of these obligations whether in time of peace or war, their non-derogation under ‚states of emergency,' and universal jurisdiction over perpetrators of such crimes.[36]

On states specifically, the International Law Commission in the commentary to the Draft Articles on State Responsibility points out that "it is necessary for the Articles to reflect that there are certain consequences flowing from the basic concepts of peremptory norms of general international law and obligations to the international community as a whole within the field of State responsibility."[37] Article 41 of the Draft Articles imposes a positive duty on states to "cooperate to bring to an end through lawful means any serious breach." The Commentaries note that

---

[33] E. Voyiakis, *International and Comparative Law Quarterly* 2003, pp. 297–332 at pp. 322–323.

[34] *Furundzija, supra* note 9, at paras. 155–157.

[35] K. Bartsch and B. Elberling, *supra* note 20, p. 20.

[36] M. C. Bassiouni, *supra* note 31, p. 63.

[37] *Commentaries to the Draft Articles on the Responsibility of States for International Wrongful Acts, Report of the International Law Commission on the work of its Fifty-Third session*; Official Records of the General Assembly, Fifty-sixth session, Supplement No. 10 (A/56/10) (November 2001) at Chapter II (7) at 281; it should be noted that Chapter III addresses what the International Law Commission refers to as "serious breaches of obligations arising under peremptory norms" defined under Article 40 (2) as involving "a gross or systematic failure by the responsible state to fulfil the obligation."

a range of ways in which to bring to an end the violation may be available, and as a result, the Draft Articles do not prescribe the means[38] but lay out the obligations on the part of the state primarily responsible as: "to cease the wrongful act, to continue performance and, if appropriate, to give guarantees and assurances of non-repetition, … and entails a duty to make reparation."[39]

Some commentators have argued that state immunity does not impact upon jus cogens norms, such as the prohibition of torture, because state immunity, as a procedural rule, cannot interact with a substantive rule such as a jus cogens norm. As a result, they argue that the underlying responsibility of the state is not removed. Rather, procedural rules only determine when and where a claim is heard.[40] For example, in the Arrest Warrant case, the International Court of Justice found that the foreign minister of the Democratic Republic of Congo (DRC) enjoyed immunity from the jurisdiction of foreign courts for so long as he remained in office (when a claim is heard) but in the meantime could be prosecuted before the courts of the DRC or before an international forum (where a claim is heard).[41] However, the available alternative forums must not be theoretical or illusory but practical and effective. Theoretically, the courts of the state in which the violation took place should be available; states can waive their immunity before foreign courts, and states can bring cases against the violating state before an international forum. In practice, however, the courts of the state in which the crimes took place are very often unavailable for a variety of practical, political, and legal reasons; states do not waive their immunity in cases concerning serious international crimes; the concept of *implied waiver* has faced many challenges in domestic courts; states have rarely brought cases against offending states before an international forum for crimes under international law; and individuals can only access a limited number of forums at the international level. As a result, there may be no alternative forum before which to bring a claim against the state primarily responsible.

---

[38] Id., at 286–287.

[39] Id., at 291; see also *The Legal Consequences of the Construction of a Wall in the Occupied Palestinian Territories*, ICJ Advisory Opinion, 2004, para. 159.

[40] See H. Fox QC, *The Law of State Immunity* (2002), p. 525, arguing that "state immunity is a procedural rule going to the jurisdiction of a national court. It does not go to substantive law; it does not contradict a prohibition contained in a jus cogens norm but merely diverts any breach of it to a different method of settlement. Arguably, then, there is no substantive content in the procedural plea of State immunity upon which a jus cogens norm can bite." See also A. Zimmerman, *Michigan Journal of International Law* 1994/ 1995, pp. 433–440 at p. 438, arguing that "it seems to be more appropriate to consider both issues as involving two different sets of rules which do not interact with each other."

[41] Case concerning the *Arrest Warrant of April 11, 2000 (Democratic Repubic of Congo v. Belgium)*, *supra note* 1, paras. 60–61; see also A. Orakhelashvili, *German Yearbook of International Law* 2002, pp. 227–267 at p. 227.

III. Why the Approach of the Courts of Dualist States Must Be Brought into Compliance with International Law

In dualist states such as Canada, the United Kingdom and the United States, international law is not directly incorporated into domestic law. Because all three states have domestic legislation on state immunity, the courts have respectively found immunity to be available in cases concerning jus cogens norms. The judgments have focused on the comprehensiveness of the domestic statutes, despite the courts' acknowledgment of the peremptory status of the jus cogens norms.

1. Canada

In *Bouzari v. the Islamic Republic of Iran*, Mr. Bouzari, an Iranian citizen, brought civil proceedings against the Islamic Republic of Iran. He alleges that following his refusal to accept the assistance of the then Iranian president for a commission of $50m while working on an oil and gas project in the Persian Gulf, he was tortured in state prison by methods such as fake executions, beatings with cables, and being hung by his shoulders.

Acknowledging the existence of the Canadian State Immunity Act 1985 and its provision for a general rule of immunity, Mr. Bouzari argued that the case fell within one of the three enumerated exceptions or, in the alternative, that a "further exception should be read into the Act to permit a civil action for damages for torture against a foreign state."[42] However, the Ontario Court of Appeal found no appropriate exception to apply to Mr. Bouzari's case. It found that section 18, which excludes criminal cases from the reach of the State Immunity Act, did not apply because the mere seeking of punitive damages does not make the claim criminal.[43] The commercial exception did not apply under section 6 because, although the purpose of the torture may have been for commercial gain, the applicable test focuses on the nature of the act which was in tort.[44] The tort exception also did not apply because the injury took place outside the territory of Canada, the plaintiff's continuing posttraumatic stress disorder notwithstanding.[45] The court also held that an implied human rights exception to state immunity did not exist, despite its recognition of the peremptory status of the prohibition of torture under international law.

On the basis of a comparative study, the court argued that no evidence exists in state practice to demonstrate that the violation of a jus cogens norm means that state immunity does not apply.[46] Further, the court found that even if Canada's international obligations required the provision of a civil remedy for torture committed extraterritorially—which it found they did not—its domestic law would still

---

[42] *Bouzari v. Islamic Republic of Iran*, Ont. C.A. (2004).
[43] Id., at para. 44.
[44] Id., at paras. 48–55.
[45] Id., at paras. 46–47.
[46] Id., at para. 88 (citing the lower court's decision at para. 63).

take precedence in cases of inconsistency. Here, the court argued, the State Immunity Act deals with the issue comprehensively and as it does not provide for a human rights exception and no other enumerated exceptions apply, the general rule of state immunity applies.[47]

Mr. Bouzari was subsequently denied leave to appeal to the Supreme Court of Canada. However, as discussed below, the Committee against Torture found in its consideration of Canada's state party report that the failure of Canada to provide a civil remedy to all torture survivors did not comply with its obligations under the Convention against Torture. Mr. Bouzari has now lodged a new civil claim in Ontario against the individuals allegedly responsible for his torture. The suit names Akbar Hashemi Rafsanjani (the former President of Iran between 1989 and 1998), his second eldest son, a former prosecutor, and four intelligence agents.[48]

2. The United Kingdom

In the United Kingdom, the issue of whether a human rights exception applies to state immunity has been addressed in two cases.

In *Al-Adsani v. Kuwait*,[49] the plaintiff, Mr. Al-Adsani, a dual national of the United Kingdom and Kuwait, brought a civil claim before the English courts against individual officials and the state of Kuwait for his alleged torture in the Kuwaiti State Security Prison through methods such as holding him underwater in a pool full of corpses and putting him in a room with mattresses doused in petrol and set alight. His claim against the Kuwaiti State was based on the doctrine of vicarious liability, the characterization of which the Court of Appeal accepted and a default judgment was entered against the Sheikh.

However, the Court of Appeal held that the state of Kuwait was entitled to immunity even in a case involving allegations of torture on the basis of the State Immunity Act 1978, which it referred to as a "comprehensive code." It found that any exception to the general provision of immunity must be enumerated within the Act itself and because the alleged torture took place in Kuwait, it did not fall under the exception of section 5, which provides that death or personal injury must be caused by an act or omission within the United Kingdom. Although the court conceded that torture, as "a violation of a fundamental human right, it is a crime and a tort for which the victim should be compensated," it rejected the argument put forward by Mr. Al-Adsani that the jus cogens status of torture resulted in an implied exception to the State Immunity Act and that immunity would only be provided where the state acted within the Law of Nations. The court also referred to the "practical consequences of the Plaintiff's submission," citing the difficulty the court would face in attempting to assess the genuineness of allegations of torture

---

[47] Id., at para. 67.
[48] Filed in the Superior Court of Justice in Toronto on May 30, 2005; see *Toronto Star*, June 15, 2005.
[49] *Al-Adsani v. Government of Kuwait and Others*, CA 12 March 1996; 107 ILR 536.

made by asylum seekers and refugees coming to the United Kingdom. The House of Lords refused to grant Mr. Al-Adsani permission to appeal.[50]

Mr. Al-Adsani then brought a case before the European Court of Human Rights (ECtHR). In a judgment of 9-8, the court reached the same result as the English Court of Appeal.[51] The majority first noted the importance of the prohibition of torture, which had reached the level of a peremptory norm, under international law. It pointed out that

> the existence of this corpus of general and treaty rules proscribing torture shows that the international community, aware of the importance of outlawing this heinous phenomenon, has decided to suppress any manifestation of torture by operating both at the interstate level and at the level of individuals. No legal loopholes have been left.[52]

Yet, it failed to conduct a detailed analysis of the significance of the jus cogens nature of torture. Rather, the majority simply upheld the English Court of Appeal's decision to grant Kuwait immunity, with blanket effect.[53] In addition to the Pinochet judgment, an amendment to the Foreign Sovereign Immunities Act (FSIA) in the United States (that allows suits to be brought against states designated by the State Department as state sponsors of terror[54]) was also deemed insufficient to demonstrate a crystallization of a shift in international law to mean that immunity no longer applied in cases of torture and other serious crimes.[55] The court reasoned that the very need for the FSIA amendment at all served to demonstrate that, as a general rule of international law, state immunity can be claimed even in respect of violations of jus cogens norms such as officially-sanctioned torture.[56]

In addressing this conflict, the minority of the court found that it was widely accepted that state immunity did not belong to the category of peremptory norms, as evidenced by the fact that states have on occasion chosen to waive their right to immunity.[57] As a result, should the prohibition on torture come into conflict with a claim of state immunity, it found that, "the procedural bar of State immunity is automatically lifted, because those rules, as they conflict with a hierarchically higher rule, do not produce any legal effect."[58]

---

[50] October 27, 1996.

[51] *Al-Adsani v. The United Kingdom, supra* note 19.

[52] *Al-Adsani v. The United Kingdom, supra* note 19, at para. 30 (citing *Furundzija, supra* note 9, at para. 146).

[53] *Al-Adsani v. Government of Kuwait and Others, supra* note 49.

[54] 28 U.S.C. 1605 (a) (7).

[55] *Al-Adsani v. The United Kingdom, supra* note 19, at para. 24.

[56] Id., at para. 64.

[57] But see L. Caplan, *American Journal of International Law* 2003, pp. 741–781 at p. 771, arguing that "a presumption should be made against the availability of state immunity because state immunity is an exception to the jurisdictional authority of the forum state that would otherwise exist." However, he argues that, ironically, those in support of the normative hierarchy theory presume that there is an inherent right to state immunity.

[58] Joint Dissenting Opinion of Judges Rozakis et al., *Al-Adsani v. The United Kingdom, supra* note 19, at para. 3.

The issue of state immunity did not end with the ECtHR's decision in Al-Adsani. In *Ron Jones and Ors. v. Saudi Arabia*,[59] the claims of three British citizens and one dual national who allege that they were tortured in Saudi Arabia were joined. Mr. Jones initiated civil proceedings against the individuals allegedly responsible for the torture and the Kingdom of Saudi Arabia itself. The other three claimants brought civil proceedings against the named Saudi officials only. The Court of Appeal dismissed the claim against the Kingdom of Saudi Arabia on the basis of state immunity. The court referred to the Al-Adsani judgments before the Court of Appeal and the ECtHR and the subsequent application of the ECtHR's decision in Al-Adsani to the Bouzari case in Canada to find that although "international law is in the course of continuing development,"[60] "as of yet, no evidence exists to show that the peremptory status of jus cogens norms means that immunity should not apply."[61] In addressing Article 14 (1) of the United Nations Convention Against Torture, however, the court found that both the individual and the perpetrating state should be held responsible for the act of torture, but questioned whether this resulted in an obligation upon the forum state to hold the foreign state responsible. However, the court did deny the individual officials the protection of immunity. The appeal and cross-appeal to the House of Lords is scheduled to be heard in April 2006.

3. United States

Although the earlier case of *Von Dardel v. Union of Soviet Socialist Republics* found that immunity does not apply "where the foreign state defendant has acted in clear violation of international law,"[62] the United States Supreme Court in Amerada Hess[63] held that the FSIA provides the exclusive basis for jurisdiction; any exceptions to the general rule of immunity had to fall within those enumerated under the Statute. The approach adopted in Amerada Hess was upheld in Siderman de Blake, where the Court of Appeal held that

> we do not write on a clean slate. We deal not only with customary international law but with an affirmative Act of Congress, the FSIA. ... The Court [in Amerada Hess] was so emphatic in its pronouncement, "that immunity is granted in those cases involving alleged violations of international law that do not come within one of the FSIA's exceptions" ...that we conclude that if violations of jus cogens committed outside the United States are to be exceptions to immunity, Congress must make them so.[64]

The student note in the California Law Review (discussed above in the section on implied waiver), accepted the comprehensiveness of the FSIA but argued that

---

[59] *Jones v. Ministry of Interior Al-Mamlaka Al-Arabiya (The Kingdom of Saudi); Mitchell and others v. Al-Dali* (2004) All ER (D) 418 (Oct).

[60] Id., para. 16.

[61] Id., para. 17.

[62] *Von Dardel v. Union of Soviet Socialist Republics*, 623 F. Supp. (D.C.D.C. 1985) at 246.

[63] *Argentine Republic v. Amerada Hess Shipping Corp.*, 109 S Ct. 683 (1989).

[64] *Siderman, supra* note 26, at 718–719.

within its terms, developments in international law could be taken into account through the *implied waiver exception.*

Statutory codifications of international law doctrines should leave room for developments in international law. The concept of sovereign power is constantly evolving, as demonstrated by the substantial limitations placed on this power since World War II. To freeze the development of sovereign immunity law at one point in time forecloses the responsiveness of U.S. law to further evolutions in the scope of sovereign power.[65]

However, as discussed, the District Court in *Princz v. Germany*, rejected this argument. Similarly, the terms of the FSIA have generally suppressed any attempts to use the "trumping" argument.[66]

The common thread to the approach in Canada, the United Kingdom, and the United States is the comprehensiveness with which the domestic statutes on immunity are treated. The courts of all three countries have refrained from analyzing how jus cogens norms impact upon state immunity because the respective domestic legislation does not expressly address the issue. However, under international law, the "comprehensiveness" or clarity of the terms of domestic law provides no basis or justification for the failure to take international law into account.[67] As a result, even in dualist countries, courts must analyze how jus cogens norms relate to state immunity, instead of simply acknowledging that the prohibition of torture, for example, constitutes a jus cogens norm, and then pointing to the comprehensiveness or exclusivity of the state immunity legislation as the reason for failing to conduct a closer investigation and resolution between the two issues.

IV. Attempts to Distinguish between the Availability of Immunity on the Basis of the Type of Proceeding, Civil or Criminal

Despite the fact that both Prefecture of Voiotia and Ferrini concerned civil proceedings, the courts of dualist countries such as the United Kingdom and Canada

---

[65] A. C. Belsky, M. Merva and N. Roht-Arriaza, *supra* note 10, pp. 397–398.

[66] *Chuidian v. Philippine National Bank*, 734 F. Supp. 415 (DC 1990); *Boshnjaku v. Federal Republic of Yugoslavia*, 2002 WL 1575067 (N.D. Ill. July 18, 2002); *Garb v. Republic of Poland*, 207 F. Supp. 2d 16 (E.D.N.Y. 2002); *Abrams v. Societe Nationale des Chemins de Fer Francais*, 175 F. Supp. 2d 423 (E.D.N.Y. 2001); *Joo v. Japan*, 172 F. Supp. 2d 52 (D.D.C. 2001); *In re World War II Era Japanese Forced Labor Litigation* 164 F. Supp. 2d 1160 (N.D. Cal. 2001).

[67] See I. Brownlie, *Principles of Public International Law*, 6th ed. (2003), p. 34, who purports, "A state cannot plead provisions of its own law or deficiencies in that law in answer to a claim against it for an alleged breach of its obligations under international law"; see Human Rights Committee, *General Comment 31*, CCPR/C/21/Rev.1/Add.13 (adopted on March 2004): "Where there are inconsistencies between domestic law and the Covenant, article 2 requires that the domestic law or practice be changed to meet the standards imposed by the Covenant's substantive guarantees."

have attempted to distinguish the availability of immunity based on the type of proceeding, civil or criminal, involved.

In Al-Adsani, the majority of the ECtHR distinguished the case before it—as a civil claim—from the authority it cited as evidence of the jus cogens status of the prohibition of torture, such as Furundzija and Pinochet, which related to criminal proceedings.[68] On the basis of this distinction, the court concluded that

notwithstanding the special character of the prohibition of torture in international law, the Court is unable to discern in the international instruments, judicial authorities or other materials before it any firm basis for concluding that, as a matter of international law, a State no longer enjoys immunity from civil suit in the courts of another State where acts of torture are alleged.[69]

Similarly, in Bouzari, the Ontario Court of Appeal found that the text of the Convention Against Torture "does not provide clear guidance" on the territorial reach of Article 14 (1). It then cited the lack of state practice interpreting Article 14 (1) as requiring the provision of a civil remedy for torture committed extraterritorially to demonstrate that no obligation exists.[70]

However, in Al-Adsani, in their joint dissenting opinions, Judges Rozakis, Caflisch, Wildhaber, Costa, Cabral Barreto, and Vajic, disputed the majority's division between criminal and civil proceedings. Rather, they held that the type of proceeding—whether criminal or civil—is irrelevant and inconsistent with the nature of a jus cogens norm, which relates to the underlying act.[71] The key issue is the conflict between a peremptory norm and another norm under international law.[72] Notably, the United Nations Committee against Torture addressed the implications of Article 14 (1) within its consideration of the Canadian legal system, following the Bouzari case. It criticized "the absence of effective measures to provide civil compensation to victims of torture in all cases"[73] and recommended that Canada "review its position under Article 14 of the Convention to ensure the provision of compensation through its civil jurisdiction to all victims of torture."[74]

The history, rationale, and practice on immunities in the other contexts demonstrates that the availability of immunity has never been determined on the basis of the type of proceeding involved, whether administrative, criminal, or civil. Rather, courts have focused on the nature of the underlying act, for example, commercial acts, or torts. Although immunity is not a concept divisible by the type of proceed-

---

[68] Id. at para. 61.

[69] *Al-Adsani v. The United Kingdom, supra* note 19, at para. 61.

[70] *Bouzari v. Islamic Republic of Iran, supra* note 42, at paras. 68–95.

[71] Joint Dissenting Opinion of Judges Rozakis and Caflisch, joined by Judges Wildhaber, Costa, Cabral Barreto and Vajić, in *Al-Adsani v. The United Kingdom, supra* note 19, at pp. 29–31.

[72] Dissenting Opinion of Judge Loucaides, in *Al-Adsani v. The United Kingdom, supra* note 19, at p. 34.

[73] Committee against Torture, *Consideration of Reports Submitted by States Parties under Article 19 of the Convention: Conclusions and Recommendations of the Committee against Torture*, 34th Session (May 2005), CAT/C/CO/34/CAN at para. C (4) (g).

[74] Id., at D (5) (f).

ing used, in traditional cases on immunity, the particular "exception" involved will often correlate to civil or criminal proceedings. For example, in cases involving the commercial "exception," the parties involved demonstrate a clear preference for the use of civil suits. However, the courts do not determine the availability of immunity in these cases based on the type of proceeding used; rather, they look at whether the acts in question constitute *acta jure imperii* or *jure gestionis*.

In the context of crimes under international law, both civil and criminal proceedings offer equal means by which to achieve accountability. In common law countries, the type of proceedings used is usually determined by the person or official body bringing the case. In criminal cases, the ability to initiate the case usually lies within the domain of the Attorney-General who has discretion as to whether to initiate proceedings. In contrast, in civil proceedings, the victim or the victim's family is usually the party to bring suit. In civil law countries, clear divisions do not exist due to the *partie civile* system which allows victims and sometimes other interested parties to participate in criminal proceedings and bring civil claims for compensation within the same proceedings. As a result, the arguments advanced in support of a split on the basis of the type of proceeding involved seem to relate less to legal principles underlying jus cogens norms or immunity and arguably more to an attempt to protect states, which, at least under current thinking, can only be held accountable in the courts of a foreign state in civil rather than criminal proceedings.[75]

V. Conclusion

The debate over whether immunity should be available in cases concerning crimes under international law is not new: since the decision of the US Supreme Court in Amerada Hess in 1989, courts have been considering the issue repeatedly. State immunity is not a static concept inextricably tied to its historical origins. Rather, it has been characterized as "a classic subject of international law in perennial need of adjustment to contemporary notions of State and the rule of law."[76] As has already been demonstrated by the restriction of state immunity in areas such as commerce, the doctrine is capable of responding to the changing conception of statehood. The "commercial exception" emerged out of the perceived unfairness that state immunity caused by preventing the party contracting with the state from adjudicating disputes. On this logical basis, the unfairness rendered by the potential availability of state immunity in cases concerning crimes under international law is even more evident as the survivor does not voluntarily transact with the state and the lack of an alternative forum in which to bring a claim, may mean that in practice, impunity flows from the provision of immunity. As a result, state immunity must respond to the inequities its availability produces.

---

[75] See Chapter III (6) of the *Commentaries, supra* note 37, at 280.
[76] M. Gavouneli, *State Immunity and the Rule of Law* (2001), p. 19.

Universal Jurisdiction: Developing and Implementing an Effective Global Strategy

Christopher Keith Hall

What is required to develop and then implement an effective global strategy to enforce international criminal law by the use of universal jurisdiction in national courts? Three questions should be answered.

I. What Is the Purpose of Universal Jurisdiction?

There are two fundamentally different answers to this first question that have been suggested by non-governmental organizations and lawyers representing victims of crimes under international law. The choice of answer will determine what strategy those acting in the interests of such victims are likely to adopt.

For some, litigation in national courts based on universal jurisdiction is simply a useful way to make a political point, to embarrass the target, to press for law reform by demonstrating the weakness of existing legislation, or to cry in desperation when all other avenues have failed, even if the case would pose a serious risk of undermining the legal framework that would enable other victims and their families to obtain a measure of justice and reparations. When the judicial system of an oppressive government is completely unresponsive to demands of victims of crimes under international law for justice, truth, and reparations to which they are entitled as of right, filing hundreds or thousands of complaints with no hope of winning, may well be a legitimate tactic to shame the judiciary, the legislature, or the executive into action. However, even under the apartheid system in South Africa, the strategic use of carefully chosen, well-documented, and clearly argued civil suits was able to make an impact by frustrating some of the worst initiatives, shedding light through inquests, and laying the foundation for the establishment of the rule of law in the future.

For others, like Amnesty International, universal jurisdiction since the first prosecution involving post-Second World War crimes in Denmark in 1994 has been one legal tool for states acting as agents of the international community to bring as many of those responsible for conduct amounting to crimes under international law to justice as possible.[1] Viewed from that perspective, every effort must be made to ensure that police, prosecutors, and investigating judges in every country in the world have effective legislation and interstate cooperation agreements, that they and those who decide whether such legislation can be used have the knowledge, experience, and political will to use it, and that cases be carefully chosen for their likeliness to succeed and strengthen the legal framework for other victims and their families, rather than weaken it.

II. What Are the Obstacles That Victims, Their Families, Police, and Prosecuting Authorities Face and How Should They Be Overcome?

There are three types of obstacles to the exercise of universal jurisdiction: the lack of effective legislation, practical problems in implementing the legislation, and the backlash against universal jurisdiction since the high-water mark in 1999 of the second decision on the merits by the House of Lords in the *Pinochet* case.

1. The Absence of Legislation or Effective Legislation

As the Amnesty International global study of state practice at the international and national levels concerning universal jurisdiction in 125 countries published in 2001 demonstrates, almost two-thirds of all states have some legislation permitting their courts to exercise universal jurisdiction over conduct amounting to genocide, crimes against humanity, war crimes, torture, and other crimes under international law.[2] However, much of that legislation is seriously flawed, for example, by failing to include all crimes under international law (often relying on ordinary crimes, such as murder, in their criminal codes), defining crimes in a manner that is not consistent with international law, defining principles of criminal law (such as command or superior responsibility) in a manner inconsistent with international law, and including defenses (such as superior orders) prohibited by international law. In addition, particularly when universal jurisdiction is applied to ordinary crimes under national law, it is subject to other legislative obstacles,

---

[1] In November 1994, a Danish court convicted Refik Sarić of grave breaches of the Geneva Conventions for assault and aggravated assault on detainees in a detention camp in Bosnia and Herzegovina. *Public Prosecutor v. N.N.*, judgment, *Ostre Landsrets* (Eastern High Court), 3rd Div., November 25, 1994, *aff'd, Public Prosecutor v. T.*, judgment, *Jojesteret* (Sup. Ct.), August 15, 1995.

[2] Amnesty International, *Universal jurisdiction: The duty of states to enact and implement legislation* (2001), AI Index: IOR 53/002–018/2001. This 750-page study, the first global survey since the *Harvard Research in International Law* (*American Journal of International Law* Supp. 1935, p. 435), has recently been confirmed with regard to war crimes by the International Committee of the Red Cross, J.-M. Henckaerts and L. Doswald-Beck, *Customary International Humanitarian Law* (2005).

including statutes of limitation, dual-criminality, *ne bis in idem* prohibitions, amnesties, and official immunities, which are inappropriate with regard to crimes under international law.[3]

In developing an effective global strategy, Amnesty International has focused much of its effort on long-term lobbying of governments to enact or amend criminal law, criminal procedure, and universal jurisdiction provisions as part of its work for effective legislation to implement the Rome Statute of the International Criminal Court.

2. Practical Obstacles

There are numerous practical obstacles, including slow and ineffective arrest procedures that have permitted suspects in France and Switzerland to escape arrest and inadequate knowledge of the forum state's criminal procedure by those filing criminal complaints or civil suits. Few states have special investigations and prosecution units for these crimes. Indeed, members of the criminal justice systems of most states are not familiar with international law, particularly regarding universal jurisdiction. Political will may be lacking to enact effective legislation or to amend it. Usually, the law enforcement authorities are hesitant to use universal jurisdiction. Even worse, in some countries political officials, not prosecutors, determine whether to open a criminal investigation based on universal jurisdiction and may prevent the opening of, or even terminate, such an investigation. Political officials of the forum state may even assist a suspect to flee home. Some states continue to exercise extraterritorial jurisdiction through military courts or executive bodies called military commissions, with all the due process and sham trial concerns they present.

Persuading states to extradite accused persons is particularly difficult in cases involving crimes under international law because few states have effective extradition agreements covering these crimes.

Obtaining evidence abroad can pose problems. Mutual legal assistance agreements are the exception, not the norm, and they often are themselves weak. States where witnesses or evidence is located, which are not only the states where the crimes occurred, may be reluctant to cooperate with a foreign state. This can be a particular problem for defendants. Even witnesses testifying by audio or video links can enjoy immunities, have testimonial privileges, or commit perjury in the foreign state. It is often difficult to obtain documentary and physical evidence abroad. Problems may include inaccurate translations of documents, authentication of documents, restrictions on export of certain items, excavations of grave sites, and other searches. In addition, some states even insist that a foreign prosecutor or investigating judge acting pursuant to a *commission rogatoire* submit for approval a list of questions before asking them of a witness.

---

[3] For an extensive discussion of legal and practical obstacles to the effective exercise of universal jurisdiction and ways to overcome them, see Amnesty International, *supra* note 2, Chapter Fourteen, (AI Index: IOR 53/017/2001).

As part of Amnesty International's global strategy, in addition to pressing for legislative solutions, it has strongly supported efforts by REDRESS and the Fédération Internationale des Ligues des Droits de l'Homme (FIDH) to persuade states within the European Union, and now members of Interpol around the world, to increase practical interstate cooperation in investigating and prosecuting crimes under international law.[4] It has also recommended the drafting of United Nations extradition and mutual legal assistance treaties for crimes under international law, subject to fair trial guarantees and the prohibition of the death penalty.[5]

3. Backlash

Since 1999—partly as a result of complaints filed apparently without any strategic vision, primarily against serving high-level officials such as heads of state, heads of government, foreign ministers, and defense ministers—national courts have rejected universal jurisdiction complaints in high-profile cases, usually on the grounds that the official has immunity from criminal prosecution or civil suit in a foreign court for crimes under international law, a concept previously rejected in every international instrument dealing with crimes under international law. These judgments have set back the promising national jurisprudence concerning universal jurisdiction that had been emerging in Austria, Belgium, Canada, Denmark, France, Israel, Germany, Paraguay, Senegal, Spain, Switzerland, and the United Kingdom.

They have also led to the public becoming increasingly disenchanted with universal jurisdiction, which was portrayed as simply a national and political, rather than an international and legal, tool. States, for example, Belgium, have weakened legislation after criticism of cases filed against such high-level officials, which nevertheless rarely lead to a formal investigation. Judges of the International Court of Justice expressed restrictive or even hostile views in a case challenging the exercise of universal jurisdiction against a serving foreign minister.[6] Police and prosecutors became more reluctant to investigate and prosecute. The press has become critical, and academic public international lawyers and even some nongovernmental organizations have advanced restrictive interpretations of universal jurisdiction. Some academics have supported official immunity from prosecution in foreign national courts for serving heads of state, heads of government, and foreign ministers for genocide and other crimes to avoid disrupting diplomatic rela-

---

[4]   REDRESS and FIDH, *Legal remedies for victims of "international crimes": Fostering an EU approach to extraterritorial jurisdiction* (2004), at http://redress/reports.html; Interpol, *Genocide, War Crimes, and Crimes against Humanity: The Investigation and Prosecution of Genocide, War Crimes, and Crimes against Humanity* at http://interpol.int/public/crimesagainsthumanity/default.asp.

[5]   Amnesty International, *Justice and the rule of law: The role of the United Nations – Statement by Amnesty International* (2004), AI Index: IOR 40/014/2004.

[6]   Case concerning the *Arrest Warrant of 11 April 2000* (*Democratic Republic of the Congo v. Belgium*), judgment of February 14, 2002, *ICJ Reports* 2002.

tions.[7] Others have supported preventing courts from investigating crimes committed by suspects abroad who have never been in the forum state, even though this was authorized by the Geneva Conventions more than half a century ago.[8] Scholars, one national court, and even a United Nations commission of inquiry have also called for victims and prosecuting authorities to prove that the state where the crime occurred was unable and unwilling to act, a difficult and sometimes impossible burden to meet.[9] In part, these views have been shaped by myths—dispelled by the Amnesty International study in 2001—such as the supposed lack of legislation providing for universal jurisdiction and the supposed indispensable link between the seriousness of the crime and universal jurisdiction.

It will be crucial to address these attitudes and misconceptions in a wide variety of fora, including law journals, which are more likely to be read by legal advisers in foreign ministries than reports of non-governmental organizations. However, it will also be essential to develop and implement a global litigation strategy designed to convince the public and decision makers of the legitimacy and necessity of universal jurisdiction. These attitudes can also be changed by a careful strategic choice of cases by victims and by prosecuting authorities.

III. How Should Cases Be Chosen and Litigated?

One model, which Amnesty International favors, is for non-governmental organizations and lawyers representing victims to agree on a set of informal guidelines outlining a long-term series of stages in carefully chosen jurisdictions, building incrementally on each previous step, and stopping to assess at each stage and with each issue whether the benefits of this particular approach is working. This was the incredibly successful approach initiated in the United States of America before the Second World War by the NAACP Legal Defense and Educational Fund in its campaign to dismantle segregation and later by the American Civil Liberties Union/New York Civil Liberties Union Mental Health Law Project to vindicate the rights of mentally ill persons, many of whom were caged in huge, impersonal, an-

---

[7] See, for example, D. Akande, *American Journal of International Law* 2004, p. 407 at pp. 409–410.

[8] See, for example, A. Cassese, *Journal of International Criminal Justice* 2003, p. 589 at p. 594, claiming, without citing any evidence, that "the presence of the accused on the territory of the prosecuting state is the crucial test for the exercise of universal jurisdiction."

[9] For example, a UN commission of inquiry asserted, contrary to international law, that universal jurisdiction could not be exercised unless the suspect was present in the forum state and that the forum state must request the state where the crimes occurred and the state of the suspect's nationality "whether [they are] willing to institute proceedings against that person and hence prepared to request his or her extradition. Only if the State or States in question refuse to seek the extradition, or are patently unable or unwilling to bring the person to justice, may the State on whose territory is present initiate proceedings against him or her." *Report of the Commission on Inquiry on Darfur to the United Nations Secretary-General*, Geneva, January 25, 2005, para. 614.

tiquated institutions without due process and subjected to forced and often harmful medication.[10]

Elements of such a litigation strategy for universal jurisdiction would include focusing on low-level suspects who have no arguable claim to immunity; using a wide variety of jurisdictions—not just the same few—to avoid creating a misleading impression that the courts are overloaded, even though most complaints do not lead to formal investigations; selecting easier legal obstacles for attack *after* assessing the forum's legal and political receptivity to such challenges; and filing complaints in the South against suspects from the North and South, to deflect the bizarre charge that the North's use of courts to investigate and prosecute persons responsible for mass murder in the South is an attack on the South.[11] Every organization or lawyer filing a complaint would be encouraged to undertake an international risk assessment in consultation with experts to weigh whether the chances of setting back the law for other victims would outweigh the possible benefits to an individual victim.

Had such a global strategy been in existence in 1999, one might well wonder whether the string of complaints filed in Spain and Belgium against heads of state, prime ministers, and senior government officials would have been made at this stage in international law development. However, these issues were discussed before the filing of the complaint here in Germany against the current US Secretary of Defense, and, yet, the decision was made to proceed despite concerns that, even though there was a solid jurisdictional basis under German law to proceed, the high profile of the main suspect this case would lead to dismissal under overt political pressure with serious damage to the independence of the prosecutor and German law and harm to universal jurisdiction elsewhere.[12]

The German Federal Prosecutor declined in February 2005 to prosecute, citing the previously discredited doctrine of horizontal subsidiarity between states invented by a Spanish court in 2000 in a proceeding against several former Guatemalan presidents and generals and rejected on appeal by the Supreme Court three years later.[13] He contended that the German universal jurisdiction provision ap-

---

[10] For the history of the development and implementation of the desegregation strategy, see R. Kluger, *Simple Justice: The history of Brown v. Board of Education, the epochal Supreme Court decision that outlawed segregation, and of black America's century-long struggle for equality under law* (1977). For a brief note on Bruce J. Ennis and the American Civil Liberties Union/New York Civil Liberties Union Mental Health Law Project, see New York Civil Liberties Union, *Championing Civil Rights and Civil Liberties for Fifty Years* (2003), p. 19.

[11] These claims have no merit because the complaints were filed by victims from the South who had failed to obtain justice from criminal justice systems in their own states.

[12] The intention of the drafters of the legislation was to permit the prosecutor to decline to prosecute a case where another national prosecutor was actually doing so in fair proceedings, which are not a sham—not on the basis that it was not demonstrated that the state of the suspect's nationality or the state where the crime occurred would not do so. See S. Wirth, *Journal of International Criminal Justice* 2003, p. 151 at pp. 159–160.

[13] *Tribunal Supremo, Sala de lo Penal, Sentencia N°327/2003*, de 25 de Febrero de 2003 (available in English at: http://www.derechos.org/nizkor/guatemala/doc/stsgtm.html).

plied only when the state of the suspect's nationality declined to investigate the allegations and that it had not been demonstrated in this case that it would not do so.[14] Whether the choice made by the complainants to file the complaint in Germany has strengthened or weakened the use of universal jurisdiction in German courts and other national courts was considered in the panel titled, Conclusions from the German Case against Donald Rumsfeld. The decision by the Federal Prosecutor on March 31, 2006, that he would not prosecute Zakirjon Almatovich Almatov, the Uzbekistan Minister of Interior, for torture and torture as a crime against humanity based on a complaint made in four months earlier in December 2005, on the grounds that the suspect had left Germany after the complaint and was not likely to return and that the current government of Uzbekistan was not likely to cooperate with the investigation, is not a particularly auspicious omen.

IV. Is the Proposed Global Strategy Feasible?

One may doubt it. Individual clients, as opposed to organizations, may wish to press on regardless of the risks that defeat will pose for other victims as—understandably—they see that universal jurisdiction in their case is their last possible hope of justice and reparations. Lawyers for individual victims will often be constrained by client-based ethics rather than by general public interest considerations that organizations working on behalf of all victims would have. The more constricted legal arena in which the NAACP Legal Defence and Educational Fund and the American Civil Liberties Union/New York Civil Liberties Union Mental Health Law Project operated with virtual monopolies over the issues is a far cry from the global arena where victims and lawyers everywhere have instant access to legal developments in all countries through the Internet.[15] Of course, that should not stop those concerned with justice for victims from trying to develop a global

---

[14] On 10 February 2005, German Federal Prosecutor Kay Nehm dismissed the complaint on the ground that he believed that the US would investigate the allegations and stated that "there are no indications that the authorities and courts of the United States of America are refraining, or would refrain, from penal measures as regards the violations described in the complaint." On September 13, 2005, the 5th Chamber for Criminal Matters of Stuttgart Court of Appeals (Oberlandesgericht) dismissed the appeal of this decision on the ground the prosecutor has almost complete discretion under Sec. 153f of the Code of Criminal Procedure to dismiss the complaint (*Zeitschrift für internationale Strafrechtsdogmatik* 2006, pp. 143 et seq., available at http://www.zis-online.com). The texts of both decisions are reproduced with English translations at http://www.ccr-ny.org. See also the contributions of W. Kaleck and F. Jessberger in this volume.

[15] All of the developments in the field of universal jurisdiction, including links to the texts of court decisions, legislation, scholarly literature, and non-governmental organization reports, were reported and analyzed in the excellent UJ-Info website, established by REDRESS and the Center for Justice and Accountability, until foundations regrettably shifted their priorities. The Swiss Association against Impunity (TRIAL) has partially filled the gap, but it is largely limited to daily press reports and case summaries, rather than court decisions or legislation.

strategy; what is at stake is too important. However, there is a serious risk that there will be a steadily increasing erosion of all the accomplishments in persuading national police, prosecutors, and investigating judges to act as agents of the international community in enforcing international law.

All is not bleak, however. Non-governmental organizations and lawyers representing victims have been discussing the drafting of informal checklists of good practice and manuals to assist in deciding whether to use universal jurisdiction and, if so, how to do so most effectively. Support for Amnesty International efforts to include effective universal jurisdiction provisions in implementing legislation for the Rome Statute of the International Criminal Court is starting to have an impact on draft and enacted legislation. As noted above, the EU, through its system of contact points, and Interpol, with its working group on crimes under international law, are encouraging police and prosecutors to cooperate more effectively. More of the complaints are starting to focus on lower-level suspects, particularly those who are no longer in office or whose governments have been replaced. This approach is starting to bear fruit in courts in Belgium, Canada, France, Mexico, the Netherlands, Spain, the United Kingdom, and the United States.[16] If these positive, low-profile, time-consuming, and laborious efforts continue, the prospects that universal jurisdiction will become an effective tool for national courts to enforce international criminal law will be bright.

---

[16] Belgian courts convicted two Rwandese businessmen, Etienne Nzabonimana and his half-brother, Samuel Ndashyikirwa, on June 28, 2005, of 81 charges of war crimes and murder committed in Rwanda in 1994; Canada arrested Désiré Munyaneza, a former Rwandan official, on October 19, 2005, on two charges of genocide in Rwanda in 1994; the Danish Assistant Prosecutor General Plum Lans Nunk was reported in February 2006 to be engaged in the investigation of persons in Denmark suspected of genocide in Rwanda during 1994; a French court convicted Ely Ould Dah, a Mauritanian soldier, on July 1, 2005, in a trial in absentia of torture and sentenced him to ten years' imprisonment; a Mexican court ordered the extradition of Ricardo Miguel Cavallo to Spain to face charges of genocide and terrorism; on April 7, 2004, the Rotterdam District Court in the Netherlands convicted Sebastien Nzapali, a former commander of the Zaire (now the Democratic Republic of the Congo) *garde civile* of torture and sentenced him to two and a half years' imprisonment; another Dutch court in The Hague convicted Habibullah Jalalzoy and Heshamuddin Hesan, two former Afghan generals, on October 14, 2005, of war crimes, including torture, during the 1990s and sentenced them to nine and twelve years' imprisonment respectively; a Spanish court convicted Aldofo Scinglo, a former Argentine naval commander, on April 19, 2005, of murder, illegal detention, and torture in Argentina and sentenced him to 640 years in prison; an English court convicted Zardad Khan, a former leader of an armed group, on July 19, 2005 of torture in Afghanistan and sentenced him to 20 years' imprisonment; and a United States District Court in on November 18, 2005, held Colonel Nicolás Carranza, a former Vice-Minister of Defence, civilly responsible for extrajudicial executions and torture in El Salvador. In another, unrelated positive development, on October 5, 2005, Spain's Sala Segunda del Tribunal Constitucional (Constitutional Court, Second Chamber) in the Guatemala case overruled in part previous decisions that had restricted the scope of universal jurisdiction under Spanish law by requiring links between the case and Spain.

German International Criminal Law in Practice: From Leipzig to Karlsruhe

Wolfgang Kaleck

The German Code of Crimes Against International Law (*Völkerstrafgesetzbuch*, or VStGB) has been viewed by the German federal government, legal scholars, and human rights organizations as a model criminal code for national prosecution of international human rights violations in the era of the International Criminal Court (ICC). In the explanatory memorandum of the law, one of its purposes is formulated as "promoting international humanitarian law and contributing to its spread by creating an appropriate set of national rules."[1] Federal Minister of Justice Zypries has claimed that the VStGB "reflects the most modern stage in the development of international humanitarian law and international criminal law."[2] It has been translated into eight of the world's most widely spoken languages.[3] But by summer 2006, the Federal Prosecutor's office in Karlsruhe[4] had not opened a single investigation under the VStGB, either on his own authority (*propio motu*) or on the basis of the approximately fifty complaints lodged so far. There thus seems to be a gap between the ideal and the reality of international criminal law in Germany.

This discrepancy will be considered in the following sections. At the heart of these reflections is the Federal Prosecutor's handling of complaints lodged under the VStGB. But first, we will look at the practice of international criminal law in Germany in the years from 1919 to 1995. In this period, international criminal law was forming at the international level, especially once the first milestone was

---

[1] *Bundestags-Drucksache* 14/8524, p. 12.

[2] Speech on June 27, 2003, reprinted in http://www.bmj.de/enid/0,0/Juni/Berlin__27_06_2003__Völkerrechtsverbrechen_fa.html?druck=1.

[3] See http://www.iuscrim.mpg.de/forsch/online_pub.html#legaltext.

[4] In the express desire of the legislature, jurisdiction over trials under the VStGB in accordance with Secs. 142a (1), 120 (1) No. 8 of the Court Constitution Law (*Gerichtsverfassungsgesetz*) lies with the Federal Prosecutor attached to the Federal Supreme Court, as the "highest national appeals organ, which guarantees a high level of legal qualification. This concentration of jurisdiction also does justice to the special significance and gravity of crimes under the Code of Crimes Against International Law" (according the Stuttgart Court of Appeals in a decision on September 13, 2005, in the *Rumsfeld* case, *Neue Zeitschrift für Strafrecht* 2006, pp. 117 et seq.).

passed in the Nuremberg trials. The legal treatment of the century's crimes, including World Wars I and II and the extermination of European Jewry, has been considered in depth elsewhere.[5] Yet it would be remiss to completely ignore the German legal system's treatment of these crimes committed by Germans when considering the practical application of international criminal law in Germany (I). Although German criminal law prior to 2002 offered significantly fewer possibilities than the VStGB in regard to the prosecution of crimes against international law, German prosecutors used the former laws to thoroughly investigate two major sets of human rights violations abroad: crimes by Bosnian Serbs against Bosnian Muslims and human rights violations by the Argentine military during the dictatorship from 1976 to 1983. Both cases will be treated briefly (II). The aforementioned analysis of the practical application of the VStGB (III) will be followed by a preliminary assessment of the practice of international criminal law in Germany and its future prospects (IV).

I. The Leipzig Trials, the Nuremberg Trials, and Beyond: 1919 to 1995

During the long years from 1919 to 1995, international criminal law had almost no practical application in Germany.

1. It is true that German war crimes in World War I were the subject of numerous investigations and of one trial before the Reich Court in Leipzig.[6] During the war, and especially following the sinking of the passenger ship *Lusitania* on May 7, 1915, by a German submarine, which caused the death of 1198 people, the Allies already hoped to try German war criminals—including former Kaiser Wilhelm II, who had fled to Holland—before military tribunals.[7] The legal basis for these trials was to be primarily the norms of the Fourth Hague Convention on the Laws and Customs of War on Land. The main incidents they had in mind were the mass shootings in Belgium, frequent abuse of prisoners, and the use of unrestricted submarine warfare—that is, the sinking of both hostile and neutral ships without prior warning. The aim of punishing German war criminals was found in the Versailles Treaty.[8] Following this line, the Allies on February 3, 1920, de-

---

[5] See generally H. Kreicker, in A. Eser and H. Kreicker (eds.), *Nationale Strafverfolgung völkerrechtlicher Verbrechen, Vol. I: Deutschland* (2003), pp. 85 et seq., 426 et seq; G. Hankel, *Leipziger Prozesse. Deutsche Kriegsverbrechen und ihre strafrechtliche Verfolgung nach dem Ersten Weltkrieg* (2003); R. Huhle et al., *Von Nürnberg nach Den Haag. Menschenrechtsverbrechen vor Gericht. Zur Aktualität des Nürnberger Prozesses* (1996); J. Perels, *Die Zeit*, January 26, 2006; I. Müller, *Furchtbare Juristen* (1987); J. Perels, *Kritische Justiz* 1998, pp. 84 et seq.; J. Perels, *Entsorgung der NS-Herrschaft? Konfliktlinien im Umgang mit dem Hitler-Regime* (2004); J. Friedrich, *Die kalte Amnestie. NS-Täter in der Bundesrepublik* (1994).

[6] See generally G. Hankel, *supra* note 5.

[7] Ibid., pp. 23 et seq.

[8] In Articles 227 et seq.

manded that the Reich government surrender some 900 persons. This demand was not met.[9] The Allies did not insist, but instead accepted the promise that Germany would follow up on the allegations. Indeed, the Reichstag adopted a law for the punishment of war crimes and misdemeanors on 18 December 1919, and in early 1920 they sent the Allies a list of 45 names of persons whom they wished to investigate.[10]

The subsequent Leipzig Trials before the Reich Court are, first of all, evidence of a state's difficulty in dealing with war crimes before its own courts. The trials also illustrate the strong influence of anti-Republican forces within the Reich military and the justice system in the Weimar Republic. From January 1921 until November 1922, a total of 17 trials took place, of which seven ended in acquittal and the rest in sentences between six months and four years, some of which, for killings.[11] In all, between 1921 and 1927, 1,700 people were investigated. The soldiers were often credited with momentary mistakes or of being unaware that they were doing wrong. The concepts of military necessity, customs of war, and acting under orders were broadly interpreted.[12] Ultimately, a legal concept emerged affirming the permissibility of acts of war, with disastrous effect (*Not kennt kein Gebot*).[13] The German judiciary thwarted an adequate reckoning with war crimes, thereby creating the conditions under which, at the end of World War II, the Allied victors no longer trusted the German justice system to investigate and try German war crimes. Thus in the preparatory phase of the Nuremberg trials, the American view was, "What can we learn from Versailles and Leipzig? Above all, that the United Nations must not again trust that the Germans will do justice to their war criminals. In their eyes, they are heroes."[14]

2. As we know, the Nuremberg Trial and the follow-up trials involved Allied and US military tribunals. The Nuremberg trial of the major war criminals, held by all the Allies on the basis of the Nuremberg Charter from November 1945 until the judgment in October 1946, was followed between April 1947 and April 1949 by twelve subsequent trials of Nazi elites, held under American auspices under Control Council Law No. 10. The trials targeted a total of 185 defendants; they dealt with medical and legal crimes and punished leaders of the *Einsatzgruppen*, generals, members of the Foreign Office, and economic leaders of IG Farben, Krupp and Flick.

Even decades later, the German justice system and German legal scholars were skeptical of the laws created by Nuremberg.[15] Criticism culminated in the dictum of "victors' justice," thereby taking up the Nuremberg defense's *tu quoque* argu-

---

[9]   G. Hankel, *supra* note 5, pp. 41 et seq.

[10] Ibid., pp. 54–55.

[11] Ibid., pp. 97 et seq.

[12] Ibid., pp. 228 et seq.

[13] Ibid., pp. 151 et seq., 507 et seq.

[14] S. Glueck, cited by G. Hankel, *supra* note 5, p. 11 note 5.

[15] In regard to the crime of aggression, see the opinion by Carl Schmitt written on behalf of Friedrich Flick in 1945, later published as *Das internationalrechtliche Verbrechen des Angriffskrieges und der Grundsatz "Nullum crimen, nulla poena sine lege"* (1994); for critical comment, see N. Paech, *Kritische Justiz* 1996, pp. 251 et seq.

ments. The defense had fundamentally objected to the trials on the basis that the Allies had also waged a war of aggression and committed war crimes. Thus, they argued, it was an expression of victors' justice for the victorious side to place the losing side on trial. Further, they said, the charges of crimes against peace and crimes against humanity contained in the Nuremberg Charter violated the prohibition on retroactivity.[16] The verdict of "victors' justice" has held to this day, and has led to a situation in which the term is used even today, and not merely by revisionists, radical right-wingers, and nationalists.

3. To this day, Germany maintains a reservation to Article 7 (2) of the European Human Rights Convention that allows this article to apply only within the bounds of Article 103 (2) of the Basic Law (*Grundgesetz*, the German constitution). Article 7 (2) of the European Human Rights Convention, reflecting the principle of *nulla poena sine lege*, provides, "No one shall be held guilty of any criminal offence on account of any act or omission which did not constitute a criminal offence under national or international law at the time when it was committed." However, this does not include the trial or punishment of any person "for any act or omission which, at the time when it was committed, was criminal according to the general principles of law recognized by civilized nations." This wording was intended as an express, if retroactive, legitimization of the Nuremberg Trials through the European Convention.[17]

4. While the entire world and, as seen on the sixtieth anniversary of the trial in 2005, now even Germany's political establishment celebrated Nuremberg as the birth of the Nuremberg Principles, the Nuremberg Trials, and a new world law or international criminal law,[18] Nazi crimes were actually prosecuted inadequately by the German justice system. As Kreicker[19] summarizes, the German legal system "largely failed in the task of dealing with Nazi injustice, quite simply by not undertaking investigations or trials at all or doing so with insufficient commitment." The Amnesty Laws of 1949 and 1954, as well as the supposedly coincidental reform of Sec. 50 (2) of the Criminal Code (*Strafgesetzbuch*) in 1968,[20] were expressions of a widespread mood. Some politicians even demanded a general amnesty for Nazi criminals.

Perels[21] thus describes as "truncated" the "prosecution of Nazi state crimes— despite important trials such as the Auschwitz trial." Despite extensive preliminary investigations of 600 suspects, he points out, possible prosecutions of the Reich Security Main Office (*Reichssicherheitshauptamt*) on the basis of this material were never undertaken. So-called accomplice jurisprudence, in particular, was the

---

[16] For a nuanced view, see G. Werle, *Völkerstrafrecht* (2003), margin notes 24 et seq.; H. Kreicker, *supra* note 5, pp. 85 et seq.

[17] See J. A. Frowein and W. Peukert, *Europäische Menschenrechtskonvention, Kommentar*, 2nd ed. (1996), Art. 7, margin note 8.

[18] See, e.g., the essays in R. Huhle et al., *supra* note 5.

[19] *Supra* note 5, p. 87.

[20] See J. Perels, *Die Zeit*, January 26, 2006.

[21] Ibid.

subject of numerous critical debates.[22] It provided that conviction for murder was possible only if it could be proven that the defendant internally approved of the policy of exterminating the Jews. A commission of the German Jurists' Organization comprised of leading criminal law scholars criticized this jurisprudence for "strikingly low penalties" and demanded punishment of additional groups of perpetrators as perpetrators rather than accomplices.[23]

The jurisprudence of German postwar courts on the Nazi euthanasia program was particularly scandalous: the defendants were given the opportunity to plead an insurmountable, blameless legal error because people might have held different views on the permissibility of killing disabled people. A collision of duties was constructed in regard to some of the participants in the program, because they had assisted in the killing of certain groups of people, but had rescued others.[24] Writer Jörg Friedrich refers to an "acquittal of the Nazi judiciary" and a "cold amnesty."[25] In a leading case, the German Federal Supreme Court (*Bundesgerichtshof*) acknowledged the "overall failure to prosecute Nazi judicial crimes."[26] One cause of this may have been the continuity in the work of the same judges and prosecutors who had formerly applied Nazi laws, and later sat in judgment over themselves and those like them.[27] According to recent statistics from the Ludwigsburg Central Office of the State Judicial Administration for the Investigation of Nazi Crimes, after May 8, 1945, the West German justice system opened investigations and preliminary investigations of 106,496 suspects. Only 6,495 were convicted, 157 of them to life imprisonment.

5. In a study of international criminal law practice in Germany, one could more thoroughly investigate the prosecution of crimes committed by East German officials. For legal reasons, such prosecutions occurred only on the basis of West German law and the East German Criminal Code (Sec. 315). It was to some extent a subject of controversy whether East German government crimes could be considered international crimes.[28] Especially in the aftermath of the European Court of Human Rights decision of March 22, 2001 in the case of *Stelitz, Kessler, and Krenz*,[29] there has been much debate on the applicability of the principle of retroactivity.[30]

---

[22] See especially the pieces by F. Kruse and by B. Just-Dahlmann and H. Just, *Kritische Justiz* 1978; J. Perels 2004, *supra* note 5, pp. 148 et seq.

[23] See J. Perels 2004, *supra* note 5, pp. 157 et seq.

[24] Ibid., pp. 163 et seq.

[25] These are the titles of two of his books, published in 1983 and 1984.

[26] Judgment of December 13, 1993, *Neue Juristische Wochenschrift* 1994, pp. 529, 531.

[27] See I. Müller, *supra* note 5; J. Perels 1998, *supra* note 5, pp. 84 et seq.; J. Perels 2004, *supra* note 5; J. Friedrich, *supra* note 5.

[28] For a negative response, see H. Kreicker, *supra* note 5; for the opposite view, see G. Werle, *Neue Juristische Wochenschrift* 2001, pp. 3001, 3005, with further citations, who overall sees the East German border regime as a crime against humanity.

[29] *Neue Juristische Wochenschrift* 2001, pp. 3035 et seq.

[30] See J. Arnold, in E. Samson et al. (eds.), *Festschrift für Gerald Grünwald zum siebzigsten Geburtstag* (1999), pp. 31 et seq.

II. Yugoslavia and Argentina: Exceptions for the German Justice System

1. The Legal Situation and Its Problems before 2002

Germany is a member of the Geneva Convention[31] and the Genocide Convention.[32] Despite acknowledged shortcomings in penalization, however, there was no sense that special provisions on international crimes were needed. Even the explanatory memorandum of the VStGB emphasizes that "most actions included in international criminal law ... were heretofore punishable under the German Criminal Code."[33] But this only partially describes the reality. Jessberger[34] accurately describes the situation as follows: "Traditionally, there has been little love between the Germans and international criminal law." He then describes the difficulties with "pre-Rome" law, taking as an example German prosecutions of the Argentine military after 1998, which will be discussed below. Under the prior law, particularly significant gaps existed in the prosecution of crimes against humanity. In addition, because of the applicability of the usual statutes of limitations for crimes that occurred in the past, only murders could be prosecuted. They are especially difficult to prove under criminal regimes, because it is difficult to determine the details of the fate of imprisoned and tortured opponents of a regime, given the closed nature of the repressive apparatus, especially in the case of disappearances.[35] Previously, the only international core crime in the German Criminal Code, the crime of genocide (Sec. 220 et seq.), was not applied until the mid-1990s.

2. Yugoslavia

According to the federal prosecutor's office, in the 1990s about one hundred investigations were opened by German prosecutors involving crimes in Bosnia.[36] In addition, on the basis of the April 10, 1995, Law on Cooperation with the International Criminal Tribunal for former Yugoslavia,[37] German prosecutors worked closely with the ICTY and responded between 1996 and 2001 to about five hundred letters rogatory from the Yugoslavia Tribunal.[38] The investigations led to a

---

[31] Geneva Convention of August 12, 1949, *Bundesgesetzblatt* 1954 II, p. 781.
[32] Convention on the Prevention and Punishment of the Crime of Genocide of December 9, 1948, *Bundesgesetzblatt* 1954 II, p. 730.
[33] *Supra* note 1, p. 12 ; see also H. Kreicker, *supra* note 5, p. 88.
[34] F. Jessberger, *Finnish Yearbook of International Law* 2001, pp. 281 et seq.
[35] See C. Grammer, *Der Tatbestand des Verschwindenlassens einer Person. Transposition einer völkerrechtlichen Figur ins Strafrecht* (2005); W. Kaleck at http://www.menschen-rechte.org/Koalition/Artikel/Rechtliche%20Probleme.htm.
[36] See http://www.generalbundesanwalt.de/aufgabe/vmord.php.
[37] *Bundesgesetzblatt* 1995 I, p. 480.
[38] See G. Werle, *supra* note 16, margin note 219.

number of prosecutions, and especially to a series of decisions affirmed on appeal to the Supreme Court and the Federal Constitutional Court (*Bundesverfassungsgericht*). However, the applicability of the principle of universal jurisdiction under Sec. 6 (1) of the Criminal Code was restricted when the Supreme Court, in a highly controversial decision,[39] demanded the presence of an unwritten element of the crime, a "special legitimizing link." In the unambiguous words of Sec. 6 of the Criminal Code, the crimes listed in Sec. 6 are subject to universal jurisdiction, regardless of the nationality of the perpetrator, the law of the place of the crime, or the place the crime was committed. Nevertheless, as an unwritten condition, the court developed the requirement of a "legitimizing domestic link," whereby prosecution must have a direct domestic relationship in order to justify German jurisdiction. Only if this is present may German jurisdiction be exercised. This was the case if the perpetrator himself, though neither the victim nor a witness, was present in Germany. However, in a later decision on December 12, 2000,[40] the Federal Constitutional Court left open the question whether an additional legitimizing domestic link was necessary at all. In a 2001 judgment,[41] the Supreme Court found that the perpetrator's permanent residency in Germany formed a direct link to domestic prosecution, but leaned towards no longer requiring any "legitimizing link in individual cases going beyond the wording of Sec. 6 of the Criminal Code," at least for Sec. 6 (9).[42]

The first convictions handed down by German courts for the crime of genocide, Sec. 220 a of the Criminal Code, occurred in the course of the Yugoslavia trials. The sentencing of Nicola Jorgic, a Bosnian Serb, to life imprisonment on eleven counts of genocide by the Düsseldorf Court of Appeals (*Oberlandesgericht*) on September 26, 1997, was affirmed by the Federal Supreme Court[43] and later by the Constitutional Court.[44] In a leading case, the Constitutional Court determined that "As the most serious violation of human rights, ... genocide is the classic case for

---

[39] For critical views, see A. Eser, in A. Eser et al. (eds.), *Strafverfahrensrecht in Theorie und Praxis* (2001), pp. 3 et seq.; G. Werle, *Juristen-Zeitung* 1999, pp. 1181, 1182 and *Juristen-Zeitung* 2000, pp. 755, 759; R. Merkel, in K. Lüderssen (ed.), *Aufgeklärte Kriminalpolitik oder Kampf gegen das Böse?, Vol. 3* (1998), pp. 237 et seq.

[40] *Neue Juristische Wochenschrift* 2001, pp. 1848 et seq.

[41] Judgement of February 21, 2001, 3 StR 372/00, pp. 20-21.

[42] Because of the entry into force of the Code of Crimes Against International Law and Sec. 153f of the Code of Criminal Procedure, this problem became less serious or shifted from the justification of German criminal authority to the determination of prosecutorial discretion. This once again unmistakable legislative assessment has been interpreted unanimously in the literature as a "clarification" rather than something new (see the explanatory memorandum, *supra* note 1; W. Beulke, in P. Rieß (ed.), *Löwe-Rosenberg, Strafprozessordnung*, 25th ed. (2003), Sec. 153c, margin note 1, Sec. 153f margin note 2), and a retreat from the jurisprudence apparently abandoned by the Supreme Court itself; it must then also be considered in interpreting Sec. 6 (1) No. 1 and 9 of the Criminal Code, such that no domestic link is any longer necessary for older cases as well. (W. Beulke considers the question still "uncertain," referring to A. Zimmermann, *Zeitschrift für Rechtspolitik* 2002, pp. 97, 100.)

[43] Decision of April 30, 1999, *Neue Zeitschrift für Strafrecht* 1999, pp. 396 et seq.

[44] Decision of December 12, 2000, *Juristen-Zeitung* 2001, pp. 975 et seq.

application of universal jurisdiction, ... the function of which is to make possible the most complete possible prosecution of crimes against particularly important legal values of the international community."[45]

3. The German Criminal Trial of the Argentine Military and the Pinochet Case

Also under prior law, since 1998 the Nuremberg-Fürth prosecutor has brought a complex of criminal cases against former members of the Argentine military for crimes committed under the military dictatorship between 1976 and 1983. Since 1998, a coalition of non-governmental organizations, called the Coalition against Impunity,[46] has been working to have German criminal law authorities investigate and prosecute the cases of Germans and people of German origin victimized by the Argentine military dictatorship. The coalition was formed at the initiative of German family members of victims of the dictatorship in Argentina and Argentine Nobel Peace Prize recipient Adolfo Perez Esquivel. It consists of church, human rights and lawyers' organizations. Between 1998 and 2004, a total of 39 complaints were lodged by victims against 89 members of the Argentine military and a German-Argentine manager at Mercedes-Benz, now Daimler-Chrysler AG.[47]

In a series of jurisdictional decisions, the Federal Supreme Court first found that the State Court of Nuremberg-Fürth had jurisdiction over the relevant complaints, under Sec. 13 (a) of the Code of Criminal Procedure (*Strafprozessordnung*, or StPO).[48] German jurisdiction was justified in most cases under the passive-personality principle provided for in Sec. 7 (1) of the Criminal Code, since the victims were Germans or could be treated as such.[49]

The Nuremberg-Fürth prosecutor's office then took over various parts of the investigation, some of which continue to this day. After a hesitant beginning, some eighty witnesses and experts were deposed, either at the prosecutor's office in Nuremberg-Fürth or through consular hearings at the German embassy in Buenos Aires. Two legal opinions were commissioned from the Max Planck Institute for Domestic and Foreign Law in Freiburg.[50] In the course of the investigations, the federal government sent several letters rogatory to Spain, Italy and Argentina.

Ultimately the district court in Nuremberg issued several arrest warrants for a total of five former members of the military, including one on November 28, 2003, against former military junta chief and State President Jorge Rafael Videla,

---

[45] Ibid., p. 980.

[46] See http://www.menschenrechte.org/Koalition.

[47] See http://www.menschenrechte.org/Koalition.

[48] Unpublished decisions 2 AR 80/98.

[49] See generally, and on the particular problem of descendants of Jewish Germans whose citizenship was revoked, F. Jessberger, *supra* note 34, pp. 293 et seq.; K. Ambos, in *Münchner Kommentar StGB und Nebenstrafrecht, Vol. 1* (2003), § 7, margin notes 19 et seq.

[50] K. Ambos, G. Ruegenberg and J. Woischnik, *Europäische Grundrechte-Zeitschrift* 1998, pp. 468 et seq.

already under house arrest in Argentina for other crimes.[51] The reason given for this was that the suspects

> had created a terror regime, including an apparatus of repression with a hierarchical command structure … with the aim of systematically killing people with different political views, so called subversives. Based on their authority over this apparatus of organizational power, knowledge of its functioning, and absolute power of command, they initiated more or less regular sequences of events that led to the killing of the victims named below, taking advantage of the absence of a chain of command, especially to General Suarez Mason, Videla's immediate subordinate.

On the elements of murder, regarding the case of the kidnapped German student Käsemann, it stated:

> They had Elisabeth Käsemann killed within the framework of their organizational authority by the security services, bound by their orders, with the intention of covering up crimes previously committed against Elisabeth Käsemann (deprivation of liberty, bodily harm). The suspects, who ordered the physical extermination of people solely because of different political opinions on the basis of the command situation that was created, acted out of base motives.

In this remarkable decision, the Nuremberg District Court followed a September 9, 2002, legal opinion by the Max Planck Institute for Foreign and International Criminal Law[52] submitted by the complainants. It reached the following conclusions:

> In this case, it is to be investigated in the cases of the living suspects Jorge Videla and Emilio Massera whether, using specific organizational conditions, they contributed to the crime through which regular sequences of events were initiated that led more or less automatically to the murder of Elisabeth Käsemann. The suspects must have known of the aforementioned conditions and the initiated regularity, and have had the intent to carry out the crime. The necessary conditions for application of the doctrine of organizational authority are present in the form of an apparatus of repression within the security forces, whose aim was the "elimination of subversive elements." There is strong suspicion that Jorge Videla is responsible for the murder of Elisabeth Käsemann as an indirect perpetrator based on organizational authority. He modified, influenced and exploited the state apparatus of repression, using his command authority as junta member and commander of the army, in such a way that members of this apparatus kidnapped and eliminated people suspected of subversion. He thus contributed to the crime in such a way that regular sequences of events were initiated within the described context, specifically the "elimination of subversive elements," among which Elisabeth Käsemann was counted. Jorge Videla also knew the method by which this apparatus of repression functioned and intended the crimes as a result of his own actions.

On the basis of an arrest warrant issued by the Nuremberg District Court, the Federal Republic of Germany is the only country so far to demand the extradition of the former military junta leader, although Spain, France, and Italy have initiated in some cases significantly more comprehensive investigations of former members

---

[51] 57 Gs 13320-13322/03, see, http://www.justiz.bayern.de/olgn/presse/info/fr_aktuell.htm.
[52] Unpublished in Germany, see K. Ambos and C. Grammer, in T. Vormbaum (ed.), *Jahrbuch der Juristischen Zeitgeschichte, Vol. 4* (2003), pp. 529 et seq.

of the military. The German government most recently appealed a decision by the Argentine government and courts refusing extradition. The appeal was successful, and the Camara Federal decided that the Argentine court has to trial the case again in an open and public hearing with the participation of the German government.

In contrast, former Chilean military dictator Augusto Pinochet Ugarte was only briefly investigated in Germany following his arrest in London on October 16, 1998, under an arrest warrant issued by the Spanish Audencia Nacional. Three German victims did press charges against him for torture suffered in Chile after 1973.[53] The German Supreme Court transferred the investigation and decision of the case to the Düsseldorf State Court under Sec. 13 of the Code of Criminal Procedure.[54] The prosecutors there began an investigation, but transferred the case to the Chilean criminal authorities shortly after Pinochet's departure for Chile. The Düsseldorf prosecutors apparently believed there were no deficiencies in prosecuting crimes in Chile once several cases had been opened against members of the military responsible for the dictatorship's crimes. In any case, they believed investigations were better undertaken there. This approach contrasts with that of the Nuremberg-Fürth prosecutor in the Argentine case, who continued the investigations, at least in part, and maintained the request for extradition until further notice, despite the resumption of prosecutions following the lifting of the amnesty under the current Kirchner regime in Argentina.[55] In any case, the cases in Chile have not progressed very far, to the detriment of the German complainants.

III. Practical Application of the Code of Crimes Against International Law (VStGB)

1. The Concept Behind the VStGB

Starting in the second half of the 1990s, the German federal government developed an increasingly positive attitude toward international criminal law. This was expressed most clearly in the important role played by German representatives in the creation of the International Criminal Court in The Hague. Efforts were also made to compensate for the legal shortcomings in national law. A group of experts was set up for this purpose in the Federal Ministry of Justice; their draft of a Code of Crimes Against International Law ultimately led to the VStGB that was adopted on June 30, 2002. This for the first time makes possible universal prosecution of crimes against humanity and, in Sec. 1, provides for universal prosecution of crimes against international law in Germany, regardless of the person of the perpetrator or the victim and regardless of the place of commission. To prevent unbri-

---

[53] See generally, K. Thun, in H. Ahlbrecht and K. Ambos (eds.), *Der Fall Pinochet(s). Auslieferung wegen staatsverstärkter Kriminalität?* (1999), pp. 18 et seq.

[54] See, e. g., the decisions 2 ARs 471/98 and 2 Ars 474/98, in H. Ahlbrecht and K. Ambos, *supra* note 53, pp. 100 et seq.

[55] See http://www.justiz.bayern.de/olgn/presse/info/fr_aktuell.htm.

dled prosecution, a Sec. 153f was added to the Code of Criminal Procedure, providing the Federal Prosecutor's office in Karlsruhe (which has sole jurisdiction) with rules regarding which cases require an investigation to be opened or closed and what standards to use in deciding.

So far, no investigations have been initiated under the VStGB. This is on the one hand understandable, as the law is only applicable to cases that occurred following its entry into force on 30 June 2002. For crimes committed earlier, the old laws apply. On the other hand, one needs only read the daily papers or the reports of human rights organizations to know that numerous serious crimes under international law have been committed since then that would allow the German investigative authorities to act, and in some circumstances would require it.

The VStGB was expressly created for cases in which international crimes would otherwise go unpunished. This includes countless crimes, even in the age of the permanent International Criminal Court. The ICC only has jurisdiction over cases that occur in signatory states, are committed by citizens of a signatory, or are referred to the ICC by the UN Security Council, which has so far happened only in the case of Sudan. Numerous powerful states in which significant crimes occur, such as China, Russia, Pakistan, Iran and Iraq, did not sign the treaty, nor did the United States. In addition, the capacity of the newly formed court is limited, and the few cases in which investigations are taking place at present have pushed it to the limits of that capacity. Domestic prosecutions thus continue to play a major role. Since it must still be assumed that prosecutions will not occur in most states of commission, it is the states that are most able to prosecute, financially and in terms of infrastructure, that are called upon at least to open investigations, if not to prosecute. Because of its legal infrastructure and its Code of Crimes Against International Law, the Federal Republic of Germany is predestined to offer at least start-up assistance.

So far, few cases have been publicly discussed in which the Federal Prosecutor's office has been asked to open a criminal investigation under the VStGB. But the public discussion often overlooks the fact that under the principle of compulsory prosecution, Sec. 152 of the Code of Criminal Procedure, the Federal Prosecutor is not only authorized, but in some cases even required, to initiate an investigation. There has been no explanation as yet from the Federal Prosecutor of why no investigations have been undertaken by the prosecutor's office. Some of the roughly fifty criminal complaints made so far under the VStGB involve actions that clearly do not fall under the jurisdiction of German courts and occurred before the VStGB came into force. I will briefly discuss below the few remaining examples in which complainants received long explanations from the Federal Prosecutor of the grounds for closing an investigation, or notifications that no investigation would be initiated.

2. Torture in Abu Ghraib

The Federal Prosecutor (*Generalbundesanwalt*, or GBA) attached to the Federal Supreme Court refused on February 10, 2005, to open an investigation of war crimes against US Secretary of Defense Donald H. Rumsfeld[56] and nine other suspects under the VStGB for the abuse of prisoners in Abu Ghraib prison in Iraq between 2003 and 2004.[57] Of the ten accused, at least three were stationed in Germany at the time the complaint was lodged. The GBA justified its decision on the grounds that, under Sec. 153f StPO, there was no way for German investigative authorities to take action, given the principles of subsidiarity of the German legal authorities and non-intervention in the affairs of foreign countries, since the accusations were being prosecuted in the United States. The complainants, including the respected civil rights organization Center for Constitutional Rights in New York[58] and a total of seventeen victims from Iraq, appealed this decision and requested that charges be brought against Rumsfeld et al., or alternatively that an investigation of the accused persons at least be initiated.[59] In addition, they requested that, in view of an expert opinion on international law by M. Bothe and A. Fischer-Lescano,[60] an opinion be obtained from the Federal Constitutional Court, under Art. 100(2) of the Basic Law, regarding the relationship between the principle of universal jurisdiction (Sec. 1 VStGB) and Sec. 153f StPO. In a September 13, 2005, decision, the 5th criminal law panel of the Stuttgart Court of Appeals found inadmissible the request for a court decision forcing the prosecution to take up the case (*Klageerzwingungsverfahren*).[61]

The Stuttgart Court of Appeals found the request to force the prosecutor to pursue the case inadmissible (Sec. 172 (2), (3) StPO in conjunction with Sec. 153f StPO). It said the legislature had not intended such a use of the Klageerzwingungsverfahren in cases in which a case is dropped under the so-called principle of discretionary prosecution, including cases under Sec. 153f. In the court's view, when the VStGB was introduced, the legislature purposely refrained from establishing a process in the law for court review of the Federal Prosecutor's decisions. The Stuttgart Court of Appeals thus rejected the complainants' legal interpretation, which argued that the conditions of a crime under Sec. 153f were not present, and that therefore, as an exception, a Klageerzwingungsverfahren would be admissible. The complainants had argued that a domestic link was present due to the presence of at least three of the suspects and the temporary stays that could be ex-

---

[56] See generally http://www.rav.de/ag_voelkerrecht.htm; http://www.diefirma.net/index.php?rumsfeld.

[57] Reprinted in *Juristen-Zeitung* 2005, pp. 311 et seq.; thereto see the contribution of F. Jessberger in this volume; see also J. A. Hessbrugge, *ASIL Insights*, December 2004; for a critical view, see A. Fischer-Lescano, *German Law Journal* 2005, pp. 689 et seq.

[58] See http://www.ccr-ny.org.

[59] The text of the appeal is available at http://www.rav.de/download/kaleckKlageerzwingungsantrag.pdf.

[60] Available at http://www.rav.de/download/RumsfeldKurzgutachten1.pdf.

[61] *Neue Zeitschrift für Strafrecht* 2006, pp. 117 et seq.; for a critical view, see D. Basak, *Humanitäres Völkerrecht – Informationsschriften* 2005, pp. 85 et seq.; R. Keller, *Goltdammer's Archiv für Strafrecht* 2006, pp. 25 et seq.; M. Kurth, *Zeitschrift für internationale Strafrechtsdogmatik* 2006, pp. 81 et seq.; T. Singelnstein and P. Stolle, *Zeitschrift für internationale Strafrechtsdogmatik* 2006, pp. 118 et seq., available at http://www.zis-online.com; A. Fischer-Lescano, *International Legal Materials* 2006, pp. 115 et seq.

pected on the part of further suspects, so that the case could not have been suspended in the way it was. In addition, extensive expert opinions[62] and factual presentations provided evidence that criminal prosecutions in the United States had been limited to roughly a dozen lower-level soldiers, and that charges of command responsibility on the part of civilian and military superiors for the systematic torture at Abu Ghraib were not, in fact, being investigated in the United States. The Stuttgart Court of Appeals did not recognize this argument in any way nor did the Federal Prosecutor in the prior February 10, 2005, decision. Additionally, according to the Stuttgart Court of Appeals, the "(actual) discretionary decision by the Federal Prosecutor cannot be legally rejected," as it had not crossed the line into arbitrariness. The Federal Prosecutor's broad discretion was justified in this case, the court added, because "otherwise an unbridled extension of domestic criminal prosecution, which is questionable under international law," was to be feared.

The decision by the Stuttgart Court of Appeals may be criticized from the perspectives of both criminal procedure and legal policy.[63] In the end, the Stuttgart court essentially permitted the Federal Prosecutor to open investigations under the VStGB based on doubtful criteria, or to close cases from the start, as long as the decision is not obviously arbitrary in the court's view. The refusal to undertake substantive review of the Federal Prosecutor's decisions reveals a legal gap that cannot be reconciled with the rule of law created under the Basic Law.[64] As a result, victims of the most serious crimes remain without effective legal protection in Germany. The Center for Constitutional Rights, along with other human rights organizations, in February 2006 submitted a complaint to the UN Special Rapporteur on the Independence of Judges and Lawyers, Leandro Despouy, asking that he censure the US and German governments for impermissible intervention in the decisions of the German Federal Prosecutor.[65]

Substantively, the decision has been criticized in the literature primarily on the grounds that a duty to prosecute exists under Sec. 153f (1) sentence 1 StPO, because the majority of the suspects were found in Germany, especially the soldiers stationed there, and therefore conditions for the exercise of broad discretion on the part of the Federal Prosecutor were not present.[66] In addition, it is argued that the precedence of the state closest to the crime, which in itself is acceptable, was based on "abstract assumptions" and that the Federal Prosecutor refrained from "monitoring," for example, through inquiries or its own investigation.[67] Since the official explanation of the VStGB itself does not allow apparent prosecution to derogate from the principle of compulsory prosecution, the United States would

---

[62] See, inter alia, http://www.rav.de/StAR_290105_Horton.htm.

[63] For a critical view, see R. Keller, *supra* note 61; M. Kurth, *supra* note 61.

[64] See T. Singelnstein and P. Stolle, *supra* note 61, for agreement.

[65] See the joint press release by the complainants at http://www.rav.de/StAR_270206_Presseerklaerung.htm.

[66] See, e. g., M. Kurth, *supra* note 61, p. 84; T. Singelnstein and P. Stolle, *supra* note 61; A. Fischer-Lescano, *supra* note 61.

[67] See R. Keller, *supra* note 61, pp. 36 et seq.

have had to make it clear that "even the military courts they themselves appointed were making efforts at serious criminal prosecution."[68]

Based on the results of the courts martial in the United States that are now available, which were mainly limited to a dozen directly involved soldiers, and based on more recent information about the direct involvement of members of government, government lawyers, and high-ranking military officers in the planning and use of prohibited methods of interrogation,[69] a criminal complaint will once again be lodged in the foreseeable future.

It should also be noted that criminal complaints have been lodged repeatedly against German politicians for preparation of a war of aggression, especially by members of the peace movement who cite Sec. 80 of the Criminal Code, Art. 26 (I) of the Basic Law. In its January 26, 2006, decision—3 ARP 8/06-3—the Federal Prosecutor's office affirmed its well-known view of the law:

> Under the express wording of the provision, only the preparation of aggressive war, and not aggressive war itself, is criminal, so that taking part in a war of aggression planned by others is not criminal (Tröndle/Fischer, StGB, 53rd ed., Sec. 80 margin note 13). No analogy may be made in criminal law to the effect that, if preparation of a war of aggression is criminal, then this must also apply to its implementation (BVerfGE 26, 41, 42; 47, 109, 121 ff.). Nor can Art. 26 (1) of the Basic Law, which extends beyond the scope of Sec. 80 of the Criminal Code, be consulted in the interpretation. Article 103 (2) of the Basic Law prohibits the application of a criminal law provision beyond its express wording. Thus no one who became involved in the war-making enterprise only when war broke out or afterwards can be seen as a possible perpetrator (LK-Laufhütte, Criminal Code, 11th ed., Sec. 80 margin note 7).

This discussion again indicates how controversial, nationally and internationally, the criminalization of aggression is.[70] The ICC Statute lacks a definition of the crime, although the court's jurisdiction over the crime of aggression is established in Article 5 (I) (d). There is no provision of German international criminal law that extends universal jurisdiction to the crime of aggression. The commission of war crimes laid out in Part II of the VStGB may be universally prosecuted. Otherwise, only German participation in a war of aggression is criminal, and the prevailing interpretation of the term is very narrow. In this view, it includes only wars in contravention of international law that aim to annex or subjugate another country.[71]

3. Crimes of Torture in China Against Falun Gong Members

In a decision dated June 24, 2005, following a year and a half of preliminary investigation, the Federal Prosecutor's office in Karlsruhe refused to open a case

---

[68] D. Basak, *supra* note 61.

[69] See K. J. Greenberg and J. L. Dratel (eds.), *The Torture Papers: The Road to Abu Ghraib* (2005); K. J. Greenberg (ed.), *The Torture Debate in America* (2005).

[70] See the discussion in G. Werle, *supra* note 16, margin notes 1137 et seq.

[71] Ibid., with additional citations.

against Chinese government members for human rights violations against practicing members of Falun Gong in China (including torture and inhuman treatment in work camps, as well as killings). In November 2003, criminal complaints were submitted in the name of an association close to Falun Gong and a total of 40 individual complainants, some of them victims, from various nations.[72] The crimes alleged in the complaint, some of which were committed before and some since the VStGB came into force, included genocide, crimes against humanity, torture and other crimes, and named former Chinese President Jiang Zemin, further members of the Chinese government, and other high-ranking functionaries.

The grounds given in the prosecutor's announcement of the decision to close the case included, inter alia, that the suspects could not be expected to spend time in Germany. The complainants had shown that in the period since the complaint was lodged alone, two of the suspects had visited Germany. The prosecutor further explained that no successful investigation by German criminal authorities would be possible because the crimes had occurred in China.

In addition, he argued that the prosecutor's office assumed that the former President of the People's Republic of China, Jiang Zemin, enjoyed immunity under Sec. 20 (2) of the Court Constitution Law. The VStGB, unlike the Rome Statute of the ICC, contains no special immunity provisions, so that Secs. 18–20 of the Court Constitution Law (*Gerichtsverfassungsgesetz*) remains applicable. Without providing a more specific justification, the Federal Prosecutor's office claimed the existence of a rule under international law that not only sitting but also former heads of state and government enjoy immunity before foreign states' courts, at least for actions during their time in office. The court said that this state practice had been affirmed in the International Court of Justice decision in the case of the Democratic Republic of Congo against Belgium. In a further, as-yet-unpublished decision on April 28, 2005,[73] the Federal Prosecutor refused on similar grounds to initiate an investigation of Chechen Vice-President Ramzan Kadyrov and applied the claimed international legal rule to deputies of heads of state and government and to Chechnya, an autonomous republic within the Russian Federation.

This very broad interpretation of immunity as a bar to criminal prosecution by the Federal Prosecutor contradicts the prevailing view in the literature and in case law, especially the referenced ICJ decision in the *Yerodia* case on February 14, 2002.[74] In the above-mentioned study of the subject by the Max Planck Institute for Foreign and International Criminal Law, Kreicker explains:

> From these reasons for immunity *ratione personae*, however, it also follows that it cannot outlast the individual's term in office. Following the end of their function, heads of state and members of government no longer enjoy any special immunity. They can, however, call upon general sovereign immunity for official acts attributable to their state. But for crimes under international law, as shown, there is an exception. State practice confirms

---

[72] Available at http://flgjustice.org/dmdocuments/GermanComplaintJiangGe20031121.pdf.

[73] 3 ARP 35/02-2.

[74] Case concerning the *Arrest Warrant of 11 April 2000* (*Democratic Republic of the Congo v. Belgium*), judgment of February 14, 2002, *ICJ Reports* 2002, especially number 61, also available at http://www.icj-cij.org.

this statement ... For Germany, this means that sitting heads of state and government and ministers of foreign states enjoy complete immunity in Germany from criminal accountability, with no exception for crimes against international law. However, once they cease this function, they enjoy no special international legal exemption from criminal accountability—even for acts committed in their official capacity during their time in office. Without restriction the international legal immunity can hold them accountable.[75]

In a legal opinion[76] entitled "Immunity for Foreign State Officials Suspected of International Crimes," Professor Antonio Cassese limited this interpretation such that ministers do not enjoy personal immunity per se outside of the country, especially immunity from criminal prosecution for both official and private acts under general international law. They might be granted personal immunity, under special circumstances, if they are on an official mission abroad and thus represent their country. But even national law can only grant broader immunity to foreign officials to a certain extent. A grant of immunity cannot lead to immunity for international crimes. In this view, foreign officials who travel to Germany for private reasons do not enjoy immunity under Sec. 20 of the Court Constitution Law.

---

[75] H. Kreicker, *supra* note 5, pp. 350 et seq.—Sovereign immunity is based on two ideas: the sovereign equality of all states and the maintenance of the functioning of interstate communication. Two types of immunity are distinguished: immunity *ratione materiae* (substantive immunity) and *immunity ratione personae* (functional immunity); see K. Ipsen, *Völkerrecht*, 5th ed. (2004), Sec. 26, margin notes 35 et seq.; A. Cassese, *European Journal of International Law* 2002, pp. 853 et seq. See also the contribution of L. McGregor in this volume.

Immunity ratione materiae exists for sovereign acts by officials in their official capacity. The sovereign act is attributed only to the state; that is, only the state is responsible under international law, not the official. Thus immunity ratione materiae prevents the emergence of substantive individual (criminal) accountability; that is, even after the end of tenure in office, an official acting in an official capacity cannot be held personally responsible. Immunity ratione materiae is thus substantively limited; it applies only to sovereign acts in an official capacity but has no temporal limits.

Immunity ratione personae, in contrast, is granted to certain persons who represent a state for all acts for the duration of their tenure in office. It prevents trials of representatives of a state during their tenure in office, in order to ensure the ability of the state they represent to function. Immunity ratione personae is therefore temporally limited to the duration of the term in office, but its effect is absolute; that is, for acts committed either in an official or a private capacity, before and during one's term in office. Immunity ratione personae is only granted to a limited number of people, namely heads of state, diplomats (Article 31 of the Vienna Convention on Consular Relations), heads of government, and foreign ministers (case concerning the *Arrest Warrant of 11 April 2000* (*supra* note 74), margin note 51). These persons also, of course, enjoy immunity ratione materiae for their actions in an official capacity; that is, it is crucial for criminal prosecution after the end of one's term in office whether the act was done in an official or a private capacity.

[76] This opinion, submitted by the complainants in preparation of the complaint to be considered below against *Almatov et al.*, remains unpublished.

4. The Criminal Complaint against Former Uzbek Minister of the Interior Almatov et al. for the Andijan Massacre and Systematic Torture

On December 12, 2005, a criminal complaint was lodged with the Federal Prosecutor in Karlsruhe against Uzbek Minister of the Interior Zakir[77] Almatov and eleven other leading members of Uzbek security forces who appear on a list of people denied entry in a November 15, 2005, joint European Union position, 205/792/GASP, regarding restrictive measures.[78] The complaints were lodged by the US human rights organization Human Rights Watch[79] and eight Uzbek citizens, of whom four were in exile. The complaints alleged torture and crimes under Sec. 7 (10) (1), (5), (8), (9) and (10) of the VStGB; grievous bodily harm, Sec. 223, 224 of the Criminal Code; and murder and manslaughter, Secs. 211 and 212 of the Criminal Code in conjunction with Sec. 1 VStGB, 6 no. 9 of the Criminal Code, and the UN Torture Convention. The crimes charged relate to several cases, described in detail, of torture and of a massacre in the eastern Uzbek city of Andijan on May 13, 2005. The suspect Zakir Almatov had spent time in a special clinic in Hanover for cancer treatments in November 2005 until shortly before the complaint was lodged, and then left suddenly, for as yet unknown reasons. He has since been removed as Uzbek Minister of the Interior.

In a decision on March 30, 2006, the Federal Prosecutor refrained from initiating a case against *Almatov et al.* under Sec. 153f StPO, and for incidents occurring before June 30, 2002, under Sec. 153c StPO. According to the decision, the principle of compulsory prosecution applies only to a limited extent for crimes under the VStGB. Since neither the perpetrators nor the victims were located in Germany, an investigation could only be initiated "if significant success can be achieved in investigations by German investigative authorities to lay the groundwork for later prosecution (in Germany or abroad)." In the Uzbek case, this was not the situation; significant success could only be achieved by investigations in Uzbekistan itself. The prosecutor added that German officials would be unable to determine whether "one can assume tolerance or promotion of systematic torture by the Uzbek government that would justify prosecution under Sec. 7 VStGB." Thus the strong suspicion necessary to issue an arrest warrant was not present. Furthermore, a "significant loss of evidence resulting from the failure of German investigative authorities to act" was not to be feared, since

many facts have already been comprehensively documented by non-governmental organizations and the United Nations. ... The view that a German investigation must document according to procedural standards and systematically evaluate evidence existing worldwide, based on an unlimited principle of universal jurisdiction (Sec. 1 VStGB), is a mistake. It would lead to purely symbolic prosecutions. These were not wanted by the legislature, even for crimes under international law, especially since it would lead to long-term commitment of the prosecution's already limited personnel and financial resources, to the detriment of other prosecutions that hold greater promise of success.

---

[77] Also written as Zokirjon.
[78] See the text of the complaint at http://www.zeit.de/online/2005/51/anzeige_almatov.
[79] http://www.hrw.org.

With this decision, the brief spring of international criminal law in Germany seemed to be over before it had really begun. Under this restrictive interpretation, the VStGB can apparently only be applied in the rare cases in which perpetrators who enjoy no immunity in the broadest sense spend enough time in Germany for investigations to be carried out without the perpetrators' knowledge that can lead to results justifying strong suspicion. Almatov, who was one of those responsible for the massacre in Andijan in which hundreds of civilians lost their lives and is on the list of those prohibited from entering the EU, was nevertheless able to enter Germany unmolested under a humanitarian exception and to remain for private reasons, without any investigation being undertaken by the Federal Prosecutor. The criminal complaints lodged by non-governmental organizations, which called attention to him only after he had entered the country, were then rejected on the grounds, among others, that the suspect was no longer in Germany at the time of the decision and that an investigation therefore had little chance of success and, because of the absence of the suspect, would be purely symbolic.

One of the complainants' important arguments for prosecution of the former Uzbek minister by German prosecutors is the obvious lack of punishment in Uzbekistan itself for torture and systematic violence against the civilian population. Even under the broadest interpretation of the principles of subsidiarity and complementarity, the prosecutor would, according to its own legal interpretation, be obliged to take action. A year before, in refusing to open a case against US Secretary of Defense Donald Rumsfeld for the mistreatment of prisoners at Abu Ghraib, the Federal Prosecutor had primarily relied on the fact that cases were already pending in the United States against individual perpetrators. Thus in the view of the Federal Prosecutor, there could be no talk of impunity for violations of human rights in the case of the United States. This view did not even apply to the civilian and military superiors, especially Rumsfeld, against whom the complaints were lodged in Germany because no cases had been brought in the United States for command responsibility.[80] In the case of Uzbekistan, this argument does not apply in any case, since not even lower-level direct perpetrators have been prosecuted.

IV. Prospects

For many reasons, prosecutions for serious violations of human rights are always preferable in the state of commission, or if possible in the country of origin of perpetrators and victims, rather than in uninvolved third states. These reasons include the difficulty of obtaining evidence, the unlikelihood of achieving the questionable but established goals of punishment such as positive and negative special and general prevention, and the questionable effects on the affected population and the

---

[80] This has now been strongly criticized by numerous US human rights organizations, for example in Human Rights First, *Command's Responsibility: Detainee Deaths in US Custody in Iraq and Afghanistan* (2006); Center for Human Rights and Global Justice, Human Rights First and Human Rights Watch, *By the Numbers: Findings of the Detainee Abuse and Accountability Project* (2006).

public. Thus national and regional human rights protection systems should be created, such as the European Court of Human Rights and the inter-American human rights system. To avoid longer-lasting impunity for such crimes for the affected individuals and societies, however, a practice of international criminal prosecution has developed over the last ten years that resembles a patchwork quilt. In addition to the UN Tribunals for former Yugoslavia and Rwanda, with jurisdiction over specific regions; the mixed, national/international tribunals for Sierra Leone, Cambodia, and Bosnia-Herzegovina; and the International Criminal Court in the Hague—with jurisdiction only over incidents after July 1, 2002, in the signatory states and in exceptional cases over others—a number of mainly Western European countries such as Spain, Belgium, France, and the Netherlands have pending or completed prosecutions against suspected perpetrators of serious violations of human rights from third states on the basis of universal jurisdiction.[81] Despite the pre-eminent role claimed by Germany in the creation of the ICC and despite the adoption of a Code of Crimes Against International Law that seems to reflect "the most modern stage in the development of international humanitarian law and international criminal law,"[82] no significant practical application of international criminal law can be observed in Germany.[83]

The reasons for this lack of practice are, among other things, political opportunism in regard to foreign policy and economic goals; a lack of political will on the part of criminal authorities and their superiors at the Federal Ministry of Justice; lack of knowledge and understanding of international criminal law practice in the Federal Prosecutor's office; and also an understandable reluctance, given the above-mentioned problems in carrying out investigations.

So far, the international law scholars charged with developing the draft of the VStGB have had little to say about the practice of the Federal Prosecutor's office or about the possible reasons for its general passivity. Criminal law scholar Rainer Keller sees a fundamental danger of political selectivity in the use of universal jurisdiction and "an element of arbitrariness that calls the admissibility of universal jurisdiction into question," if "members of powerful states are systematically exempted from assignments of blame."[84] Thus he would prefer to limit its application generally to those present in the country, and also considers it inadmissible without a domestic link if "the officials using universal jurisdiction" are not guaranteed "complete independence from instructions and monitoring on the part of the respective national executive."

Contrasting with this are the demands of human rights organizations for an increase in response to serious human rights violations by means of the criminal law. This approach at times fails to acknowledge that, for national prosecutors in

---

[81] See the recent Human Rights Watch Report, *Universal Jurisdiction in Europe* (2006), available at http://www.hrw.org.

[82] *Supra* note 2.

[83] See especially the criticism of the Federal Prosecutor's decision in the *Abu Ghraib* case, *supra* III.2.

[84] R. Keller, *supra* note 61, pp. 30 et seq. Thereto see also the contribution of P. Stolle and T. Singelnstein in this volume.

third states, the possibilities for investigation and prosecution are limited, given their own need to take account of nationally and internationally recognized standards of fair procedure. Therefore, no quick results can be achieved. International criminal law is not a cure-all. The demand for retroactive criminal sanctions for human rights violations should continue to be made, but attention should be paid to the worldwide establishment of civil restitution rules. In addition, the focus of the work of human rights organizations should lie in the areas of prevention, avoidance of human rights violations, and the building of rule of law and democratic structures throughout the world. Furthermore, continuing education is necessary to create awareness among (potential) perpetrators, victims, criminal lawyers, prosecutors, and law enforcement agencies of the fact that even perpetrators of macrocriminality, often government officials, may be subject to individual criminal prosecution.

The Pinochet Effect and the Spanish Contribution to Universal Jurisdiction

Naomi Roht-Arriaza

If you had asked in 1995 about the prospects for bringing to justice those responsible for killings, disappearances, and torture in the Southern Cone of Latin America (Argentina, Chile, and Uruguay), most observers would have been deeply pessimistic. Amnesties and/or pardons were in place in all three countries, the "end of the transition" had been decreed, human rights groups were marginalized.

Ten years later, the situation is far different in all three countries. The amnesty laws have been annulled in Argentina and major cases have been reopened; the surviving leaders of the repression are in jail awaiting trial. In Chile and Uruguay, the amnesty law has been at least to some degree sidelined and limited. General Pinochet faces trial on both human rights and corruption charges, his immunity stripped. The head of the notorious secret police, DINA, and other operatives are in prison or face long prison terms. A government-appointed Commission has investigated widespread torture throughout the dictatorship years and proposed reparations. In Uruguay, numerous investigations are now underway.

What happened? The answer is a complex interplay between domestic factors, including political change and judicial reform, and external factors. Foremost among the latter, and where I will focus my remarks, is the effect of transnational cases—that is, cases brought in one state's national courts regarding events that took place in another state—as catalysts for domestic prosecutions and investigations. I look specifically at the cases, based on universal jurisdiction, begun in Spain in 1996 against the leadership of the Argentine and Chilean military dictatorships, and the evolution of Spanish jurisprudence on the issue of universal jurisdiction. I argue that in choosing what kind of transnational cases to bring, it is important to consider the potential for catalytic effects within the territorial state and the type of catalytic effects that have characterized the Southern Cone cases. It is also important to consider the converse: the potential for a backlash against an ambitious case or an overload of controversial cases to close off possibilities for future complainants and of future development of the law. In other words, it is important to be strategic.

Part I will discuss the Spanish cases that led up to, most famously, the detention of Pinochet in London in 1998, and the subsequent evolution of those cases. Part

II will trace the backlash in the Spanish courts. Part III considers the most recent reaffirmation of a broad principle of universal jurisdiction by the Spanish Constitutional Court in October 2005, and concludes with some thoughts for the future.

I. The Early Cases

In April 1996 members of the Spanish Union of Progressive Prosecutors filed a complaint in Spanish federal court (Audiencia Nacional) accusing members of the Argentine military junta of genocide, terrorism, and other crimes regarding the detention and subsequent disappearance during the 1970s of a number of Spanish citizens and citizens of Spanish descent.[1] Spanish law allows public interest organizations, as well as aggrieved individuals, to file and maintain criminal complaints even without the backing of, and in this case over the strenuous opposition of, the state prosecutor's office. This complaint, and other similar complaints later filed in Belgium, France, Italy, Switzerland, Germany, and elsewhere, would profoundly influence the legal process within Chile and Argentina.

Article 23.4 of the Spanish Judicial Law allows prosecution of non-Spanish citizens for some crimes committed outside Spain, among them genocide, terrorism, and other crimes under international law contained in treaties ratified by Spain. The law does not limit prosecutions to Spanish citizens, but applies to victims of any nationality. Nor does it, by its terms, create any hierarchy of jurisdictions. The case was by law assigned to the Audiencia Nacional, the court with jurisdiction over international crimes. By lot, the case fell to Judge Baltazar Garzón.

In 1998 Garzón issued an international arrest warrant for retired General Galtieri and nine other Argentine officers, later expanding indictments to encompass over a hundred officers.

Meanwhile, in July 1996 a second complaint accused General Pinochet and others of the deaths and disappearances of Chileans, and was assigned to a different judge.[2] Judge Garzón began looking into Operation Condor, a coordinated effort by the South American militaries to assassinate and disappear opponents across borders in Latin America, Europe, and the United States. The two cases were later consolidated within a single investigation under Judge Garzón. It was Garzón who, in the course of the Operation Condor investigation, issued an arrest warrant and a request for extradition of General Pinochet when he arrived in London for medical treatment. The UK House of Lords eventually held, twice, that Pinochet had no immunity from prosecution for torture and other international

---

[1] *Denuncia de la Asociación Progresista de Fiscales de España con la que se inicia el juicio por los desaparecidos españoles en Argentina, de fecha 28 marzo de 1996*, (complaint), found at http://www.derechos.org/nizkor/arg/espana/inicial.html. A detailed discussion of the Spanish cases can be found at R. J. Wilson, *Human Rights Quarterly* 1999, p. 927.

[2] See http://www.derechos.org/nizkor/chile for copies of the relevant complaint and legal decisions in the Spanish case.

crimes as a former head of state, and that he could be extradited to Spain.[3] As is well known, he was eventually released by the political branch of the UK government on humanitarian grounds, based on his ill-health, and returned to Chile in March 2000.

There, as mentioned, his parliamentary immunity has been stripped several times and he has faced multiple indictments. While several of these were eventually dismissed based on his health, as of November 2005 he faces trial for kidnappings and murder as well as for income tax evasion and fiscal fraud. In addition, some 300 other cases are either pending or have resulted in convictions, and the 1978 amnesty law has been partially limited through judicial interpretation, although not annulled. As a result of subsequent investigation into Pinochet's money-laundering activities, the executives of US-based Riggs Bank were forced to create a $9 million fund for victims of the military regime.[4]

The Argentine investigation has also produced concrete results. In addition to annulment of the due obedience and *punto final* laws and the resumption of large-scale investigations into the army and navy's participation in criminal activities, many of the most notorious operatives of the dictatorship period, including General Videla, are under arrest. A pair of navy officers have also been detained in Spain. Adolfo Scilingo, a former navy captain who confessed to throwing prisoners alive from airplanes into the sea, was detained in October 1997 after traveling to Madrid. He was eventually tried before a 3-judge panel and sentenced to over 200 years in prison on April 19, 2005, convicted on charges of crimes against humanity. Another navy officer, Miguel Angel Cavallo, was detained in Mexico on a Spanish warrant stemming from Judge Garzón's investigation. After the Mexican Supreme Court denied his legal challenges, he was extradited to Spain and his trial is now scheduled for 2006.[5]

In addition to these direct impacts, there are a number of indirect impacts. The cases pushed governments, judges, and advocates to acknowledge the need for, and legitimacy of, prosecutions for the deaths, torture, and disappearances of the 1970s and '80s. Most importantly, they cases demonstrated the limits of local amnesty laws, especially those that do not enjoy international legitimacy. The Spanish courts held that they did not need to take the Chilean or Argentine amnesty laws into account because they were not acquittals or pardons as required under Spanish law and were otherwise illegitimate under international law. The Court based its decision in part on the jurisprudence of the Inter-American Commission

---

[3] *Regina v. Bartle and the Commissioner of Police for the Metropolis and Others ex parte Pinochet*, November 25, 1998, 3 WLR 1456 (*Pinochet I*); *Regina v. Bartle and the Commissioner of Police for the Metropolis and Others ex parte Pinochet*, March 24, 1999, 2 WLR 827 (*Pinochet III*). The decisions and other documents relating to the UK and Spanish cases are collected in R. Brody and M. Ratner (eds.), *The Pinochet Papers: The Case of Augusto Pinochet in Spain and Britain* (2000).

[4] "Riggs to Pay Victims Of Pinochet," *Washington Post*, February 26, 2005.

[5] Decision of Judge Juan García Orozco, Judge of District B of "Amparo" of the Federal District Criminal Court, March 22, 2002; Suprema Corte de Justicia, *Caso Cavallo*, June 10, 2003, available at http://www.scjn.gob.mx/inicial.asp.

and Court.[6] This reduces the value of a local amnesty, since a transnational or international prosecution may proceed even in the face of one.[7] These cases also helped to prompt a reexamination of Spain's own past, with a Parliamentary Commission established and increasing calls for exhumations of the thousands still unclaimed after Spain's Civil War. In Mexico as well, in the wake of the Cavallo affair the Mexican Supreme Court found that disappearance cases are not subject to a statute of limitations, and the Mexican government (largely for internal reasons, admittedly) created a Special Prosecutor's Office to look into the emblematic crimes of previous governments, including the 1968 Tlatelolco student massacre.

II. The Backlash

The other indirect result was to give new hope to victims worldwide that they could use transnational justice mechanisms in cases where justice was unavailable at home. Complainants began bringing dozens of cases, most of them to the two most well-known and welcoming forums: Belgium and Spain. Some involved high-profile defendants, including sitting heads of state and figures from powerful states, and many of them involved cases where neither the complainants nor the defendants had any tie with the forum state. Predictably, states reacted, creating pressure to reform or shut down the possibility of using these forums. The backlash took a number of forms. First, legislative as well as jurisprudential efforts inserted and tightened the required links between the complainant and the forum state in the name of avoiding "chaos" in the international system. Second, access to the universal jurisdiction-based forum was made dependent on a showing that the case could not be brought in the territorial jurisdiction; conversely, cases were to be dismissed where the quality of justice in the territorial state was deemed adequate. Third, some states enacted, and others began discussing, limits on complainants' ability to go directly to an investigating judge, requiring that cases be brought solely through a state prosecutor, in order to give the executive branch an early check on which cases could proceed. Altogether, between 1998 (the high point of enthusiasm for universal jurisdiction) and 2004, there was a significant reduction.

In Belgium, under intense US pressure, a 2003 legislative reform severely limited Belgium's earlier broad universal jurisdiction statute. The most important changes concern the need for links to the forum, executive discretion, and the relationship to the territorial jurisdiction. A case cannot be opened unless there is a link between the crime and Belgium: either the suspect must be Belgian, the vic-

---

[6] The French Cour de Cassation has come to a similar conclusion in the *Ould Dah* case, October 23, 2002, available at http://www.legal.apt.ch/MECHANISMS/International_ Justice/Universal%20Jurisdiction/France%/20-%20Germany%20-%20UK/fr-ca%20e;u-%20ould.htm. See also the contribution of J. Sulzer in this volume.

[7] The establishment and decisions of the Special Court for Sierra Leone have also eroded the value of local amnesties, of course.

tim must be Belgian or reside in Belgium for at least three years, or a treaty (i.e., the Torture Convention) must require prosecution, for example, when the suspect is present in Belgium. Victims can now file suit directly (as *partie civile*) only if the accused is Belgian or lives in Belgium. Otherwise, the decision to investigate lies entirely with the state prosecutor, or in some cases the office of public prosecutions. The prosecutor is obligated to proceed unless, among other reasons, in the interests of justice and in keeping with Belgium's international obligations, the case should instead be brought to another jurisdiction, where the administration of justice is independent and impartial. The decision not to proceed cannot be challenged. A few pending cases were "grandfathered in" because the investigations were at an advanced stage, but most were not.

In Spain as well, the law was tightened up along various axes, although here the job was done through the courts rather than the legislature. The Guatemalan case was the leading example. In 1999, Nobel Peace Prize winner Rigoberta Menchú along with others brought a complaint in Spanish courts alleging genocide, torture, terrorism, summary execution, and unlawful detention perpetrated against Guatemala's Mayan Indians and their supporters. The suspects included five generals, two police chiefs, a colonel, former presidents, and former defense and interior ministers. On March 27, 2000, Judge Guillermo Ruíz Polanco accepted the complaint and agreed to open an investigation. In his ruling, the judge noted that several of the victims were Spanish or had died on Spanish territory. "The events reported clearly show the appearance of genocide. And that is sufficient for now," said the judge's ruling. The genocide charges included both the targeting of ethnic Mayans and the intended elimination of a part of the "national" group due to its perceived ideology, a gloss on the definition of genocide already accepted by the Audiencia Nacional in earlier cases involving Chilean and Argentine defendants.[8] The judge, like Judge Garzón in the Southern Cone cases, found that Spanish jurisdiction was appropriate because the local courts had not acted. The lower courts had thus introduced the notion of *subsidiarity* into the law, the idea that universal jurisdiction was required because the domestic courts had not properly done their jobs. That notion was to prove problematic as the case moved through the courts.

In December, 2000, the full Audiencia Nacional, acting as an appeals court, ruled against the Guatemalans.[9] It held that "for the moment" Spanish courts had no jurisdiction over the alleged crimes and that the case should be closed. The judges gave two reasons. First, while the Spanish courts could consider genocide and terrorism committed elsewhere by non-Spaniards, any such inquiry had to be subsidiary to the state where the crimes took place. Other national courts could act only if there were clear legal impediments to prosecution there, or if judges there were "subject to pressure from official or de facto powers that create a climate of intimidation or fear making it impossible to carry out the judicial function with the

---

[8] See Autos (Decisions) of November 4 and 5, 1998, reproduced in R. Brody and M. Ratner, *supra* note 3.

[9] Decision of the Audiencia Nacional (Sala de lo penal) of December 13, 2000 (*genocide in Guatemala*), available at http://www.icrc.org/ihl-nat.nsf and http://www.derechos.org/nizkor/guatemala.

serenity and impartiality required." Second, the court applied its test to Guatemala. Since the UN-sponsored truth commission had only published its report in 1999, and the Guatemalan Law of National Reconciliation permitted genocide prosecutions, there was insufficient evidence in the record that the Guatemalan courts were not able or willing to do the job themselves. Therefore, Spanish courts should stay out of the case.

On February 25, 2003, over two years after the AN decision, the Spanish Supreme Court, by a vote of 8-7, tightened even further the requirements for a universal jurisdiction-based case. The majority held, in short, that only cases with a clear link to Spain could proceed. The case was reopened and remanded to pursue investigations into the possible torture of Spanish citizens in the 1980 Embassy massacre, and the torture of four Spanish priests killed by the military from 1980 through 1982, but all the genocide and terrorism charges, and the torture charges against non-Spaniards, were dismissed.

The majority opinion first quickly found that the AN's inquiry into the availability of an alternative forum was inappropriate. "Basing subsidiarity on the real or apparent inactivity of local courts implies a judgment of one state's courts about the ability to administer justice of the similarly situated organs of another sovereign state." While such an "unable or unwilling" inquiry might be appropriate for an ICC, national courts should not be making these kinds of judgments, which could have an important effect on foreign relations and should be left to the political branches.

Next, the majority construed the 1948 Genocide Convention. The court found, as in the Southern Cone cases, that Article 6 of the Convention was not limited to territorial and international criminal jurisdictions. However, Article 8 directs states to respond to genocide occurring outside their borders by going to the UN, not by exercising universal jurisdiction. The presence of a UN mission showed that the UN knew about conditions in Guatemala, yet had failed to create an ad-hoc tribunal along the lines of Yugoslavia or Rwanda.

The heart of the matter, for the majority, was that Article 23.4 of the Organic Law of State Power (LOPD), despite its apparent clarity, could not be so open-ended as to allow criminal investigations based on news of crimes being committed anywhere in the world. Extraterritorial jurisdiction, when not authorized by the UN or specifically regulated by treaty, required a point of contact with the nation or with national interests. The majority cited cases from the German and Belgian courts, and the ICJ's *Arrest Warrant (Congo v. Belgium)* case, in support of these propositions.[10] The court pointed to the "extradite-or-prosecute" provisions of a number of treaties, including the Torture and Terrorism Conventions, as requiring the presence of the defendant to proceed when there is no other type of national interest (like the protective principle or active or passive personality principles) involved. A connection to a state interest, the majority opined, creates legitimacy and rationality in international relations and respect for the non-intervention prin-

---

[10] The judgment concerning the *Arrest Warrant of 11 April 2000 (Democratic Republic of the Congo v. Belgium)*, February 14, 2002, holds that a sitting foreign minister has personal immunity from criminal jurisdiction in national courts.

ciple. What is more, this connection to a national interest should exist in the principal charges against the defendant, not just in related or ancillary ones. For that reason, all the genocide charges were thrown out—none of the defendants were present and there was no allegation genocide had been aimed at Spaniards as a group. Only the torture charges, to the extent they involved Spanish citizens, could stand because the Convention against Torture allows for passive personality jurisdiction.

The seven dissenters argued the position that universal jurisdiction in cases of genocide was necessary to avoid impunity and that in such cases the state acted in representation of the international community. The majority's view was too restrictive and, therefore, "incompatible with the treatment of this grave crime in our internal law and in international law."

Rather, any limits had to come from a flexible, prudential rule of reason aimed at practical concerns like the potential effectiveness of an investigation and extradition request or a potentially high burden on the Spanish courts. For the dissenters, a tie to Spain was merely an aid in applying this rule of reason, not a jurisdictional prerequisite. In this case, they found more than enough links to Spain to justify the Spanish courts' intervention. Historic, social, linguistic, and jurisprudential ties linked the countries. The crimes at issue involved Spanish citizens, not as victims themselves of genocide, but as victims targeted because they were defending others from genocide. This case was a paradigmatic example of those where Spain should exercise its jurisdiction: there would never be a more compelling case. "If there is no nexus in this case, then a nexus requirement becomes a mere pretext to exclude or suppress universal jurisdiction in all genocide cases." That, the dissenters argued, should not be done.

Subsequent cases involving Chile and Peru reiterated the Supreme Court's majority holding, giving it precedential weight. It seemed that the Spanish forum had partially closed, although the two cases involving Argentine torturers moved forward because at least one of the victims had Spanish nationality.

III. A New Turnaround?

Since 2004, the courts and prosecutors offices have been giving mixed signals about the continued viability of universal jurisdiction cases. On the one hand, the German prosecutor's decision not to proceed in the Rumsfeld case and in the Falun Gong cases,[11] and a lower French courts' decision not to proceed in the Massacre on the Beach cases from Congo Brazzaville[12] are continuing setbacks, and particularly indicative that prosecutors and courts, even with ostensibly broad le-

---

[11] Ruling of the Attorney General not to institute proceedings against *Jiang Zemin et al.*, June 24, 2005, Case 3 ARP 654/03-2 (on file with author). The decision is on appeal.

[12] The case was dismissed in February 2005 and is on appeal before the Court de Cassation. See http://www.lemessager.net; FIDH, *Affaire des disparus du Beach: La justice française instrumentalisée, les victimes insultées* (November 23, 2004). See also the contribution of J. Sulzer in this volume.

gal authority, are not willing to take on the powerful of powerful countries. On the other hand, a number of cases are more hopeful. These include a number of cases against perpetrators found within the forum state (and so, legitimate under even the restrictive "links" requirement), including the convictions of Afghans in the UK and the Netherlands, and of a Congolese military officer in the Netherlands,[13] as well as the Belgian prosecutor's decision to move forward on the Habré case. That case, involving the ex-head of state of Chad, was one of three cases grand-fathered in under the pre-2003 Belgian universal jurisdiction law; so, arguably, it too fits within the new, narrower scope for universal jurisdiction. However, the September 26, 2005, ruling of the Spanish Constitutional Court in the Guatemala case, along with other cases from Spanish courts, provides a direct challenge to the narrower, *links-* and *subsidiarity*-based analyses.

The Spanish change in attitude towards universal jurisdiction cases can be traced in part to the election of Socialist José Luís Rodríguez Zapatero as Prime Minister in 2004. As a result, the Public Prosecutor's Office, which had been hos-tile to universal jurisdiction cases from 1996 on, changed its tune and began sup-porting victims' groups in litigating the existing cases. The first concrete results of this change appeared in the Spanish courts in April 2004, when the Prosecutor's office argued for conviction and a lengthy sentence in the Scilingo case. Recall that Scilingo had been charged with genocide and terrorism and jailed when he ar-rived in Spain in 1997. A three-judge panel found on April 19, 2005, that Scilingo was guilty of crimes against humanity. Although the legal figure of crimes against humanity was not made part of the Spanish Penal Code until well after the events at issue, and although the original charge was genocide, the panel found that by the 1970s crimes against humanity constituted a part of customary international law. It was therefore applicable by local courts directly without violating the prin-ciple of *nullum crimen sine lege*. Genocide was a subspecies of crimes against humanity. The panel relied extensively on ICTY jurisprudence to reach its conclu-sion, which will make it much easier to bring cases before the Spanish courts based on allegations of crimes against humanity, without need to prove the spe-cific intent and limited racial, religious, national, or ethnical group requirements of genocide.

The Constitutional Tribunal's decision in the Guatemala case, handed down in September 2005, largely mirrors the dissent in the (lower) Supreme Court. The Tribunal began with the plain language and legislative intent of Article 23.4 of the Organic Law of State Power (LOPD). As the Tribunal pointed out, the law itself establishes only a single limitation: the suspect cannot have been convicted, found innocent or pardoned abroad. It contains no implicit or explicit hierarchy of poten-tial jurisdictions; it focuses only on the nature of the crime, not on any ties to the

---

[13] Hesamuddin Hesam, 57, and Habibullah Jalalzoy, 59, a former head of Afghan intelli-gence and his deputy, were convicted of torture in October 2005 by the Dutch courts. Sebastian Nzapali, a former colonel in the Zairian army under Mobutu, was tried and convicted on torture charges in Rotterdam in March 2004. Faryadi Sarwar Zardad, an Afghan accused of torture and hostage-taking, was convicted in the UK's Old Bailey court on July 19, 2005.

forum; and it establishes concurrent jurisdiction. Given the lack of textual support, restrictive interpretations of the law were overly strict and unwarranted. Moreover, the Constitutional Tribunal found that both the AN and the Supreme Court's subsidiarity requirements put complainants in an untenable position, having to prove that no case could be brought at home.

The Constitutional Tribunal rejected the lower court's analysis of the Genocide Convention. The Convention's silence on alternative jurisdictions beyond the territorial and an international court cannot be read as an implicit limit. Rather, Article VI of the Convention simply establishes the minimal obligations on states. The obligations to avoid impunity found in customary international law (and even as a jus cogens norm) are incompatible with such a limited reading of the Convention and would, perversely, create a limit on state action for parties to the Convention that did not apply to non-parties, which could rely on a universal jurisdiction founded in customary international law.

The Supreme Court majority had found in customary international law a need for a "connecting nexus," which might include the presence of the defendant, the nationality of the victims, or some other point of contact with national interests. The Constitutional Tribunal strongly disagreed. "We think it is highly debatable that the requirement of a nexus is to be found in customary international law, especially because the cases cited by the Supreme Court do not support that conclusion." The Tribunal pointed out that a number of other countries have broad jurisdictional grants that do not require any link, citing among others the German Code of Crimes Against International Law.

The Supreme Court had also cited a number of treaties containing "extradite-or-prosecute" obligations when the defendant is present as evidence that the defendant's presence was required. The Constitutional Tribunal found that such a restriction might be applicable when jurisdiction was based on Article 23.4 (g), which extends jurisdiction to unenumerated crimes where so required by treaty. But it surely did not apply to the rest of the Article, which enumerated specific crimes like genocide and terrorism. While the defendant's presence was necessary for trial (Spain forbids trial in absentia), it was not needed to open the case. Extradition could be used to achieve the goal of universal jurisdiction: prosecution and punishment of crimes that affect the entire international community.

Similarly, limits based on the nationality of the victims or on protective principles were contrary to the language of the statute and would abrogate it in practice. Nationality-based limits were especially absurd in cases of alleged genocide, since not only would the victims have to be Spanish, but the specific intent of the defendant would have to encompass the destruction of Spaniards as a group, which the court found an improbable reading of the statute. The national interest or protective criteria were equally baseless, and irreconcilable with the very foundation of universal jurisdiction, which is based solely on the nature of the crime. "Prosecution and punishment of crimes that affect not only the specific victims but the international community as a whole are not only a shared commitment but also a shared interest of all states, and therefore their legitimacy cannot depend on the particular interest of any one state."

For those reasons, the Constitutional Tribunal found that the right to an effective judicial remedy had been abridged, in that the lower courts had created a crabbed interpretation of the law, in violation of principles of proportionality between means and ends.

The practical effect of the decision is to send the Guatemala case back to the investigating magistrate to reopen it in line with the Tribunal's judgment, admitting the bulk of the claims involving genocide against Guatemalans. It also erases the prior doctrine enunciated by the Supreme Court, affecting other pending cases as well, at least where local courts are not actually prosecuting. The most important of these is a case involving Chinese government officials' acts in Tibet.[14]

In light of the strength of the backlash against "pure" universal jurisdiction cases, the reversal of this trend at the level of Spain's highest court is significant. The decision takes on some of the thorniest issues, those involving links to the forum state, and the relationship between the forum state and the territorial state. A presence-of-the-defendant requirement, for example, changes the nature of universal jurisdiction from a doctrine providing for prosecution and punishment, to a doctrine that provides "no safe haven" but little more. Few defendants are likely to hang around while judges investigate their cases or complainants amass requisite evidence. Moreover, allowing the defendant's presence for trial to be sought through extradition may, under certain treaty obligations, trigger a duty to prosecute domestically if extradition is denied. Similarly, demanding a nexus through victim nationality or residence requirements or through "national interest," ignores universal jurisdiction's fundamental claim that suppressing certain heinous crimes affecting international order is in the interest of all states; it reduces universal jurisdiction to a variant on passive personality jurisdiction. The Tribunal's jettisoning of these limits is to be welcomed.

The question of the relationship between the forum investigating the crimes and the territorial forum is more complicated. Investigations based on universal jurisdiction, if they are successful, can serve as a catalyst for domestic investigations; indeed, I argue elsewhere that the potential for such catalytic effects is one of the primary ways to evaluate the promise of such efforts.[15] The calculus of how real or effective domestic prosecution efforts are is often not easily answerable and changes over time; the simple opening of an investigation at home may not be enough and should not, by its terms, oust jurisdiction in another forum. Moreover, at some point considerations of judicial economy and "sunken"—that is, already incurred, costs counsel continuing a prosecution where it has begun, even if at some point later a domestic forum becomes available. This was one of the argu-

---

[14] The Tibet complaint was filed in June 2005 by three Tibet-related organizations. It names seven high-ranking Chinese government officials, including ex-President Jiang Zemin and former Prime Minister Li Peng. The decision of the lower court, dated January 10, 2006, relies on the Constitutional Court decision and finds that the facts submitted on Tibet constitute prima facie substantiated allegations of genocide. Decision of the Audiencia Nacional, 4th section, Criminal Chamber, January 10, 2006, Case No. 196/05; available at http://www.derechos.org/nizkor/espana/doc/tibet.html.

[15] See N. Roht-Arriaza, *The Pinochet Effect: Transnational Justice in the Age of Human Rights* (2005).

ments in favor of keeping the Scilingo and Cavallo prosecutions in the Spanish courts despite changes in the availability of an Argentine forum. On the other hand, concurrent prosecutions could be duplicative and lead to inconsistent results. Moreover, if a goal is to eventually strengthen domestic legal systems, complainants and advocates must actually use them to try cases.

Beyond counseling self-restraint by complainants and improved judicial cooperation, courts may find it necessary to develop doctrines of prudential abstention or conditional suspension in cases where concurrent investigations would be wasteful or confusing. But the Spanish Tribunal helps clarify that such accommodations are neither jurisdictional nor required—the ICC's "unable-or-unwilling" requirement does not apply to national courts.

Of course, the sweep of this decision may itself push the pendulum back the other way. Courts may well choose to adopt a version of the Supreme Court minority's "prudential" test, asking whether the case could be effectively litigated in Spain even if in theory the courts do have jurisdiction. Or, if a flood of cases descend on the Spanish courts anew, momentum for legislative limits may grow. It will be up to advocates to act responsibly and strategically, bringing cases that will minimize the potential for backlash while maximizing the potential to dislodge blockages to action at the domestic level and to create good outcomes. Both boldness and self-restraint, in equal measures, will be needed to ensure the continuing viability of a broad view of universal jurisdiction.

Implementing the Principle of Universal Jurisdiction in France

Jeanne Sulzer

I. Scope of Universal Jurisdiction in France

Although French law has incorporated universal jurisdiction based on treaty obligations, in respect of certain offenses, absolute universal jurisdiction based on customary international law has not been established. As a result, universal jurisdiction cannot generally be exercised in French courts over certain *jus cogens* crimes, including crimes against humanity and crimes of genocide. A limited exception is provided by Law No. 95-1 of January 2, 1995, and Law No 96-432 of May 22, 1996, which allow for the exercise of absolute universal jurisdiction in relation to international crimes committed in Yugoslavia and Rwanda respectively. These were enacted in order to adapt French law to the requirements of UN Resolutions 827 (Yugoslavia) and 955 (Rwanda), adopted by the United Nations Security Council to establish the two ad hoc International Criminal Tribunals.

1. Extent of Treaty-Based Universal Jurisdiction before French Courts

Article 689 of the French Code of Criminal Procedure (CCP) defines the mechanism of universal jurisdiction before French courts in the following terms:

> Perpetrators of or accomplices to offenses committed outside the territory of the Republic may be prosecuted and tried by French courts either when French law is applicable under the provisions of Book I of the Criminal Code or any other statute, or when an international Convention gives jurisdiction to French courts to deal with the offense.[1]

Article 689-1 CCP provides that persons guilty of committing any of the offenses under the international conventions listed in the subsequent paragraphs (689-2 to 689-9 CCP), can be prosecuted and tried by French courts, whatever their nationality, if they are present in France.

---

[1] All translations of the French Criminal Code and Code of Criminal Procedure are taken from the official site of the French government, *Legifrance*, available at http://www.legifrance.gouv.fr/html/codestraduits/liste.htm.

In addition to the crime of torture (a), three categories of offenses can be distinguished: those relating to the physical protection of nuclear material[2]; those concerning the protection of the communities' financial interests and the fight against corruption involving officials of the European communities or officials of member states of the European Union[3]; and those defined as terrorist acts. The failure to implement the Geneva Conventions, which are not referred to under Article 689 despite the fact that they require the exercise of universal jurisdiction, makes it difficult, if not impossible, to rely on them before French courts (b).

a) Universal Jurisdiction for Crimes of Torture

The provisions of the Convention against Torture and Other Cruel, Inhuman or Degrading Treatment adopted by the General Assembly on December 10, 1984 which entered into force on June 26, 1987,[4] require states, first, to adopt legislation criminalizing torture, and second, to provide for the exercise of universal jurisdiction to prosecute perpetrators of torture. Torture is defined under Article 1 of the UN Convention against Torture.[5]

France ratified the Convention against Torture on February 18, 1986. According to Article 4 of the Convention, States Parties have a duty to ensure that all acts of torture are criminal offenses under national law. The same applies to attempts to commit torture and to any person's acts which constitute complicity or participation in torture. States Parties are obliged to make these offenses punishable with appropriate penalties reflecting their grave nature. French law conforms to these provisions: under Article 222-1 CCP, the subjection of a person to torture or to acts of barbarity is an offense punishable by fifteen years' imprisonment.

Article 5, paragraph 2 of the Convention against Torture provides for the exercise of universal jurisdiction: States Parties are obliged to prosecute crimes of torture even when the crime has no direct link to the state. The only requirement in such a case is the presence of the alleged offender in the territory of the State

---

[2] France ratified the Convention on the Physical Protection of Nuclear Material of 1987 on September 6, 1991. Article 8 para. 2 provides for the exercise of universal jurisdiction regarding offenses defined in Article 7 of the Convention. Article 689-4 CCP transposes the provisions of the Convention.

[3] The Convention against Corruption of May 26, 1997 and the Protocol of September 27, 1996, which protects the European Communities' financial interests, aim to define the offenses of active and passive corruption committed by EC or national civil servants. Article 689-8 CCP transposes the provisions of these conventions.

[4] General Assembly Resolution 39/46 of December 10, 1984.

[5] The term *torture* means "any act by which severe pain or suffering, whether physical or mental, is intentionally inflicted on a person for such purposes as obtaining from him or a third person information or a confession, punishing him for an act he or a third person has committed or is suspected of having committed, or intimidating or coercing him or a third person, or for any reason based on discrimination of any kind, when such pain or suffering is inflicted by or at the instigation of or with the consent or acquiescence of a public official or other person acting in an official capacity. It does not include pain or suffering arising only from, inherent in or incidental to lawful sanctions."

Party. After the ratification by France of the Convention against Torture, and in accordance with the obligations it imposes, national legislation was enacted in order to implement the principle of universal jurisdiction for the crime of torture in French courts. The combined provisions of Articles 689-1 and 689-2 CCP provide that "a person guilty of committing [torture as defined in Article 1 of Convention against Torture] outside the territory of the Republic and who happens to be in France may be prosecuted and tried by French courts."

The principle of universal jurisdiction in respect of crimes of torture was recognized in France in the case of *Ely Ould Dah,* first on appeal and more recently by the Supreme Court (Cour de cassation). In its October 23, 2002, judgment the Cour de cassation found that the application of the Mauritanian amnesty law by French courts would annul the principle of universal jurisdiction. The Court concluded that "with regard to the principle of the application of national law, only an amnesty granted by the French authorities could be taken into consideration, otherwise the principle of universal jurisdiction would be deprived of any effect."[6]

Captain Ely Ould Dah, a Mauritanian national accused by victims in France, was arrested for crimes of torture and acts of barbarity on the basis of Article 689-2 CCP. On May 25, 2001, the investigating judge decided to remit the case to the Cour d'assises, recognizing the principle of universal jurisdiction:

> Article 682-2 introduced into the Code of Criminal Procedure by the Law of 30 December 1985 implemented the principle of universal jurisdiction into French law by authorizing the investigation and prosecution in France of all persons who are present in French territory who are suspected of committing acts abroad which constitute crimes of torture under the Convention. ... It is therefore the duty of France, as a State Party to the New York Convention, to prosecute acts which are not subject to amnesty or statutes of limitation in France which fall within the field of application of the Convention, whatever the situation in Mauritania regarding the existing outstanding indictments and statutes of limitation and amnesties.[7]

The Supreme Court confirmed this position in the October 23, 2002, judgment remitting the case to the Cour d'assises in Nimes for Ely Ould Dah to be judged in absentia. On July 1, 2005, the Cour d'assises in Nîmes reached a historic decision, sentencing Ely Ould Dah to ten years in prison for torturing black African members of the military in 1990 and 1991. FIDH and its affiliated organization in Mauritania, AMDH, and in France, LDH, emphasized that although Ely Ould Dah was tried in absentia, he had legal representation. The Court convicted him on all charges of torture committed directly, ordered or organized at the "Jreïda Death Camp." This case, the first time universal jurisdiction was applied in France, represented a significant step forward in the fight against impunity.

b) Gaps in French Law Regarding Prosecution of War Crimes

Grave breaches of the Geneva Conventions of 1949 are subject to universal jurisdiction. As a result, France has an obligation to apply these provisions. According

---

[6]   Unofficial translation.
[7]   Unofficial translation.

to Article 55 of the French Constitution of 1958, which confirms the superiority of treaties duly ratified and approved over national law, international conventions should be applied in French law. However, in the case of the Geneva Conventions and grave breaches, this position has never been accepted by French courts.

Currently, under French law war crimes are crimes like any others. There are no specific provisions defining war crimes, either in the Criminal Code or in the Code of Military Justice. Thus, war crimes can only be prosecuted under the ordinary provisions of the Criminal Code, for example, as murder, torture, rape, or attacks on physical integrity. On July 20, 1993, Bosnian nationals Javor, Kusuran, Softic, and Mujdzic brought a complaint with an application to join proceedings as a civil party (*partie civile*) for torture, war crimes, crimes against humanity, and genocide. The complainants had escaped from Serb detention camps. The Tribunal of First Instance (Tribunal de Grande Instance) in Paris, on May 6, 1994, ruled that it had partial jurisdiction and accepted the victim's application to participate as partie civile. Reversing this decision, the Court of Appeal (Chambre d'accusation) of Paris gave two reasons for its ruling: Firstly, the Court considered that the Convention against Torture of 1984 was not applicable, since the partie civile had failed to provide sufficient evidence of the presence of the alleged perpetrators in France. Secondly, the Court found that the Geneva Conventions were not directly applicable in national law and that no implementing legislation had been introduced. The Supreme Court reexamined this last argument, after the legislation implementing the Statute of the ICTY was introduced.

The Court of Appeal's interpretation of the application of universal jurisdiction in accordance with the Geneva Conventions continues to apply and prevents any application of the Geneva Conventions by the French courts. This is of particular concern since, at the time it ratified the ICC Statute, France issued a declaration under Article 124 of the Statute refusing the jurisdiction of the ICC for war crimes for a period of seven years, starting on July 1, 2002. The ICC, applying the principle of complementarity, will not be able to fill the gap left by French legislation, and potential war crimes tried in France will not be punished as such.

2. The Absence of Universal Jurisdiction for Crimes Against Humanity and Genocide

a) From 1945 to 1994: French Courts Recognize Crimes against Humanity Committed by Agents of the Axis Powers during the Second World War

In France, at the time of the *Barbie*, *Touvier* and *Papon* cases, the Criminal Chamber of the Supreme Court (Chambre criminelle de la Cour de cassation) clarified the conditions for the application of Article 6 of the Charter of the International Military Tribunal, annexed to the London Agreement of August 8, 1945, which defines crimes against humanity. In the *Touvier* case,[8] the Court stated that "cri-

---

[8] Criminal Chamber of the Supreme Court, February 6, 1975, *Bulletin des arrêts de la Cour de cassation* 42.

mes against humanity are crimes under ordinary law, committed in certain circumstances and on certain grounds, specified in the provisions which define them."[9] These grounds are "political, racial, or religious." Crimes can be committed "individually or as members of an organization" by persons acting "on behalf of the European Axis countries."

After the adoption of the 1964 law, which provides that statutes of limitations are inapplicable to crimes against humanity, the Supreme Court confirmed this position in its judgment in the Barbie case of January 29, 1984. On April 1, 1993, in the case of Boudarel,[10] the Supreme Court considerably reduced the scope of application of this offense by limiting prosecution to atrocities committed by those bearing greatest responsibility within the Axis powers and by ruling that complaints in relation to acts committed "after the Second World War cannot be defined as crimes against humanity."

b) Case Law since 1994

Article 212-1 of the new 1994 French Criminal Code penalizing crimes against humanity, introduced a broader definition, which confirmed the existence of the customary international notion of crimes against humanity. In the case of French General Aussaresses,[11] the Supreme Court, rejecting the charge of crimes against humanity, emphasized that at the times of the events, the acts committed by General Aussaresses could not be classified as crimes against humanity, in view of the absence of any provision in the French Criminal Code. Furthermore, the Court confirmed the ruling of the investigating judge, which stated that international custom cannot make up for the absence of criminal legislation defining crimes against humanity, in respect of the facts of the complaint made by the partie civile.

In this case, the Supreme Court missed an opportunity to fill the legal gap that still exists for crimes against humanity committed between 1945 and 1994. The first step towards the reversal of this position was taken in a complaint of a partie civile of October 26, 1998, made by the beneficiaries of Enrique Ropert, executed in September 1973 by agents of the Chilean State, during the period of terror formulated and orchestrated by General Augusto Pinochet.

The Indictment Division (Chambre d'Instruction) of the Court of Appeal in Paris delivered a judgment reversing the ruling of March 22, 2000, which had dismissed the case for lack of evidence, and remitting the case to another investi-

---

[9] Unofficial translation.

[10] *Boudarel Sobanski et Association nationale des anciens prisonniers internes d'Indochine c. Georges Boudarel, Bulletin des arrêts de la Cour de cassation* 143, Gaz. Pal. June 24, 1993, p. 14, Dr. penal 1994.38, obs J-H. Robert (unofficial translation).

[11] FIDH lodged a complaint with an application to join proceedings as partie civile on May 29, 2001, for crimes against humanity by General Aussaresse, the 1957 coordinator of the Information Services in Algeria under General Massu, and all other persons identified in the inquiry. The complaint was based on the revelations made by General Aussaresses in his book *Services spéciaux Algérie 1955-1957* (2001), in which he describes acts of torture and summary executions committed in this period in Algeria, which he claims were justified.

gating judge of the Tribunal of First Instance in Paris to pursue the investigation. The court found that since the case concerned the definition of crimes against humanity, the judge was "obliged to investigate in order to determine if the accusations constitute such an offense and to examine whether they were punishable under treaty provisions and on several other legal bases raised by the partie civile."[12]

c) The Absence of Universal Jurisdiction for Genocide

Although France ratified the Convention on Prevention and Punishment of the Crime of Genocide of 1948, in October 1950, it was only with the new Criminal Code of 1994 that a specific definition of the crime of genocide was introduced into French law.[13]

The *Javor* case ruling on May 6, 1994, referred to Article 6 of the Convention on Prevention and Punishment of the Crime of Genocide, which provides, "Persons charged with genocide ... shall be tried by a competent tribunal of the State in the territory in which the act was committed." The Court found that "as a result, French Courts cannot have jurisdiction with respect to the accusations in the current case, since they were committed outside French territory."[14] The Court of Appeal in Paris confirmed this decision on November 24, 1994, holding that "the Convention on Prevention and Punishment of the Crime of Genocide does not contain any rule of universal jurisdiction."[15]

Similarly, in March 1996, in the case of the Rwandan priest Wenceslas Munyeshyaka, a refugee in France investigated for genocide, torture, and inhuman and degrading treatment, the Indictment Division of the Court of Appeal in Nîmes found that it did not have jurisdiction to try offenses committed abroad by a foreigner against foreigners, since the Code of Criminal Procedure did not at the time provide for the jurisdiction of French courts in such a case. However, on January 6, 1998, the Supreme Court ordered the reinstatement of the proceedings in France against Wenceslas Munyeshyaka, first opened in 1995, holding that the Indictment Division had erred by only considering a rubric based on genocide when the acts committed could have been labeled crimes of torture, for which Article 689-2 CCP provides for universal jurisdiction.

---

[12] Unofficial translation.

[13] Article 211-1 of the new Criminal Code provides a definition of the crime of genocide: "Genocide occurs where, in the enforcement of a concerted plan aimed at the partial or total destruction of a national, ethnic, racial, or religious group, or of a group determined by any other arbitrary criterion, one of the following actions is committed or caused to be committed against members of that group: willful attack on life; serious attack on psychic or physical integrity; subjection to living conditions likely to entail the partial or total destruction of that group; measures aimed at preventing births; enforced child transfers."

[14] Unofficial translation.

[15] Unofficial translation.

3. Ad hoc Universal Jurisdiction for Crimes Committed in the Genocide in Rwanda and the War in Former Yugoslavia

France is the only European country to have enacted implementing legislation permitting the exercise of absolute universal jurisdiction in the limited context of the international criminal tribunals. France adopted two laws in this respect: on January 2, 1995, to implement the provisions of the Statute of the ICTY; and on May 22, 1996, to implement the provisions of the ICTR. These laws established the exercise of universal jurisdiction by French courts over war crimes, crimes against humanity and genocide in the following three cases:

- Crimes committed since 1991 in the former Yugoslavia;
- Crimes committed during 1994 in Rwanda;
- Crimes committed during 1994 by Rwandan citizens in neighboring states.

The adoption of the statutes for the ICTY and ICTR into French law had immediate consequences, as in the *Javor* case, cited above. Similarly, in the *Munyeshyaka* case on January 6, 1998, the Indictment Division of the Court of Appeal in Paris reversed its initial position, concluding that French courts were competent to investigate the full range of facts of the allegations against Wenceslas Munyeshyaka, whether constituting the crime of torture or the crime of genocide. Since this reversal, other investigations have been opened into alleged perpetrators of the Rwandan genocide.

II. Practical Considerations Concerning the Exercise of Universal Jurisdiction before French Courts

1. Burden of Proof of Presence of the Alleged Perpetrator of Torture on National Territory

If the condition of presence required by French law to exercise universal jurisdiction cannot be challenged, this is not so in respect of the condition imposed by the courts on victims to provide absolute proof of the presence of the accused in French territory. On March 26, 1996, the Supreme Court rejected an appeal on the basis that "the presence in France of the victims of such crimes is in itself insufficient to justify setting public proceedings in motion where ... the alleged perpetrators and their accomplices have not been found in French territory,"[16] as required by Article 2 of the French implementing legislation of the Statute of the ICTY.

Neither the spirit nor the letter of the December 10, 1984, Convention against Torture impose such an obligation on victims or their representatives to put in place methods of surveillance and detection to inform authorities of the movements of their torturers. A study of the *travaux preparatoires* of the Convention

---

[16] Unofficial translation.

reveals that the drafters did not make absolute proof of the presence of an alleged torturer in forum state territory a precondition for the initiation of an investigation and merely required that the state had information relating to the presence of the suspect in its territory.

The problem posed by the condition of presence lies in its implementation by the investigative authorities. Although they refer specifically to the International Criminal Tribunals (ICTR and ICTY), two memoranda from the Ministry of Justice[17] are of interest in that they indicate that, even where the alleged perpetrator of the crime is absent from the territory, prosecutors can proceed with victim interviews. In the same vein, the French National Consultative Commission for Human Rights (CNCDH) recommended that prosecutors systematically investigate violations of humanitarian law, including violations of the Convention against Torture, in order to avoid the burden of proof falling on the victims.[18]

In charge of the complaint lodged by FIDH and LDH, the Tribunal of First Instance prosecutor in Paris agreed in January 2000 to a preliminary investigation in order to confirm complainant reports that Rwandan genocide suspects were present in France. Thus, on January 25, 2000, the prosecutor referred the complaint to the national antiterrorist division to carry out a national investigation "to locate the Rwandan nationals, alleged to be perpetrators and accomplices of genocide in Rwanda, in national territory."[19]

2. When Must the Condition of Presence Be Fulfilled?

When must the accused's presence in the territory be verified in order to determine French jurisdiction? If the entire investigation is devoted to establishing the

---

[17] JO No. 44, February 21, 1995, p. 2757, NOR: JUSD9530006C (unofficial translation). Memorandum of July 22, 1996, concerning the application of the Law of May 22, 1996, which adopted the Security Council resolution establishing the ICTR into French law, states that: "French courts have been given competence to hear cases, the facts of which fall within the competence of the International Criminal Tribunal for Rwanda, where the perpetrator is present in French territory. *However, as indicated in the memorandum of February10, 1995, the limited nature of this competence does not prevent prosecutors, in the course of a preliminary investigation, from proceeding with interviewing the victims of these crimes who have sought refuge in France.* Thus, the prosecutors with competence in the areas in which the victims reside should respond to their request and proceed to take their statements." (emphasis added). Memorandum of February 10, 1995, concerning the Law of January 2, 1995, which adopted the Security Council resolution establishing the ICTY into French law, states that, "as indicated in the course of debates before the National Assembly (JO AN CR 20 December 1994, p. 9446), the impossibility of setting proceedings in motion against persons who are not present on French territory does not prevent prosecutors, as a measure of preservation and in the course of a preliminary enquiry, from proceeding with interviewing the victims of these crimes who have sought refuge in France."

[18] Advisory opinion adopted by the full assembly on February 16, 1998, concerning the adaptation of the French legal system to humanitarian law conventions

[19] Unofficial translation.

presence of the accused, there is a great risk that no prosecution will ever be undertaken. In order to prove the accused's presence, it is necessary to conduct a search, which is often helped by evidence gathered during the procedure's preparatory phase; whereas, if the search's initiation is dependent on the condition of such presence, the entire system is blocked. Professor Lombois criticizes this situation in the context of the November 24, 1994, *Javor* judgment[20]:

> Whether or not expressed, the condition of presence must be presumed for the purposes of the "search," during the course of which it will be verified. Otherwise it is a vicious circle: in order to know whether X is in hiding on our territory, it is necessary to search for him; but in order to search for him, it is necessary to have already discovered (by enlightenment or intuition) that he is present.[21]

During the first hearing before the ICJ, *Certain criminal procedures initiated in France, Congo v. France*, the Director of Legal Affairs in the Ministry of Foreign Affairs, Ronny Abraham, furthermore stressed that "the French judge can only be competent in respect of acts committed abroad by foreigners, against foreign victims, on condition that the suspect is present in French territory *at the time* of the initiation of prosecution, in other words, on the date of the prosecutor's application and not subsequently, or, if subsequently, a new application by the prosecutor will be necessary."[22]

3. Link between the Condition of Presence and the Scope of the Referral to the Investigating Judge

Can the condition of presence form an exception to the general principle of investigation *in rem*? In *The Disappeared of the Beach* case, the prosecution adopted the position that the investigating magistrate was not competent to investigate anyone other than General Norbert Dabira. The chief prosecutor argued that the scope of the investigation was limited to the person of Dabira (trigger *in personam*) and argued therefore that "although improperly filed against X" (an unknown person), could only be directed against Mr. Dabira, because CCP Article 689-1 requires the accused to be present on French territory.

The prosecution thus adopted the official position of the French Ministry of Foreign Affairs:

> Even though the complaint by the three associations referred to persons by name—the four that I mentioned—the judicial investigation was requested by the public prosecutor against unnamed persons (persons unknown) without any name being given in his application. In reality, however, the judicial investigation, at that stage, could only be directed against General Dabira, because he alone appeared to fulfill the mandatory condition laid

---

[20] Chambre d'accusation of the Cour d'appel, Paris, aff. *Javor and others*, judgment of November 24, 1994; Cour de Cassation, Chambre Criminelle, aff. *Javor and others*, judgment of March 26, 1996, *Bulletin des arrêts de la Cour de cassation* 132.

[21] C. Lombois, *Revue de Science Criminelle et de Droit Pénal Comparé* 1995, p. 401, unofficial translation.

[22] Unofficial translation (emphasis added).

down by French law for the exercise of universal jurisdiction, that is to say—I repeat and stress—that the alleged offender has to be present on French soil.[23]

However, by adopting this position, the prosecution goes against the fundamental principle of seizure *in rem*, which is one of the pillars of the criminal procedural regime in France. Article 80-1 of the CCP imposes the general principle of seizure in rem on the investigating magistrate:

The investigating judge may place under judicial examination only those persons against whom there is strong and concordant evidence making it probable that they may have participated, as perpetrator or accomplice, *in the commission of the offenses he is investigating.* [emphasis added]

Whether the preliminary application for a judicial investigation concerns named or unnamed persons, the investigating judge, who is irrevocably triggered by the facts, which are the subject of the application, can investigate all persons against whom there is evidence of participation in the targeted offenses. This is a necessary consequence of the mandate of the investigating judge, which is to investigate all the immaterial elements in the application and to establish responsibility. In particular, it is a result of this principle that the investigating judge has the necessary flexibility to arrive at the truth. Contrary to the position of the chief prosecutor, the principle of the investigating judge's seizure in rem is in no way called into question by the introduction of the mechanism of extraterritorial jurisdiction in French criminal law. Article 689-1 of the CCP, cited by the prosecution, clarifies that in the application of international conventions, any person who is accused of committing one of the offenses listed in Article 689-2 and subsequent provisions outside French territory, if present in France, can be prosecuted by the French authorities. This does not doubt the powers of the investigating judge to carry out all the necessary acts in accordance with his competence in rem, without ignoring the provisions of Article 689-1 of the CCP.

Adoption of the prosecutor's reasoning leads to restricted application of extraterritorial jurisdiction, contrary to what France has accepted in several international conventions regarding the prosecution of international crimes. It would considerably limit the scope of activities of the investigating judge, by reducing the powers granted to him under the provisions of the Code of Criminal Procedure. Abandoning the principle of competence "in rem" is all the more paradoxical in the context of prosecuting the most serious crimes. The mechanism of extraterritorial jurisdiction aims, on the contrary, to strengthen the procedural measures that may be used in the prosecution of crimes of particular seriousness for victims and the international community, as is made clear in the Convention against Torture, adopted in New York on December 10, 1984.

However, in its November 22, 2004, judgment on the application for annulment of the investigation against Jean-François Ndengue, the Court of Appeal's Indictment Division in Paris found:

[23] *Certain Criminal Proceedings in France (Republic of the Congo v. France)*, ICJ oral pleadings of April 29, 2003, official translation, available at http://www.icj-cij.org/icj-www/idocket/icof/icofframe.htm.

The application initiating public proceedings was made "against X," and therefore does not contain the necessary element to establish that the condition of the accused's presence on French territory has been fulfilled, whereas this finding is a precondition to the application of this exceptional jurisdiction.

The exceptional character of the provisions of Article 689-1 of the Code of Criminal Procedure excludes the simultaneous application of the general provisions of Article 80 of the Code of Criminal Procedure, which allow the prosecution to make an application for an investigation against named or unnamed persons.

Furthermore, in the instant case, the opening of an inquiry against X had the consequence of leading the investigating judge to have Norbert Dabira interviewed, by means of letter of request (*commission rogatoire*), who according to the prosecutor was the only person who could be investigated, whereas this is prohibited under Article 113-1 of the Code of Criminal Procedure when a person is named in the application.

An application, which fails to fulfill the legal conditions for its existence, will be nullified, as will be all subsequent proceedings.[24]

This decision came at a time when, in the course of several months, the French and Congolese authorities had been multiplying their joint initiatives aimed at putting an end to the proceedings in France in favor of opening the investigation in Brazzaville. The latter ended in August 2005, unsurprisingly, with the acquittal of all persons accused in the *Disappeared of the Beach* case.

III. The Importance of Victims' Access to Justice for the Implementation of Universal Jurisdiction

In French law, the initiation of criminal investigations is not automatic. In the case of a simple complaint, in accordance with the opportunity principle, the prosecution remains free to decide whether or not to initiate proceedings and retains this freedom of action. However, in accordance with Article 1, Paragraph 2 of the Code of Criminal Procedure, public proceedings must be initiated when the victim makes an application to join proceedings as a civil party (*partie civile*).

It is interesting to analyze the conclusions of the Magendie Report of June 2004 on the efficiency of the justice system, which suggested concrete solutions to overcome the slowness of justice in France. One of the arguments put forward is the problem of the day-to-day management of partie civile applications, which have become increasingly numerous, but are not always well-founded in law:

The legitimate irritation caused by abusive applications for partie civile must not allow us to forget the numerous applications that are not so. Everyone has in mind the recent proceedings for crimes against humanity held following the commencement of open investigations into complaints by way of applications to join proceedings as partie civile.[25]

Having recalled these principles, the Magendie Report recommends reaffirming the subsidiary nature of proceedings initiated by an injured party, by subjecting

---

[24] Unofficial translation.
[25] Unofficial translation.

the admissibility of a partie civile application to the condition that the prosecutor had decided, expressly or implicitly, to discontinue proceedings. In the context of universal jurisdiction, this solution could lead to problems for victims, or even result in justice being denied, which is obviously not the aim of the authors of the report.

Regarding the need to ensure that the prosecutor has greater independence from the partie civile, the report questions:

Why the prosecutor, who, on the basis of Article 40 of the Code of Criminal Procedure, has the discretion to decide whether to initiate prosecutions, should to a certain extent renounce this power and decide on a strictly legal basis when a complaint is lodged with an application to join proceedings as a partie civile? ... Would it not be preferable to give him the possibility of making his decision with complete independence, including in regard to considerations of appropriateness, which are usually taken into account? ... It seems curious that the complainant can, by engaging in this procedure, oblige the prosecution to undertake prosecutions that it had decided not to pursue.

However, recent universal jurisdiction use is the result of two observations by victims of the most serious crimes and by human rights organizations: (1) the incapacity or the failure of states in the fight against impunity at the national level and (2) the growing understanding that victims could force the hand of justice by lodging complaints and by confronting states with their international obligations. Victims can therefore avoid overcautious prosecutors by initiating proceedings themselves, by way of an application to join proceedings as partie civile. The use of these possibilities in pursuing universal jurisdiction is novel.

Regarding crimes which fall under the International Criminal Court's jurisdiction (war crimes, genocide, crimes against humanity), there is no provision for universal jurisdiction except where the crimes were committed in the context of the genocide in Rwanda or the war in former Yugoslavia. However, many reasons exist for the introduction of universal jurisdiction. These reasons are based mainly on the system of complementarity established by the Statute of the International Criminal Court, which aims to end impunity for crimes falling within ICC jurisdiction. This led the French Ministry of Justice to recommend establishing a mechanism of universal jurisdiction for French courts, one no longer limited to former Yugoslavia and Rwanda.

Article 10 of the draft law, which implements the Rome Statute and amends several provisions of the Criminal Code, the Code of Military Justice, the Law of July 29, 1881, on the freedom of the press, and the Code of Criminal Procedure, states:

Art. 689 – Perpetrators of offenses committed outside French territory can be investigated and prosecuted before French courts either when French law is applicable under the provisions of Paragraph 2 below, or Book 1 of the Criminal Code or any other statute, or when an international Convention gives jurisdiction to French courts to deal with the offense.

Any person who is present in France and is a national of a non state party to the Statute of International Criminal Court, Rome 18 July 1998, and who is guilty of committing one of the following offenses outside French territory, can be investigated and prosecuted before the French courts:

1. Crimes against humanity defined in Articles 211-1, 212-1 to 212-3 of the Criminal Code;
2. War crimes defined in Articles 400-1 to 400-4 of the same Code;
3. Crimes or misdemeanors defined in Articles 23 and 25 of the Law of 29 July 1881 relating to the liberty of the press where this offense constitutes incitement to commit genocide in the sense of Article 25, paragraph 3 (e) of the said Convention.

The provisions of paragraph 2 apply to attempts to commit these offenses, in every case where attempt is punishable.

The crimes and misdemeanors listed in paragraph 2 can only be investigated on the application of the prosecution.

In respect of the investigation and prosecution of the crimes and misdemenors listed in paragraph 2, the public prosecutor of the *Tribunal de Grande Instance* (Court of First Instance), the investigating judge, the *tribunal correctionnel* (criminal court), and the *Cour d'assises* in Paris have exclusive jurisdiction. Where they have jurisdiction over such offenses, the prosecutor of the *Tribunal de Grande Instance* and the investigating judge in Paris exercise their competence over the entire national territory.

The draft does not allow a partie civile application to be used to initiate public proceedings. This law quite clearly blocks the possibility for victims to lodge complaints by way of applications to join proceedings as partie civile. As a result, it grants the prosecution a monopoly. This serious attack on victims' rights is all the more unacceptable on the part of France, which for several years fought—often alone—for the rights of victims to be recognized in the Rome Statute and additional texts of the International Criminal Court, and in particular for the inclusion of provisions permitting victims to join proceedings as partie civile, as modeled by the French procedure.

Civil society organizations reacted promptly to this attempt to violate the right for victims to act as partie civile in criminal cases. After long and difficult debates between the relevant French ministries, the article was finally dropped. Because there could not be any agreement on this issue the proposed French ICC implementing legislation which has been reviewed by the Conseil d'Etat and adopted on July 26, 2006, by the Council of Ministers does not contain any reference to universal jurisdiction. A unique opportunity for victims of international crimes to seek justice in France has been missed.

The Political Funeral Procession for the Belgian UJ Statute

Michael Verhaeghe

I. The Political Funeral Procession

The Belgian law of June 16, 1993 on the punishment of serious breaches of international humanitarian law (henceforth, *UJ Statute*) initially engendered little comment in the legal doctrine, or elsewhere, for that matter. The few comments available originated from a relatively small group of scholars.[1] The first judicial decision on the UJ Statute came in November 1998, when Judge Vandermeersch ruled that he had jurisdiction to conduct a criminal investigation of Augusto Pinochet, who at that time was placed under house arrest in London. The significance of this ruling for the UJ Statute, however, was quite limited, as Judge Vandermeersch did not base his decision on that Statute.[2]

A second opportunity to develop jurisprudence on the UJ Statute came with the well-known trial of four Rwandans accused of having committed or participated in the Rwandan genocide of 1994. The case was heard before the Court of Assizes in Brussels, where the jury delivered a guilty verdict against all of the accused.[3] The verdict was not, however, based on a charge of genocide, but oddly enough on a war crimes charge.

For all of these questions, it was ultimately necessary to wait for the verdict in the Sabra and Shatila case before the Court of Appeals in Brussels, Special Investigation Chamber ("Chambre des mises en accusation"). Addressing the exact sub-

---

[1] A. Andries et al., *Revue de droit pénal et de criminologie* 1994, pp.1114–1184.

[2] The UJ Statute at that time in 1998 applied only to war crimes (the 1993 version was in fact the belated adoption of the 1949 Geneva Conventions). It was only in 1999 that crimes against humanity and genocide were added to the list of crimes subject to universal jurisdiction. Because the crimes of which Pinochet was accused were not to be considered war crimes, Judge Vandermeersch sought and found a legal basis in international customary law, more particularly the customary criminalization of the crime against humanity.

[3] Unfortunately, no records of this procedure have been published, but there is an excellent database with most of the records and a day-by-day journal of the proceedings at http://www.asf.be.

stance of the legal discussion is beyond the scope of this article on political and social developments. Suffice it to say that the Court of Appeals went against the advice of its chief prosecutor and adopted an interpretation of the Belgian criminal code that boiled down to adding a condition to universal jurisdiction: according to the Court, Belgian courts had universal jurisdiction but could only exercise this jurisdiction when the accused was present on Belgian soil.[4]

A group of senators, among them some prominent members who had approved the 1993 Statute, protested and introduced a bill to create a statute of interpretation. In July 2002, the Council of Ministers decided to back the proposed statute of interpretation, along with a second proposal designed to further adapt and streamline the UJ Statute.

Once parliamentary work was underway on the two propositions, lobbying initiatives employed various strategies. A platform of NGOs, human rights activists, and victims was formed, which led to a high-profile, influential campaign for the preservation of the fundamental principles of universal jurisdiction in Belgian law. Members of the platform had regular contact with senators and their staff. On the other end of the spectrum, heavy diplomatic pressure was mounted by Israel and the United States. Israel, for instance, provided legal advice to a senator who was an outspoken adversary of the concept of universal jurisdiction. The United States exercised clear diplomatic pressure, though not yet very openly. When Belgian Justice Minister Verwilghen met his US colleague John Ashcroft in September 2002 in Brussels, and again on January 6, 2003, in Washington, he was gently but firmly advised to find a solution to what the US Government considered a problem with the Belgian law.[5] The United States also worked indirectly: American business organizations abroad, in particular the Brussels office of the American Chamber of Commerce, convinced the Belgian Association of Enterprises (VBO) that universal jurisdiction would be harmful to its interests, which in turn motivated the VBO to begin a campaign against a broad reading of the UJ Statute.

At the beginning of November 2002, three cases dealing with the interpretation of the Universal Jurisdiction Act were scheduled to appear before the Belgian Court of Cassation, but ultimately the Court postponed its decision on this issue. At an equally high level of the Belgian judicial landscape, the Council of State, which had been asked to render an advisory opinion to parliament, delivered its advice on both proposed bills. It did not fundamentally object to the interpretative statute (on the contrary, it considered the mechanism appropriate) nor to universal jurisdiction as such.[6]

Even though the advisory opinion provided no solid legal objections to the UJ Statute, political pressure continued to rise. By July 2002 pressure reached as far as the prime minister's desk. The prime minister organized a meeting with repre-

---

[4] For more information on the subject, see, inter alia, http://www.indictsharon.net.
[5] See "Le Ministre Verwilghen sous pression américaine," *La Libre Belgique,* January 11 and 12, 2003.
[6] Advices 34.153/VR and 34.154/VR, Parl. Doc. Senate, 2002-2003, nr. 2-1255/2 and 2-1256/3.

sentatives of all government parties on January 14, 2003.[7] A new compromise was proposed, in which pending cases would be distinguished from future cases. The latter would be subject to a much stricter system for filing complaints, whereas the first group would simply continue as before.

On January 22, 2003, work resumed at the level of the Justice Commission in the Senate in accordance with the new political compromise. The opposition, in particular the Flemish Christian democrats, joined in the debate, questioning the validity of the concept of universal jurisdiction. Even Justice Minister Verwilghen overtly criticized the latest compromise in the Senate on January 22, 2003, much to the displeasure of the prime minister. Both belonged to the same political party. Generally speaking, cohesion was still sufficient for the compromise to be accepted without much difficulty in the Senate. The opposition parties abstained, apart from the extreme right Vlaams Blok party, which voted against it. The road through the House of Representatives was a much more difficult one, due to ever-increasing opposition to the very idea of universal jurisdiction. For this reason, proceedings stalled in the House.

The Belgian Court of Cassation rendered its decision in the Sabra and Shatila case on February 12, 2003. Again, much to the surprise of many observers, the court went against the advice of the Attorney General and quashed the June 26, 2002 decision of the Court of Appeals.[8] It took some time before the political world grasped the consequences of this ruling, which in fact completely reversed the situation. Partisans of universal jurisdiction were no longer in a hurry to have the modifications approved by Parliament, since the Court of Cassation's interpretation led to unlimited universal jurisdiction. Opponents, however, needed parliamentary action to limit universal jurisdiction, and were thus forced into the position of pressuring parliament as much as possible, i.e., the opposite of the stalling strategy adopted until then.

As mentioned, initial reactions to the Court of Cassation ruling of February 12, 2003, were relatively neutral and limited. The furious, if not hysterical, reaction from Israel did not give rise to any diplomatic response from the Belgian government. The party bureau of the Flemish Liberals hoped that the commotion about the case would dissipate on its own and continued its low-profile strategy on UJ: the less politicians raised the issue, the less the chance of it becoming an election issue.

The strategy failed. On March 18, 2003, a group of Iraqi refugees living in Belgium filed a complaint against George Bush Sr. for alleged war crimes during the first Gulf War. The US Government could now openly step in and side with Israel's diplomatic efforts. The pressure from the US Government was of a completely different order than the Israeli pressure. The entire economic and political

---

[7] "M. Verhofstadt veut un votre rapidement," *La Libre Belgique*, January 15, 2003.
[8] The court ruled that the UJ Statute did not encompass any restrictions on the exercise of universal jurisdiction, and that the rules of the general Code of Criminal Procedure did not apply to the UJ Statute because of its specific nature. Regarding defendant Ariel Sharon, the Court of Cassation determined that he enjoyed immunity, and hence the case was only continued against the other defendants (both Israeli and Lebanese militias).

weight of the United States was eventually deployed against the Belgian UJ Statue.[9] United States pressure was not only political, but also clearly economic. Although top officials from the US and Belgium at first denied this, rumors persisted that the US had threatened to withdraw NATO headquarters and to move them to Warsaw.[10] The US deployed not less than five different "task forces" at the level of different government agencies, including the State Department and the Pentagon, to deal with the "problem" of the Belgian UJ Statute.[11]

Out went the low-profile strategy. The file once again arrived on the prime minister's desk. During a meeting on March 25, 2003, proposals were made to specifically target the new case against Bush, in order to eliminate it. Since logical legal arguments to do so were lacking, the new mechanism, brokered by Minister of Foreign Affairs Louis Michel, allowed the Government to transfer certain cases to other countries; regardless of their willingness to try those cases, this would remove Belgium's ability to try those cases. The new clause was quickly dubbed the *Bush clause*. But while the clause was initially designed only for the new Bush case, pressure immediately came from Israel, which claimed it would be discriminatory if the new clause were not applied to the Sabra and Shatila case as well.[12] Despite informal promises by Minister Michel that the Bush clause would also apply to the Sabra and Shatila case, Parliament adopted the view that the Bush clause could only be applied to cases lodged after the entry into force of the Statute of the ICC, i.e., after July 1, 2002, which would not include the Sabra and Shatila case.

The prime minister's office was once again the scene of an all-night meeting, during which the July 1, 2002 date was dropped. A proposal by a senator that would at least have required respect for the decision of the prosecutor to start criminal investigations into a number of cases (including the Sabra and Shatila case) was declined on April 1, 2003. This political fragmentation resulted in a shift in voting in the House of Representatives. The Bush clause was adopted, as a result of support from the opposition. In the House, the socialist party even sought the advice of the Council of State as a kind of last resort, but to no avail, because the political deal had already been sealed. It is noteworthy, however, that the Council of State completely disapproved of the Bush clause as an unacceptable interfer-

---

[9] In the US House of Representatives, for instance, Congressman Gary Ackerman introduced a bill titled "Universal Jurisdiction Rejection Act of 2003," with a similar background and scope as the US bill against the ICC. Ackerman's bill was based on the position that "implicit within the very concept of universal jurisdiction is a threat to the sovereignty of the United States."

[10] Later events confirmed this threat, at least in the form of a freeze on any further investments in the headquarters, which would have resulted in their being moved in the middle term. The threat was in any case taken seriously, as demonstrated on the website of the president of the government of Brussels, Francois-Xavier de Donnéa, who expressly warned of the risk of international organizations leaving Brussels because of the UJ Statute.

[11] *De Standaard*, July 8, 2003.

[12] "Belgium curtails war crimes law; should end suit against Sharon," *Ha'aretz*, April 3, 2003.

ence by the executive branch in judicial affairs. Its remarks were swept under the carpet. The statute of April 5, 2003, was adopted.

In the American embassy in Brussels, there was also concern about the Bush clause. Legally, this clause would probably not hold water. The advisory opinion by the Council of State was drafted in such a way that a careful reader would understand that the clause ran a serious risk of being annulled by the Constitutional Court later on. The clause could indeed solve some problems temporarily, but the cases eliminated by it would very likely boomerang their way back into Belgian courts. Moreover, the political filter in the clause appeared to be its Achilles heel. The Belgian government had been rather successful in rejecting political responsibility for the cases before its courts by simply referring to the separation of powers and the independence of the judiciary. Now that the government had assumed power to terminate cases on purely political grounds, the previous argument of course fell away.

Despite the fact that they were promptly advised of the US government's objections to the Bush clause, the Belgian government firmly maintained that this clause was the best solution to all the diplomatic problems that had arisen so far. To the outside world, every effort was made to show that the matter was completely under control. One could expect no more of a government on the eve of elections.

On May 14, 2003, yet another complaint was filed. This time the complaint was aimed at the present US Government and was directed against Tommy Franks, commander in chief of the US troops that invaded Iraq in the second Gulf War. During a visit to NATO headquarters on June 12, 2003, US Defense Minister Donald Rumsfeld stated that the United States was not willing to invest in a new headquarters in Brussels as long as there was fear that US officials could be subject to criminal charges on the basis of the UJ Statute. In an interview with the *New York Times* on June 23, 2003, Rumsfeld added that he had no faith in the Bush clause and that he had given the Belgian government six months to effectively solve the problem. The tone was set for further humiliation.

At first, top Belgian politicians reacted with disbelief and stated once again that the new law provided all the tools necessary to avoid abuses (that is, to get rid of politically difficult cases). Other politicians warned of the dangers.[13] To add insult to injury, a Belgian politician filed a complaint against Belgian Foreign Minister Michel on June 20, 2003, but only to demonstrate the "absurd" character of the UJ Statute. Minister Michel responded with an angry outburst when he heard of the complaint while attending a top European Union meeting in Greece, but he could not avoid ridicule. The Associated Press made the point that the Belgian Minister of Foreign Affairs had joined the club of American officials as targets of the UJ

---

[13] Defense Minister Flahaut proposed some further modifications. Brussels Minister Vanhengel presented the results of a study he ordered showing that NATO headquarters brought revenue of more than 120 million euros per year. The former minister of foreign affairs and former NATO Secretary-General Willy Claes warned in an interview that the threat of NATO headquarters moving elsewhere had to be taken seriously. The director of the port of Antwerp said that he feared a boycott of the port.

Statute. Cartoonists targeted the statute as well, and a well-respected Belgian newspaper wrote that Belgium should turn universal jurisdiction into an export, alongside its beer and chocolate. Another Belgian newspaper came up with the term *Absurdistan* for Belgium, a term quickly copied by foreign newspapers such as the *New York Times*.

On June 22, 2003, amidst negotiations on the formation of a new government, Prime Minister Verhofstadt announced that the partners in the new government had reached a consensus on the UJ Statute. The law would be thoroughly revised. The prime minister added that the revision had nothing to do with pressure from abroad, and nothing at all to do with pressure from the United States. Equally "convincing" was his statement that even with a thorough revision of the law, Belgium would not fall behind in international justice. The prime minister conceded that the Bush clause was not a successful experiment and would certainly not be repeated. A press release on June 23, 2003, contained the major features of the modification, which were relayed to a specialists' working group.

The group worked in complete secrecy, avoiding the influence of lobby groups. Immediately after the inauguration of the new government, the statute containing the modifications was approved by Parliament without any noticeable opposition. Although some aspects of universal jurisdiction were retained, the UJ Statute was annulled upon adoption of the new Statute of August 5, 2003. The US government reacted in a positive manner, but remained skeptical and cautious.[14] They insisted on seeing whether the new statute would actually work to prevent new complaints. So far, it has done so.

II. Personal Observations by a Mourner

I fully disagree with the position, expressed by many, that the UJ Statute was the victim of its abuse (or of its success, for that matter). Undoubtedly there were abuses, as some complaints were not filed in order to achieve a criminal investigation, but merely out of political motives. Nevertheless, the vast majority of complaints were based on genuine crimes against humanity, with genuine victims, and serious indications of the guilt of a whole range of people, including officials of foreign governments. Contrary to another popular misunderstanding, Belgium was not swamped by hundreds of complaints. Apart from the dozen or so well known Rwandan cases, of which two have actually led to convictions, only 21 other complaints were actually introduced into the Belgian system. Considering the over one thousand complaints registered so far with the Office of the Prosecutor of the ICC, I am even surprised that the Belgian law, the possibilities of which were widely known among human rights activists, did not attract more complaints than it actually did. A possible explanation for this is that that a serious complaint with an investigating magistrate entails serious preparatory work and also forces the victims filing the complaint to relive their horrible experiences. Whatever the circum-

---

[14] "Encore de la méfiance à Washington," *La Libre Belgique*, June 23, 2003.

stances, I resent the idea, often portrayed in some media, that victims of serious international crimes file their complaints lightly.

Apart from this more general observation, the explanation of abuse as the cause of the UJ Statute's failure is not satisfactory and does not explain the true underlying roots of the problem Belgium faced in 2003. I am convinced that the failure of the statute was the product of a series of factors in which negative forces combined and enhanced each other. First, there were the panicked reactions of top Belgian politicians. The best example is the Bush clause, which was a product of taking a narrow view of the problem and seeking short-term solutions. It was obvious that the Bush clause would never hold up, because it so blatantly infringed on the fundamental principles of the state. Nevertheless, the solution was welcomed because it helped resolve matters on a short-term basis and gave politicians the appearance of a solution, which they apparently needed with elections on the horizon. Most probably, this move was accompanied by a conviction that the law would have to be changed again later on. Such a strategy may work for internal Belgian affairs, but was not adapted to the international dimension that had gradually begun to determine the Belgian political agenda.

A second factor was the lack of respect for the rules developed in the Statute of April 23, 2003. This statute contained rules allowing the Federal Prosecutor to dismiss a complaint, for instance, if it failed to demonstrate the necessity of Belgium as the solicited forum (in some way comparable to the *forum non conveniens* doctrine in the US). The application of these rules would indeed have entailed a judicial process, including the possibility of appeals, but they were at least not corrupted by fundamental legal shortcomings, as in the Bush clause. If the Belgian government had maintained its position on the separation of powers and the independence of the judiciary, combined with sufficient faith in the judiciary, it would have at least allowed the rules to be tested in practice.

A third factor was indeed the abuses. As has been said before, the complaint against Bush Sr. has features that indicate such abuse. The three letters that were sent by mail to the Federal Prosecutor were definitely not very serious, but they raise another question: why did the Prosecutor not simply dismiss the charges, since he had this option under the old UJ Statute?

A fourth factor was the lack of understanding, voluntary or not, by governments such as the US for the term *complaint* in Belgium. Belgium did not even attempt to explain the precise nature of a complaint before an investigative judge, which cannot simply be assimilated to an indictment as in the US. The complaint in fact retains its private character, as the expression of the plaintiff's position, until the judge formally issues warrants for the arrest of suspects or formal notices of suspicion. Until this stage, a complaint under the UJ Statute did not differ in any fundamental way from a writ of summons filed under the Alien Torts Claims Act in the US.

It is true that an information campaign would probably not have made much difference once the political problems had risen to a climax with the filing of cases against US officials. But such a campaign could and should have begun much earlier, particularly starting in the fall of 2002, when there were already clear signs of opposition from the American Chamber of Commerce, for instance.

This lack of prudence is all the more striking when one considers the UJ Statute an Belgian state experiment with international criminal law—an experiment that could have served as an example and thus created new avenues for victims of international crimes. As with all experiments, patience and a cool head were required. Both were lacking in the heat of the debate. During the last session of the April 2003 modification, one senator stated that he had been present during the initial 1993 Senate discussion, when the UJ Statute was first elaborated. He said that he had already been aware at that time of the dangers and difficulties the Statute could pose. Why, then, did the Belgian legislature and government not behave as better-qualified conductors of the experiment? Can it be that the statute was not sufficiently thought through? Or must we accept that experimental statutes can only be tested outside the lab, in the real world of plaintiffs and defendants, thus allowing for modifications and corrections only on the basis of such experience? The premature ending of the experiment will probably result in open questions like these.

Finally, we must not underestimate the effect of the ridicule to which the statute fell prey. This in fact led to a complete shift in public opinion, from one side of the spectrum (great sympathy for UJ) to the other (UJ as a useless and even economically dangerous *folie*). The most devastating effect of a campaign of ridicule is not so much the content of the ridicule as the lack of space it leaves for real debate on the issue. Ridicule contaminated the very phrase *universal jurisdiction* to such an extent that a calm discussion of its principles became next to impossible in April, May, and June of 2003.

The shift in public opinion further resulted in diminished political will for the UJ Statute. It is significant that none of the partisans of universal jurisdiction who had fought very hard in the Senate and the House in 2002–2003 began any real political campaign after July 2003 to oppose the abolition of the UJ Statute.

Universal jurisdiction as such is not a ridiculous idea. It is the result of many years of legal evolution, propelled by a history of countless atrocities and crimes against humanity. A state exercising universal jurisdiction in a genuine manner, i.e., with the purpose of contributing to the international legal order and not of shielding national interests, is not arrogant. It does not arrogate to itself a jurisdiction to which it is not entitled, but merely tries to offer solutions to impunity. In this sense, one can say that universal jurisdiction is not a formula for *gaining* jurisdiction, but one for placing the national legal order *at the service* of the international community.

Germany also has a law with strong characteristics of universal jurisdiction. The *Völkerstrafgesetzbuch* of June 26, 2002 bears resemblance to the Belgian UJ Statute, apart, of course, from the introduction of complaints to a judge directly by victims. But on a political level, this is less important. What matters, in my view, is that there was apparently never a campaign against Germany similar to the one against Belgium. The US did not threaten to close down military bases in Germany over the *Völkerstrafgesetzbuch*. I am not aware of "task forces" within US departments to monitor the evolution of the application of this German law code. I am not saying there has been no pressure or influence whatsoever, only that it did not become a campaign resembling the one against Belgium.

This leads me to my final point. Belgium must have been very easy prey for the US. Not only was Belgium sometimes portrayed as the "roaring mouse"; it was particularly vulnerable because of its international political and economic position. And last but not least, Belgium stood alone. None of its European partners, who had stood side by side in the battle for the ICC, even attempted to come to Belgium's rescue.

The Approach of the United Kingdom to Crimes under International Law: The Application of Extraterritorial Jurisdiction

Carla Ferstman

I. Introduction

All one needs to do is open a newspaper to realize that torture, crimes against humanity, and other egregious violations of human rights take place in all parts of the world with alarming frequency. For the survivors of these crimes, whether they remain in the location where the crimes occurred or manage to flee the jurisdiction, the suffering associated with such traumatic experiences can remain for a lifetime. Part of the trauma and dislocation relates to the fact that the crimes are generally perpetrated by, or at the behest of, the state. The calculated abuse of the integrity of individuals, in a way that is *designed* specifically to undermine their dignity, is particularly horrible when it is perpetrated by or on behalf of those with the very responsibility to protect individuals' rights.

Efforts to seek a remedy are particularly important in such cases. Remedies, whether they are criminal sanctions, civil remedies, or other forms of reparation, may have a deterrent effect; also, they often affirm that what was done to the victim was wrong and cannot be tolerated by the society. Nonetheless, local remedies are, by their nature, difficult if not impossible to achieve, particularly in respect of situations of systematic violations of human rights giving rise to state responsibility. It is this absence of accountability at the national level coupled with the fact that persons fleeing conflict and persecution and the alleged perpetrators, especially after a shift in regime, are present in all parts of the world, as asylum seekers, economic migrants or temporary visitors, that has made the principle and application of universal jurisdiction so vital to ending impunity for the most serious crimes.

Universal jurisdiction permits, and at times requires, states to prosecute certain crimes under international law, regardless of where they were committed, regardless of the nationality or location of the author or the victims and irrespective of any specific connection to the prosecuting state, on the basis that the crimes offend the international community as a whole and all have an inherent interest and responsibility to ensure that perpetrators of such crimes do not evade justice. The principle is not a new or novel concept in the UK or elsewhere. It has long been recognized by customary international law with respect to piracy, slavery, slave trading, and, more recently, genocide. Furthermore, in the last half-century, an expanding series of treaties has recognized universal jurisdiction over such serious international crimes as "grave breaches" of the 1949 Geneva Conventions, torture, and hijacking aircraft.

This paper explores some of REDRESS' experiences in the UK of seeking justice for survivors of torture on the basis of universal or extraterritorial jurisdiction. We have been involved in many of the recent civil and criminal cases lodged in the UK and continue to advocate for effective and enforceable remedies for torture in the UK and abroad. The paper will analyze the legislative framework, jurisprudence and institutional policies relating to the exercise of universal jurisdiction in the UK with a view to identifying existing trends and considering how the practice compares to developments elsewhere.

II. Criminal Proceedings

1. Legislation

UK law is premised upon the territoriality principle, subject to certain exceptions, most of which relate to British subjects who commit crimes overseas. There are a series of acts that allow for the exercise of universal jurisdiction. These include:

- Section 134 (1) of the Criminal Justice Act, 1988, which the UK enacted when it became party to the United Nations Convention against Torture. It provides that a person commits the offence of torture if they commit specified acts in the United Kingdom or elsewhere;
- Geneva Conventions Act 1957 as amended by the Geneva Conventions Act 1995, Section 1 (1) of which provides that "any person, whatever their nationality, who, whether in or outside of the United Kingdom, commits, aids, abets or procures the commission by any other person of a grave breach ... shall be guilty of an offence."
  The Geneva Conventions Act of 1995 extends universal jurisdiction to grave breaches of the 1st additional protocol of 1977 concerning international armed conflict. However the amended act does not apply to the 2nd protocol, which relates to merely national conflicts. This failure to account for grave breaches occurring in internal armed conflict is arguably out of step with developments in international jurisprudence;[1]
- War Crimes Act 1991, which provides the courts in England and Wales jurisdiction over the offense of homicide constituting a violation of the laws and

---

[1] *Prosecutor v. Tadić*, ICTY Case No. IT-94-1-I, Decision on the Defence Motion for Interlocutory Appeal on Jurisdiction of October 2, 1995, para. 137.

customs of war committed in Germany or German occupied territory between 1939 and 1945. It provides that the acts must have been committed by a person who, at the time of the institution of proceedings, is a British citizen or resident in the UK.

It is also possible to exercise universal jurisdiction in the UK through the Taking of Hostages Act 1982, Section 1, the Slave Trade Act 1873 as amended, which predicates universal jurisdiction on the presence within the jurisdiction of the perpetrator. There is also a more limited form of universal jurisdiction over the crimes set out in the national implementing legislation for the International Criminal Court statute—war crimes, crimes against humanity, and genocide.[2] To exercise universal jurisdiction over such crimes, they must have been committed by a UK resident at the time of either the commission of the act or the institution of proceedings.

2. The Practical Application of the Legislative Framework

Although there have been a number of allegations of torture and other international crimes committed abroad against individuals who have been physically present in the UK, there have been few arrests.[3] According to information recently given by the Home Office Minister, Baroness Scotland of Asthal, to the House of Lords, around eight cases of torture have been investigated since Section 134 of the Criminal Justice Act came into force in 1988.[4] There are only three cases where a person has been detained in the UK pursuant to this law,[5] and only a single conviction.

---

[2] International Criminal Court Act 2001.

[3] For a list of cases that are in the public domain see REDRESS and FIDH, *Legal Remedies for Victims of "International Crimes": Fostering an EU Approach to Extraterritorial Jurisdiction* (2004), p. 77, available at http://www.redress.org/publications/LegalRemediesFinal.pdf.

[4] Parliamentary answer to Lord Avebury on July 1, 2004, published by *Hansard* (official parliamentary reports), http://www.publications.parliament.uk/cgi-bin/ukparl_hl?DB=uk parl&STEMMER=en&WORDS=section+134+criminall+justic+act+J0scotland+&COL OUR=Red&STYLE=s&URL=/pa/ld199697/ldhansrd/pdvn/lds04/text/40701w02.htm#4 0701w02_wqn2.

[5] The most recent case is that of the Afghan warlord, Sarwar Zardad, who was arrested and charged with torture under Section 134 of the CJA and hostage taking in July 2003 and who was convicted of conspiracy to commit torture and take hostages in Afghanistan between 1991 and 1996 and sentenced to 20 years imprisonment in 2005. The extradition case of Pinochet turned on Section 134 of CJA, where Pinochet remained under house arrest pending the outcome of the judicial review between 1999 and 2000. Dr. Magoub, a Sudanese doctor, was charged under Section 134 of the CJA for torture in September 1997, however, the case was withdrawn during the preparation of the trial. See REDRESS, *Universal Jurisdiction in Europe Criminal prosecutions in Europe since 1990 for war crimes, crimes against humanity, torture and genocide* (1999), pp. 44–47, available at http://www.redress.org/publications/UJEurope.pdf.

When assisting torture survivors in their bid to bring the perpetrators to justice, and in particular acting as intermediary between the victim and the appropriate UK authorities, REDRESS has found that the current institutional setup in the UK does not lend itself to the swift detention of perpetrators. In principle it is possible for there to be a citizen's arrest. But in practice, cases are dealt with by the police. The main bodies dealing with cases like this are either SO 7 (1) Kidnap and Specialist Investigations Unit of the Serious Crime Group or SO13 Anti-Terrorist Branch.

a) Executive Discretion

If the case is adjudged to be appropriate to take forward to prosecution, it will be dealt with by the Crown Prosecution Service (CPS), the body that conducts all criminal proceedings started by the police. The CPS can also discontinue proceedings or change or amend charges initially preferred by the police. Before any prosecution can proceed, the Attorney General's consent is required pursuant to Section 135 of the Criminal Justice Act.[6] Similarly, under the ICC Act, no proceedings may be brought except with the approval of the Attorney General (Section 53 (3)). The same is true under the War Crimes Act 1991 (Section 1 (3)), the Geneva Conventions Act 1957 as amended by the ICC Act (Section 1A), and the Taking of Hostages Act 1982 (Section 2 (1)).

Currently, there are no published guidelines. However, the Attorney General has confirmed to Parliament that the applicable criteria he uses "are the same as for any other criminal offence. First, there must be sufficient admissible and reliable evidence to afford a realistic prospect of conviction; secondly, the circumstances must be such that it would be in the public interest for there to be a prosecution."[7]

The test requires that the evidence be admissible in a UK court of law, reliable and "more likely than not" to lead to a conviction. Section 135 of the Criminal Justice Act 1988 does not stipulate when such consent should be sought; however, in practice, the CPS, following the contact from the police, will usually seek the Attorney General's consent before the alleged perpetrator is arrested and presumably once the CPS considers that a person can be prosecuted, i.e., the case fulfills its guidelines on decisions to prosecute.[8] Consent is not needed to arrest an individual without an arrest warrant or for the competent magistrate to issue an ar-

---

[6] Section 135 of the CJA 1988 states, "Proceedings for an offence under Section 134 above shall not be begun in England and Wales, except by or with the consent of the Attorney General; or in Northern Ireland, except by or with the consent of the Attorney General for Northern Ireland."

[7] Written answer by the Attorney General to Mr. Boateng, Parliamentary question 19/07/93 published in *Hansard* (official parliamentary reports).

[8] There is no requirement for the police to contact the CPS before they have concluded their investigation and/or decided to lay charges. However, in cases such as torture, they usually liaise closely with the CPS.

rest warrant.[9] However, consent is needed if the summons procedure is used to detain a person.[10]

On September 10, 2005, a warrant for the arrest of Israeli Major General Doron Almog was issued by a senior district judge at Bow Street Magistrates' Court. The warrant was issued in response to the receipt of information regarding the destruction of houses in Rafah City (Gaza), pursuant to the Geneva Conventions Act 1957. General Almog landed at London Heathrow airport on September 11, 2005 on a flight from Tel Aviv. However, he declined to disembark from the aircraft apparently after being informed that he could be arrested. London's Metropolitan Police reportedly refused to enter the plane to effect the general's arrest and then allowed him to depart from the UK for Israel on the same aircraft on which he had arrived. Following pressure from the Israeli Government in the aftermath of this incident, the British Government is apparently considering to repeal (or amend) Section 25 (2) of the Prosecution of Offences Act, to prevent individuals from applying to the Magistrates' Court for an arrest warrant to be issued, at least in respect of "international cases."

b) Non-Retrospectivity

According to the House of Lords in the *Pinochet* case, Section 134 of the CJA is not retrospective.[11] Moreover, the majority of Law Lords found that torture was not a common law crime before Section 134 of the Criminal Justice Act came into

---

[9] Section 25 (2) (a). Section 25 of the Prosecution of Offences Act 1985 provides:
  (1) This section applies to any enactment which prohibits the institution or carrying on of proceedings for any offence except
    (a) with the consent (however expressed) of a Law Officer of the Crown or the Director; or
  . (b) where the proceedings are instituted or carried on by or on behalf of a Law Officer of the Crown or the Director; and so applies whether or not there are other exceptions to the prohibition (and in particular whether or not the consent is an alternative to the consent of any other authority or person).
  (2) An enactment to which this section applies
    (a) shall not prevent the arrest without warrant, or the issue or execution of a warrant for the arrest, of a person for any offence, or the remand in custody or on bail of a person charged with any offence; and
    (b) ...
  (3) In this section enactment includes any provision having effect under or by virtue of any Act; and this section applies to enactments whenever passed or made.
  [As quoted in District Judge Nicholas Evans' decision of April 24, 2002, to refuse an application to issue a warrant of arrest for former US Secretary of State Kissinger under the 1957 Geneva Conventions.]
[10] *R. v. Bull* (1994), 99 Cr App R 193. Confirmed in the application for the arrest of Narenda Modi, Chief Minister of the State of Gujarat, for torture under Section 134 of the CJA before District Judge Workman at Bow Street Magistrates' Court on August 20, 2003.
[11] *R. v. Bow Street Metropolitan Stipendary Magistrate ex parte Pinochet Ungarte* (3) (1999), 2 WLR 827.

force on September 29, 1988.[12] Instead the Law Lords found that acts of torture and conspiracy to commit torture, which were perpetrated prior to September 29, 1988, can only be used as evidence in a case to show that incidents of torture committed on or after that date were part of a systematic state policy.[13] An unwieldy situation arises where an individual can be prosecuted for torture under the Geneva Convention Act and the Genocide Act for torture committed prior to September 1988, but where these acts are neither a war crime nor an act of genocide, the torturer will escape prosecution, unless he/she committed further acts of torture after September 1988. As a result, torturers can evade (and have evaded) justice under Section 134 CJA, and justice and reparation are consequently denied to their victims.

c) Immunities

In the *Pinochet* case (No. 3), the House of Lords analyzed at length the applicability of immunities and concluded that immunity *rationae personae* applied to a very limited category of persons (such as heads of state) but only for the period of time in which they remained in office. Once out of office, the only immunity that was applicable was immunity *rationae materiae*, or subject matter immunity, and this could only extend to official acts. The Law Lords determined that torture could not be considered to be an official act and hence immunity *rationae materiae* could not act as a bar.

Lord Browne-Wilkinson queried in *Pinochet* (No. 3): "How can it be for international purposes an official function to do something, which international law itself prohibits and criminalizes?"[14] Further, Lord Millet noted, "The official or governmental nature of the act, which forms the basis of the immunity, is an essential ingredient of the offence. No rational system of criminal justice can allow an immunity which is coextensive with the offence."[15]

This position differs from that taken by the Yugoslav tribunal when it indicted Mr. Milosevic while he was acting head of state. Indeed, the irrelevance of official

---

[12] Ibid. Lord Millet was the only Law Lord to find that systematic practice of torture prior to September 1988 was a common law crime however, he found that a singe act of torture was not "the systematic use of torture on a large scale and as an instrument of state policy had joined piracy, war crimes and crimes against peace as an international crime of universal jurisdiction well before 1984. I consider that it had done so by 1973." (p. 103 of the judgment).

[13] Ibid. Lord Hope and Lord Browne-Wilkinson reached this conclusion. Out of the other three, Lord Millet found that torture, as part of a systematic practice, was a crime in the UK under the common law, though a single act of torture was not. Lord Hutton, Lord Saville of Newdigate and Lord Phillips of Worth Matravers all agreed with Lord Hope's analysis but made no specific comment about this.

[14] Ibid., p. 846.

[15] Ibid., p. 913.

capacity has been incorporated into the statutes of all international criminal tribunals, including the International Criminal Court.[16]

III. Civil Proceedings

1. General Principles

It is arguable that the same circumstances that make torture a crime should also give rise to a civil obligation under international law. This follows from Article 14 of the UN Convention against Torture, which sets out the obligation of state parties to ensure in their legal systems that the victim of an act of torture obtains redress and has an enforceable right to fair and adequate compensation, "including the means for as full rehabilitation as possible."[17] This means that victims must be provided with effective procedural remedies (the ability to have access to justice) as well as substantive reparation, including, as appropriate, restitution, compensation, rehabilitation, satisfaction, and guarantees of non-repetition.

Extraterritorial civil claims for torture are more frequently resorted to in common law jurisdictions because in civil law countries it is usually simpler to attach civil claims to ongoing criminal proceedings through the *constitution de partie civile* system. Most cases have proceeded in the United States where there are specific laws that allow for such claims, but increasingly cases have been lodged in the United Kingdom, Canada, Switzerland, and elsewhere. The jurisprudence in these latter countries has developed separately from the criminal jurisprudence, and in some instances different standards have been applied to questions of immunities as well as forum or nexus considerations.

In the UK, there is no specific legislative basis on which to bring an extraterritorial civil claim for torture or other crimes under international law. Civil claims are brought on the base of common law tort actions. There is no requirement under English law for a person launching a claim for a civil wrong committed abroad to be resident in the UK or to be a British national. However in claims where the injury occurred outside of the UK the claimant needs to overcome a series of procedural hurdles. In particular:

---

[16] Article 27 (1) of the ICC Statute stipulates, "This Statute shall apply equally to all persons without distinction based on official capacity. In particular, official capacity as a Head of State or Government, a member of a Government or parliament, an elected representative or a government official shall in no case exempt a person from criminal responsibility under this Statute, nor shall it, in and of itself, constitute a ground for reduction of sentence."

[17] Article 14 continues: "including the means for as full rehabilitation as possible. In the event of the death of the victim as a result of an act of torture, his dependants shall be entitled to compensation. (2) Nothing in this article shall affect any right of the victim or other persons to compensation which may exist under national law."

- Limitation periods: The time limit to bring a case for intentional trespass of the person is 6 years, however there is a discretion not to apply the limitation period when it is judged to be equitable to do so.
- Service rules: Jurisdiction will only be effective if the defendant is served in the appropriate form.[18]
- *Forum non conveniens:* The court has the inherent ability to stay the proceedings when it is satisfied that there is some other available forum having competent jurisdiction in which the case may be tried more suitably for the interests of all the parties and the ends of justice.
- Immunities: As will be discussed below, courts have taken a more expansive view of applicable immunities in extraterritorial civil proceedings than has been taken in criminal proceedings.

2. Analysis of the Case Law

There have been two main cases in the UK that have dealt with extraterritorial civil claims, and both cases turned on the preliminary issue of immunity. The first is *Al Adsani v. Kuwait,* a case involving a dual national of the United Kingdom and Kuwait, who brought a claim in UK courts against Kuwait for torture. The Court of Appeal found that the State Immunity Act 1978 was a "comprehensive code." It rejected the argument that the *jus cogens* status of torture resulted in an implied exception to the State Immunity Act. The European Court of Human Rights came to the same conclusion, perceiving a fundamental distinction between the principle of universal jurisdiction in criminal and in civil cases. Although the prohibition of torture unquestionably enjoys a peremptory status under international law, the Court was unable to find, "in the international instruments, judicial authorities, or other materials before it any firm basis for concluding that, as a matter of international law, a State no longer enjoys immunity from civil suit in the courts of another State where acts of torture are alleged."[19] The minority took a different view, and stated that it is impossible to separate the criminal and civil consequences flowing from the single act. The *jus cogens* status of the prohibition of torture attaches to the act itself, not to the criminal or civil consequences. This view is bolstered when one considers the practice of civil law countries, where civil actions are joined to criminal actions through the system of *partie civile.*

In *Ron Jones v. Saudi Arabia,*[20] the claims of three British citizens and one dual national who alleged that they were tortured in Saudi Arabia were joined before

---

[18] See REDRESS, *Challenging Impunity for Torture: A Manual for Bringing Criminal and Civil Proceedings in England and Wales for Torture Committed Abroad* (2000), pp. 125–163.

[19] *Al-Adsani v. The United Kingdom* (2002), 34 E.H.R.R. 11, at para. 61.

[20] *Ron Jones v. Ministry of Interior Al-Mamlaka Al-Arabiya (The Kingdom of Saudi Arabia) and Secretary of State for Constitutional Affairs; the Redress Trust (Intervenors); Sandy Mitchell and Ors. v. Ibrahim Al-Dali & Ors.,* Court of Appeal (Civil Division) A2 2003/2155 & A2 2004/0489 (October 28, 2004).

English courts. Mr. Jones initiated civil proceedings against the individual Saudi officials allegedly responsible for the torture and the Kingdom of Saudi Arabia itself. The other three claimants brought civil proceedings against the named Saudi officials only. The Court of Appeal dismissed the claim against the Kingdom of Saudi Arabia on the basis of state immunity. The Court referred to the *Al-Adsani* judgments before the Court of Appeal and the European Court of Human Rights to find that although "international law is in the course of continuing development,"[21] "*as of yet*, no evidence exists to show that the peremptory status of *jus cogens* norms means that immunity should not apply."[22] In addressing Article 14 (1) of the Convention against Torture, however, the Court of Appeal found that both the individual and the perpetrating state should be held responsible for the act of torture but questioned whether this resulted in an obligation upon the forum state to hold the foreign state responsible. The Court did deny the individual officials the protection of immunity. Mance LJ for the majority noted that:

> Civil proceedings have established a positive role in a domestic context where criminal proceedings have never been brought, or have been brought and have for some reason failed. The importance of civil redress is acknowledged by Article 14 of the Convention against Torture, which focuses on their compensatory function. But there are cases, and torture is among them, where the value of civil redress may be suggested to lie as much in terms of the ability to establish the truth and so to assist rehabilitation or closure as in terms of the prospect of any financial recovery. That is not to express any positive view that the truth-finding function of civil proceedings would by itself be a sufficient basis on which the courts of one state would consider it appropriate to exercise civil jurisdiction. I merely identify it as a possible factor, which, if relevant at all, could have to be balanced with other factors, including (among others) the likelihood or otherwise of the court hearing from both sides and the undoubted sensitivity of any exercise of jurisdiction in respect of torture allegedly occurring abroad. The difficulty we face is that the limited basis on which the present cases were decided below means that there was no argument there or before us about either the basis on which or circumstances in which jurisdiction could or should be exercised if state immunity is not an absolute bar to the claims against individuals.[23]

The appeal (and cross-appeal) to the House of Lords took place April 25–27, 2006, and the judgment is likely to be delivered before the end of the year.

IV. In Conclusion

The House of Lords' decisions in the Pinochet case placed the United Kingdom at the forefront of developments on universal jurisdiction, particularly in respect of the recognition that there should be no immunity (*ratione materiae*) for the most egregious crimes under international law. Nonetheless, the practice of the UK ever since, calls into question the commitment of the Government to make any real progress at all. Aside from the important prosecution of Sarwar Zardad for torture

---

[21] Ibid., para. 16.

[22] Ibid., para. 17.

[23] Ibid., p. 80.

and hostage taking, there is very little sign of commitment to universal jurisdiction, both in respect of criminal and civil cases. The continued ability of the Attorney General to disallow prosecutions on public policy grounds is highly problematic. Further, the few opportunities for victims to directly access justice by seeking an arrest warrant have not met with any success; and in fact the recent failure to implement the warrant in the case of Almog suggests outright obfuscation by the Government in order to avoid application of the law. In civil cases, immunities continue to be the principle stumbling blocks for potential claimants. Here too, the UK Government has taken a stance in direct opposition to such claims. Indeed in *Ron Jones v. Saudi Arabia*, the UK Government has intervened in support of the application of immunities in favor of the Saudi officials said to be responsible for the torture and the Saudi state itself.

Coming to Terms with Genocide in Rwanda: The Role of International and National Justice

Dieter Magsam

I will try to outline the Rwandan way of dealing with the genocide of 1994, which operates on the juridical approach on the international level and a modified juridical approach on the national level. If the attempt is made to establish individual guilt and personal responsibility, the trap of collective guilt, which inevitably falls along ethnic lines, may be avoided. But there are serious risks: the huge number of accused persons and the unprosecuted war crimes allegedly committed by some military members of the ruling RPF could endanger the reconciliation process.

I. Introduction

The 1994 genocide did not erupt from a historical vacuum. Since 1959 the Tutsi-labeled minority had lived "on probation." The Constitution of 1962 attempted to legitimate the "power of the majority," and did not even try to disguise its racist bias. In hindsight, one might even say the Constitution fostered conditions for genocide. The massacres of 1963–64 were described by—among others—British philosopher Bertrand Russell as the first genocide since the Holocaust.[1] The fact that the genocide of 1994 is increasingly seen as the "turning point" in Rwanda's history is due primarily to the military victory of the RPF on July 4, 1994. With much hesitation, the international community recognized and accepted that this military victory might have put an end to a genocide as defined by the Convention on the Prevention and Punishment of the Crime of Genocide of 9 December 1948. Mitterand's notorious phrase, "in countries like this, genocide is not very important,"[2] could have been and might still be the underlying theme of Western poli-

---

[1] N. Ellingham, *Accounting for Horror: Post-Genocide Debates in Rwanda* (2003), pp. 34 et seq.; M. Mamdani, *When Victims Become Killers. Colonialism, Nativism and the Genocide in Rwanda* (2001), pp. 103 et seq.

[2] "Dans ces pays-là, un génocide c'est pas trop important," quoted in *Le Figaro*, January 12, 1998.

cies in the Great Lakes Region.[3] UN Security Council Resolution 955 of November 8, 1994, at least provided for the establishment of the International Criminal Tribunal for Rwanda (ICTR).[4]

1. The ICTR

By establishing the ICTR, the UN Security Council acknowledged that there was no difference between a genocide committed in Africa and one in "civilized" Europe. This also applies to crimes against humanity and war crimes. The ICTR is mandated to deal with crimes committed in Rwanda or in neighboring countries between January and December 1994. This restriction in time and space is a political compromise: while the new government of Rwanda wanted to try only crimes committed in Rwanda between October 1990 (i.e., the start of the armed return of the RPF into Rwanda) and July 1994 (i.e., the fall of Kigali), the defeated government, its army, and international supporters preferred the notion of a double genocide committed against the "Hutu majority" by the RPF in late 1994, 1995, and 1996 in Rwanda and the former Zaire, to which 1.7 million Rwandans had fled.

Up to now, the ICTR has pronounced twenty-three judgments in seventeen trials, with three defendants acquitted. Trials are pending against twenty-five alleged offenders. The trials, which began no earlier than 1997, involve politicians, military commanders, directors of press and radio stations, journalists, and other private persons who had allegedly planned, organized, and executed the extermination of a part of the Rwandan population. There are fifty-seven detainees in Arusha and six prisoners serving sentences in Mali. Eighteen trials are pending against a further eighteen detainees. One can summarize the results as follows:

- It has been proven, beyond any reasonable doubt, that there was a genocide in Rwanda, planned and organized by the Rwandan "elite." Whether the targeted group, i.e., the Rwandan Tutsi, can be qualified as an ethnic group is neither probable nor important because the official ideology treated Tutsi as a racial or ethnic entity that had to be extinguished.[5] Those Rwandans registered as "Tutsi" by passport or with Tutsi fathers were considered to be Tutsi. The longer the massacres went on, the less "official" registration played a role; in time, "Tutsi" meant anyone who looked like a Tutsi, as described by the racist Hamitic thesis.[6] Leading opposition (moderate) Hutu politicians were systematically eliminated at first, in order to foster the masses' self-assessment (the feeling of being first and foremost Hutu) among the "power wing" of Hutu politics. National and local authorities then organized the genocide.

---

[3]   L. Melvern, *A People Betrayed. The Role of the West in Rwanda's Genocide* (2004), pp. 186 et seq.

[4]   All documents and judgments at the website of the Tribunal http://www.ictr.org.

[5]   *Prosecutor v. Kayishema and Ruzindana*, Case No. ICTR-95-1, judgment of May 21, 1999, para. 98.

[6]   Cf. M. Mamdani, *supra* note 1, pp. 76 et seq.

- The implication of the entire non-Tutsi population in mass atrocities was a strategic aim, in order to establish collective guilt and thus leave no one to tell the story from a neutral point of view once the Tutsi population was exterminated.
- Rape, in hundreds of thousands of cases, was conceived and used as a weapon to infect victims, destroy them physically, and symbolically undermine their ability to reproduce.

Because the mandate of the ICTR is limited, further indictments are no longer admissible since the beginning of 2005. The end of 2008 will mark the deadline for all first instance trial judgments, and the end of 2010 is the deadline for appeals cases. So it seems that some (alleged) war crimes and crimes against humanity, for which some military leaders of the RPF are blamed, will never be tried at international level. Currently, Rwanda and the ICTR are debating the transfer of 40 cases to the Rwandan judiciary. Since international justice prohibits the death penalty, the Rwandan authorities will have to assure that the death penalty will not be imposed in those cases transferred to them.

The Democratic Republic of Congo (formerly Zaire), where many alleged *genocidaires* fled after their defeat in 1994, extradited only two suspects to the ICTR, in September 2002: the former prefect of Kigali and the former mayor of Murambi. To date, no suspects have been extradited to the Rwandan authorities. There is no scientific way to measure the effects of the ICTR judgments on the reconciliation process in Rwanda or in the Great Lakes region.

The performance of the ICTR has often been criticized because of its limited output. In Rwanda, the length of the trials, as well as the "luxurious" prison conditions, have been subject to popular attack. Nevertheless, up to now Arusha has judged more genocide-related defendants than any other international tribunal since World War II, and its judgments—based on serious, fact-finding methods—provide a detailed view of how the genocide was organized and executed. Having established an international tribunal in Africa, the UN has demonstrated that genocide, crimes against humanity, and war crimes constitute a worldwide concern. Collaboration between the Rwandan prosecution service and the ICTR has improved. On the other hand, the ICTR has failed to try alleged war crimes or crimes against humanity committed by the RPF.[7] This might diminish its credibility among Rwandans who lost their families or friends during those events. This is why Belgian expert Filip Reyntjens, who for a long time collaborated with the ICTR Prosecution Service, recently withdrew from collaboration.

2. Justice on the National Level

With the Genocide Convention signed and ratified by the old regime, the new Rwandan authorities, too, were obliged and willing to establish mechanisms for legal prosecution of genocide cases. Because there is no reconciliation without

---

[7]   See A. Des Forges, *Leave None to Tell the Story: Genocide in Rwanda* (1999), pp. 726–729.

truth—and as it is up to the Rwandan judicial system to establish the latter—the quality and impartiality of judicial proceedings are crucial to the reconciliation process.

By 1996, Rwanda's prisons were overcrowded, with some 70,000 detainees. The Organic Law of August 30, 1996, covered all crimes connected to genocide and committed between October 1990 and December 1994, including not only genocide and crimes against humanity, but also related, lesser crimes such as physical injuries, theft, pillage, etc. Crimes committed by military personnel, however, were and still are to be tried in military courts.

The 1996 Organic Law created a categorization by dividing the perpetrators into four groups. A special chamber of the Supreme Court was to organize and supervise the activities of the ordinary courts, which at that time had sole jurisdiction. Any testimony, including confessions implicating other alleged perpetrators, could lead to a considerable reduction in sentence, if associated with a plea for forgiveness. However, this system did not work quickly enough. Whereas the number of persons judged increased from 346 in 1997 to almost 5,000 persons by the year 2000, the number of detainees increased to 130,000. This was why an alternative model of justice had to be established, or, *gacaca*. Under gacaca, about 250,000 "persons of integrity" were elected in 2002 to staff community-based courts with jurisdiction over categories 2–4. Offenders ranked in Category 1 (those suspected of having planned, organized and committed special atrocities like mass rapes) still await trial before the ordinary courts. At the time of this writing, gacaca courts have not yet pronounced any judgments,[8] and 90 percent of these "village courts" have not yet even started. In June 2004, a modification of the 2001 gacaca law reduced the number of gacaca judges, abolished the third category, and excluded compensation for nonmaterial damages. These changes took effect starting January 15, 2005. Since then, a few gacaca judgments have been rendered. Thus gacaca's contribution to national reconciliation is actually difficult to define or anticipate. Evaluating the results of pilot gacaca courts, having already categorized crimes committed in 10% of the country and taking into account primary findings of the database established by the National Prosecution Service and GTZ (German Technical Cooperation) Justice Project, it seems that:

- The number of Category 1 offenders to be tried by the ordinary courts will reach about 50,000.
- In total, the number of accused persons will be 500,000 to 600,000.
- There are very few confessions concerning the more than 200,000 sexual crimes alleged to have been committed.
- Lay judges do not employ methods to evaluate the credibility and probative value of confessions. The confessions often seem to be "mechanical" in content and tone, conceding nothing but those facts that are already proven or which can hardly be denied.
- Evidence provided by witnesses and accomplices or confession in general is highly suspect. In Rwanda's case, one should consider not only the ten-year in-

[8]   First judgments were pronounced in summer 2005.

terval since the events occurred, but also the lack of direct evidence. Victims rarely survived, and potential victims personally close to them only survived because they were hidden at the time. Hearsay evidence often undermines any accurate exposition of what really happened and the actual contribution of each individual defendant.

- Despite the fact that 20,000 detainees were released by presidential order in early 2003, 60,000 people remain in detention awaiting trial. Further planned releases were stopped following the murder of witnesses in Gikongoro Province in 2003.

The Constitution of 2003 established a "National Unity and Reconciliation Commission" (NURC, Art. 178f) and a "Commission to Fight Genocide" (Art. 179). The Arusha Treaties already provided for the former in 1993 (Art. 24 of the "Protocol on Power Sharing"), and it was in effect during the transition period after March 1995. Without giving a precise definition of who should be reconciled with whom, the NURC's task is only generally described as "developing national programs for unity and reconciliation" and "fighting divisionist ideology." The Commission is also responsible for *ingando* (transition camps), where prisoners and demobilized soldiers are prepared for their eventual return to civilian life. The Commission also contributes to the official curriculum on how Rwandan history should be taught at school. No official documents yet exist.

However, individuals who have gone through the education camps report that the division of Rwandan society is basically explained as a result of colonialism. They learn that German and Belgian colonialists ruled indirectly by misusing members of the "Tutsi race" as mediators, and that in the late 1950s, the Belgians and the Catholic church attempted to maintain their influence by abolishing monarchy, promoting the "Hutu majority" and excluding all Tutsi from political participation. That is why the constitutions of the First and Second Republics had already laid the foundations for the genocide of 1994. *Ingando* participants also learn that in order to assure national unity and avoid further mass killings, people should regard themselves only as Rwandans and not as Hutu, Tutsi or Twa.[9] Any political Party founded on ethnic grounds would be illegal. In contrast to this Rwandan attempt to escape an ethnically divided trap, the recently adopted Burundian Constitution and the Election Law demand the ethnic self-categorization of each Burundian citizen.

Rwanda's transition period ended in 2003. In May 2003 a referendum adopted the draft of the Constitution and was followed by presidential elections in August and parliamentary elections in October 2003. The latter were criticized, particularly for having hampered any political organizations opposed to the president's RPF party.

---

[9] See Penal Reform International, *Report on the gacaca, Report VI. From Camp to Hill, The Reintegration of Released Prisoners* (2004), http://www.penalrefom.org/download/ gacaca%VI.

II. How Best to Judge the Justice and Reconciliation Process in Rwanda?

1. The Rwandan Government must demonstrate that its methods for dealing with the genocide inside Rwanda contribute to truth and justice, and therefore to reconciliation. If not, its regional political strategies will also lack credibility. The decision to try all participants seems to be a reasonable approach. Rwanda has to deal with a "micromanaged" genocide and about half a million alleged perpetrators. This constitutes a huge difference from the Holocaust, as well as from the South African crimes of apartheid (the latter did not even constitute a genocide).

Criminal prosecution means looking for individual responsibility and trying to determine whether and why the accused persons killed unknown fellow Rwandans, or even neighbors, friends, and partners. This individual approach prevents the establishment of "collective guilt" and forestalls collective revenge. However, given the difficulties mentioned in section 1, there is some doubt as to whether this goal can be met. A report of a Parliamentary Commission in August 2004 was the first official document to mention such problems. But instead of properly analyzing the problems, the report blamed individuals and organizations—mainly NGOs critical of the government. According to this particular Commission, these NGOs had influenced the general population by spreading genocidal or "divisionist" ideology.

2. The genocide grew out of a war. Many people, especially from the North, were forced to flee the advancing RPF. Hundreds of thousands had to live in camps for IDPs (Internally Displaced Persons), where the Hutu Militia easily recruited them. For example, if we seek to understand why the son of a Byumba farmer became a killer of Tutsi, it would be helpful to know why and how his own father and other family members had been killed by RPF soldiers during the war. These inquiries would not seek to justify the genocidal crimes committed later by the surviving son, but simply to clarify and comprehend the deadly dynamics and the degree of individual guilt. Currently, no participants in gacaca even dare to speak about war crimes or crimes against humanity allegedly committed by RPF soldiers. It is said that Rwanda's military courts try them, but there is no proof of such judgments, as they are not published. Reconciliation could be facilitated by seriously investigating those alleged crimes and publishing the results of such investigations.

In general, freedom of speech in and outside the courts is vital for truth to be established and reconciliation to take root. This freedom is currently threatened by two laws that aim to punish "divisionism", "sectarianism", and/or the negation or minimization of the genocide.[10] Though the necessity of such laws cannot be questioned, it is of the utmost importance to assure that the way they are written and applied does not lead to dangerous censorship or an unacceptable limitation of the freedom of expression.

---

[10] Law 47/2001 of December 18, 2001 (Offenses of Discrimination and Sectarianism); Law No. 33 bis/2003 (Negating, Minimizing or Attempting to Justify Genocide).

3. A false accusation made against a Hutu refugee, returning from a camp in the Zone Turquoise or from Zaire, could have been enough to justify the appropriation of his or her house or land, and in many cases, the mere ethnic label "Hutu" might have been enough to send an innocent person to jail. If gacaca fails to judge such cases fairly, the feeling of being victimized by collective revenge will persist and grow, as will the "ethnic" polarization of Rwandan society. This, finally and ironically, would represent a delayed victory for the founders and supporters of the former "Hutu Republic" and the masterminds of the 1994 genocide.

4. The compensation law for survivors of the genocide—drafted long ago—is unlikely to be promulgated due to a lack of means. Since many refugees and their children now forming the new elite consider themselves also to be victims of the genocidal ideology, the lack of appropriate indemnification mechanisms could be caused by a *concurrence des victims* (Chaumont). The different interests of sometimes passive Tutsi victims inside Rwanda and those refugees and armed fighters have yet to be openly discussed.

Part III

The "War on Terror" in Particular

Military Necessity, Torture, and the Criminality of Lawyers

Scott Horton

Drawing on the works of Immanuel Kant and repudiating much of the doctrine of Carl von Clausewitz, Columbia University's Francis Lieber laid the foundations for US military doctrine for 140 years. Then, in 2002, something strange happened.

When a lawyer, particularly a government lawyer, dispenses advice that leads government officials falsely to disregard the rules of the Geneva and Hague Conventions, and this advice foreseeably causes the death, torture, or gross abuse of prisoners held in time of war, is that lawyer guilty of a war crime? This is a question of immediate importance to America in the period after publication of the government documents collectively known as the "torture papers" together with photographic evidence of the gruesome abuse that proximately resulted from them (that is my thesis) in prisons such as Guantánamo, Abu Ghraib, and Bagram. The answer to this question must be an unequivocal "yes." Moreover, the failure of criminal authorities to commence a serious investigation that might lead to prosecutions furnishes compelling evidence of the spreading corruption of the administration of justice under the Bush administration.

As Lord Justice Steyn has recently observed, America today is beset by political figures who are determined to "bend established international law to their will and to undermine its essential structures."[1] This work has been hastened on its way by a group of lawyers who have betrayed their ethical and professional responsibilities and who have dispensed opinions demonstrably at odds with the law in order to justify government lawlessness. Government lawyers who behaved in such a fashion were rightly tried and sentenced at Nuremberg. As the prosecutions at Nuremberg demonstrated, such conduct is an appropriate topic for the invocation of universal jurisdiction if American criminal authorities fail to act.

I believe a brief historical excursion is necessary to demonstrate just how radical the conduct of these US government attorneys was. It is vital to look back to the well-established norms of military doctrine, which these gentlemen violently overturned, even while they filled the news media with a smoke screen claiming

---

[1] Quoted in "Britain Accused of Creating Terror Fears," *The Guardian*, June 11, 2005.

they faced a situation that was historically unprecedented and to which prior experience gave no guidance. The news media accepted these remarks at face value. Had they scratched underneath, they would have found conscious deceit or outrageous ignorance as the only possible basis for such claims.

I. The Legacy of Washington and Lincoln

Alberto Gonzales, now Attorney General of the United States, Jay S. Bybee, now a judge of the United States Court of Appeals for the Ninth Circuit, and John Yoo, then a functionary of the Department of Justice and now a law professor at the University of California at Berkeley, are the three principal figures in this drama. Each bears heavy responsibility for overturning the nation's policy of humane treatment of prisoners in time of war and introducing a regime of barbarity of unquestioned lawlessness. In the process of their work, they ignored well-settled precedents going back to the founding of the American Army, which were subsequently codified and promulgated by Abraham Lincoln. This reflected the core of the military doctrine of the United States, a topic on which each of the writers is seemingly both ignorant and oblivious.

The American approach to the treatment of prisoners was initially articulated by George Washington, giving expression to fundamental values of the Enlightenment which belong to the underpinnings of the American republic. Following Washington's lead, at the outset of the Civil War Abraham Lincoln gave deep thought to the rules by which the war would be conducted. He was pressed by radicals in the Republican Party to deny recognition to the Confederacy as a state and to view Confederate soldiers as traitors or conspirators in a domestic insurrection. To help resolve these issues, Lincoln turned to a law professor at Columbia University named Francis Lieber. This request led to the first comprehensive statement of the US military doctrine on the law of armed conflict.

II. The Kantian Roots of American Military Doctrine

More than two hundred years ago, the sage of Königsberg wrote:

> The law of armed conflict is the single aspect of the law of nations that gives us the most trouble to conceptualize and to suggest a law for this lawless situation (*inter armes silent leges*) without contradicting ourselves; however, it would have to be this: war must be waged in accordance with such principles as will make it possible to emerge from this natural condition of states (in their external relations with one another) and progress into a lawfully ordered one.[2]

For Kant, overcoming the lawlessness of warfare was a moral imperative and an essential prerequisite to human progress and peace. A generation later, a man

---

[2] I. Kant, *Grundlegung zur Metaphysik der Sitten* (1785), p. 57 (author's translation).

whose life ties this city of Berlin with my home, New York, was much taken with Kant's thoughts about war and the imperative to tame it. His tragic experiences in war help to explain that concern. He was born, in 1798, into a middle-class Berlin family as Franz Lieber, though to us in New York and at Columbia University, he is known as Francis Lieber. Lieber was much the product of his times, though— and this is perhaps a hallmark of most greatness—he rose far above them and proved a man of exceptional vision whose thinking has provided an important guidepost for humanity on its way forward. Indeed, is it possible to conceptualize international humanitarian law today without Francis Lieber?

In the age of a betrayed idealism, the age of the Napoleonic Wars, a movement arose in Germany called "das Junge Deutschland," Georg Büchner, Ludwig Börne, and Heinrich Heine are names associated in some way with it, though to be clear the movement was a loose association. Lieber sprang from this milieu and embraced its thoughts. Though Germany had not yet properly come into being as a nation-state, Lieber was a man of strong patriotic beliefs, who volunteered at a young age to fight the Napoleonic invaders. His patriotism had a strong political content. The famous manifesto of Büchner's *Hessischer Landbote* (1834) is much like Lieber's *Manual of Political Ethics* (1838), a radical demand for democracy and freedoms of speech and press, and a rejection of the authoritarian tradition, rule and economic oppression of a stultified aristocratic class. Lieber was an outspoken radical and exponent of democracy at a time when such ideas were dangerous. He soon came under the watchful eye of the repressive regime put in place following the Carlsbad Resolutions of 1819. He quickly left Germany, fighting like Lord Byron in Greece and ultimately fled across the Atlantic to America, where he ultimately came to be engaged in the then-radical and abolitionist politics of the Republican Party, joining with other German revolutionaries of the *Vormärz* like Carl Schurz.

Today we know Lieber for one contribution above all others. Guided by Kant's moral imperative and by his own bitter memories of suffering and abuse as a soldier in the Napoleonic era,[3] Lieber waged a campaign to codify the rules of warfare. In this effort, the humane treatment of prisoners, regardless of their classification, was given a central position. His work, promulgated by Lincoln as General Orders No. 100 to the Armies of the United States in the Field, is a milestone document in the evolution of international humanitarian law. Indeed, in a profound sense the subject of international humanitarian law commences with this document.

The intellectual background of this work is significant, for it presents a fascinating dialogue with German intellectual thought of the era. The core of Lieber's analysis clearly springs from Kant, and particularly from his *Grundlegung zur Metaphysik der Sitten, Streit der Fakultäten* and the celebrated essay *Zum ewigen*

---

[3]   At the age of 18 Lieber enlisted as a soldier in the Colberg Regiment and moved under Marshal Blücher to fight Napoleon at Waterloo. After that great battle Lieber was shot twice in a skirmish with French remnants outside of Naumur and was left for dead. A Samaritan found him and carted him in a wheelbarrow to Liège, where he was hospitalized to recovery.

Frieden. Indeed, at points Lieber appears closely to paraphrase or even merely to translate the Kantian texts.

III. Clausewitz Reframed

Aside from Kant, Lieber read and had a far more critical relationship with the writings of another Prussian, Carl von Clausewitz. In his seminal work, *Vom Kriege* (1832), Clausewitz posited a notion of *Kriegsräson*, known in English as "military necessity." Under this doctrine, prosecution of a war could be justified by any measures necessary or appropriate to achieve a successful outcome. This was a quintessentially Machiavellian view under which the "ends justify the means." Lieber, while recognizing that Clausewitz was presenting things as they are rather than as they ought to be, was horrified by the untamed notion of Kriegsräson. In his view, military necessity had to be balanced by two further considerations, namely: proportionality and humanity.

Accordingly, he wrote "Men who take up arms against one another in public war do not cease on this account to be moral beings, responsible to one another and to God."[4] And he carefully redefined "military necessity" by making clear that it was *subject to law* and that it could not under any circumstance justify acts of barbarity such as *torture.*[5] "Military necessity, as understood by modern civilized nations, consists in the necessity of those measures which are *indispensable* for securing the ends of the war, and which are *lawful* according to the modern law and usages of war." Lieber uses the word "indispensable" where Clausewitz says "appropriate"—a distinction which may seem subtle, but to lawyers and military certainly is not. For Lieber, this reinforces the notion of "necessity," which is notably absent in the German text. *Kriegsräson* was coined as an adjunct to *Staatsräson,* taken from the French *raison d'état,* which might be rendered in English as "serving the interests of the state." For Clausewitz, any tactic that was appropriate to accomplish the state's military objectives was appropriate as Kriegsräson. Thus the concept was seen as trumping the rules of conduct between states or the rules governing relations between citizens and the state in time of war. Thus, when German armies crashed through Belgium on their way to engage the French and British forces on the fields of Flanders, Kriegsräson was given its ultimate exemplification. The Western powers howled about violations of sacred principles of international law, but to the German military elite, Clausewitz's rules of war had been observed.

For Lieber another important limitation on military necessity lay in the Kantian principle that humanity must strive to create an order in which the natural state of relations among states is *peace.* Paraphrasing Kant, Lieber writes that the rules of war must reinforce this by prohibiting conduct of all kinds that would undermine

---

[4] *General Orders No. 100 to the Armies of the United States in the Field* ("General Order"), Art. 15.

[5] *General Order, supra* note 4, Art. 14 (emphasis added).

the reconstruction of a just and lasting peace. "Military necessity does not admit of *cruelty*—that is, the infliction of suffering for the sake of suffering or for revenge, nor of maiming or wounding except in fight, nor of *torture* to extort confessions. It does not admit of the use of *poison* in any way, nor of the wanton devastation of a district. It admits of deception, but disclaims acts of perfidy; and, in general, *military necessity does not include any act of hostility which makes the return to peace unnecessarily difficult.*"[6] He provided that the religion of the adversary and his freedom of conscience would in all respects be protected and guaranteed.[7] Hence, *Kriegsräson* as pronounced by Clausewitz and *military necessity* as described by Lieber are quite different things. Clausewitz's notion sounds strongly of Machiavelli and Hobbes, while Lieber's view embraces the twin restraints of humanity and proportionality and thus comes close to what ultimately emerged as the Geneva Convention system at the end of World War II—indeed, on important points it even approaches the views of the Additional Protocols, with their more comprehensive protection of the civilian populace. This is hardly coincidental, since Jean Pictet's *Commentaries* make clear that the views of the Lieber Code and their advocacy by a single great power (the United States) helped to drive this strengthening and development of the Geneva system.[8]

IV. Other Kantian Elements of US Military Doctrine

Lincoln and Lieber engaged at least three other issues of moment to the United States' legal policy predicament arising from the doctrinaire prosecution of the "Global War on Terror." First, should humanitarian accommodations be available only on the basis of reciprocity between nation-states? The Civil War raised

---

[6] *General Order, supra* note 4, Art. 16 (emphasis added). Cf. I. Kant, *Zum ewigen Frieden* (1795), p. 6: "No state should permit the conduct of war through such practices as would make the confidence of the counterparty in a future peace impossible: this would include the commissioning of assassinations (*percussores*), the employment of poisons (*venefici*), the violation of terms of capitulation, fomenting acts of betrayal (*perduellio*) in the state against which war is waged, etc." (author's translation). It is remarkable that Kant's list of proscribed acts is in many respects closer to today's crisis than Lieber's. Targeted assassinations have in fact reemerged as a tool for certain Machiavellian leaders.

[7] *General Order, supra* note 4, Art. 34: "The United States acknowledge and protect, in hostile countries occupied by them, religion and morality; strictly private property; the persons of the inhabitants, especially those of women; and the sacredness of domestic relations. Offenses to the contrary shall be rigorously punished." As Lieber subsequently noted, his concern ran not only to the rights of various Christian confessions, but also to Jews and to Muslims. The importance of freedom of religion in the conduct of war and creating appropriate conditions for peace was driven home to Lieber during his participation in the Greek wars of liberation in the Ottoman Empire in 1822–1825. He believed that it would be a particular act of folly to allow war to be waged on grounds of religious intolerance, and saw the religious wars which swept France and Germany in the seventeenth century as a demonstration of the nightmarish potential of such an approach.

[8] J. Pictet, *Commentaries on the Geneva Conventions* (1960).

pointed questions on this issue, since the United States refused to acknowledge the Confederacy as a nation-state, viewing it instead as a civil insurrection. Were a highly mechanical approach to be employed, the rights of soldiers in "honorable warfare" would have to be denied, with a consequent brutalization of the war effort. On this point, the decisive policy had been adopted by George Washington, America's first commander in chief and later first president. Acting in the former capacity, on December 25, 1776, he directed the humane treatment of prisoners of war taken at the Battle of Trenton—even though the British had treated American soldiers as rebel guerillas unentitled to the advantages of "honorable warfare." Lieber embraced this view and did so for the same reasons offered by Washington: the rules were necessary for the maintenance of good order and discipline in the army, even where no expectation of reciprocity existed.[9] But beyond this, Lieber took the view that sound principles of preservation of a fragile social order demanded this step: "Where no discipline is enforced in war a state of things results which resembles far more the wars recorded in *Froissart*, or *Comines*, or the thirty-years' war, and the religious war in France, than the regular war of modern times. And such a state of things results speedily, too; for all growth, progress, and rearing, moral or material, are slow; all destruction, relapse, and degeneracy fearfully rapid."[10]

Second, would the benefits of prisoner-of-war status be offered to guerilla combatants, particularly those who fought without uniforms or other identifying insignia, as irregulars or as partisans? Again, Lieber concluded that though a distinction could be made and sustained on the basis of customary international law, it was not in the interest either of the nation or of mankind to make it. "Guerilla-men, when captured in fair fight and open warfare, should be treated as the regular partisan is, until special crimes, such as murder, or the killing of prisoners, or the sacking of places, are proved upon them."[11] Rather it was preferable to hold to a clear high standard of treatment for those brought *hors de combat*, and to eschew niggling distinctions that could be made to justify mistreatment by those likely to succumb to the brutality of war.[12]

Third, how should combatants who violate the laws of war, or other laws in times of war, be held to account? Lieber doubted the suitability of civilian courts for such a function. He was concerned that an interplay with the civilian administration of justice might undermine military discipline and the command principle. He also feared that such courts might not dispense impartial justice to captured enemy combatants. Were civilian courts the only available forum, Lieber thought, the temptation would be too great to avoid charges and trials altogether, a step which would dangerously undercut the rule of law in times of war.

---

[9] See generally D. Hackett Fischer, *Washington's Crossing* (2004).

[10] F. Lieber, *Guerilla Parties Considered with Reference to the Laws and Usages of War* (1862), pp. 33–34.

[11] F. Lieber, *supra* note 10, p. 42.

[12] "And such a state of things results speedily, too; for all growth, progress, and rearing, moral or material, are slow; all destruction, relapse, and degeneracy fearfully rapid. It requires the power of the Almighty and a whole century to grow an oak tree; but only a pair of arms, an ax, and an hour or two to cut it down." (F. Lieber, *supra* note 10, p. 34).

I must stress: these were not the idle musings of a detached academic. Because Lieber won the recognition and support of Abraham Lincoln, and because the president chose formally to promulgate them as a standing order for the nation's armed forces, these views were established as the military doctrine of the United States. Each of the points I cited and discussed above was firmly established as military doctrine in 1863, and was carried forward until the fall of 2002.

A particularly strong example is found in the United States Army's Field Manual 34–52, which continues to state this as the "default test" to be applied by officers considering the introduction and use of any new interrogation technique. This, of course, derives from the Categorical Imperative.

V. The Tradition Takes Hold: Lincoln to McKinley to Roosevelt

In the period following Lieber's death, two men were particularly responsible for the preservation and development of his legacy. The first is Francis Lieber's son, Norman, who served as chief military advisor to President McKinley and as such set the military rules in place through the arrival of the Great War.[13]

The current debate over torture marks the first time the issue has achieved such prominence in American political discussion. But it is hardly the first appearance of the issue. During the Spanish-American War, the use of certain torture techniques by US soldiers in the Philippines grabbed brief newspaper attention. Specifically, in 1902, a soldier was court-martialed for using what was called the "water cure"—forcing a prisoner to consume large amounts of water—as a technique in the interrogation of Filipino insurgents. The soldier invoked "military necessity," saying that the insurgents presented a grave threat to the safety of his troops and had to be ferreted out. At his court-martial, defense counsel advanced the traditional Clausewitz view of "military necessity" to support the defense. The court-martial found the defense unavailing and convicted the soldier.

The Judge Advocate General of the Army took an appeal from the case and addressed the claim that a "military necessity" defense could be raised to justify this conduct. He noted a General Order in effect for the U.S. forces at the time which stated that "military necessity does not admit of cruelty, that is, the inflicting of suffering for the sake of suffering or revenge … nor of torture to extort confessions." Indeed, this is the text of the Lieber Code which remained in formal force through the Great War. The Judge Advocate General's decision continues, "the [necessity] defense fails completely, inasmuch as it is attempted to establish the principle that a belligerent who is at war with a savage or semicivilized enemy may conduct his operations in violation of the rules of civilized war. This no mod-

---

[13] See N. Lieber, *The Use of the Army in the Aid of the Civil Power* (1898), a work which carries many of Francis Lieber's notions forward and which has great prescience with respect to issues of humanitarian intervention.

ern State will admit for an instant; nor was it the rule in the Philippine Islands."[14] It should be noted that, as described in contemporary accounts, this technique is similar to the practice of waterboarding or water cure that Defense Secretary Rumsfeld approved and that Bush Administration officials continue, through the date of this writing, to advocate.

The second is perhaps the greatest American lawyer and statesman of the last century, the former Bar President, Senator and Secretary of State Elihu Root. A long-time student of Lieber, Root was persuaded of the need to use the Hague process as a venue for the aggressive advocacy of Lieber's perspective of the rules of land warfare. This he did with great dedication, setting the way for the major engagement between the Lieber and Clausewitz views of military necessity that was fought in the preparatory works for the Hague Convention on Land Warfare of 1907. That effort ultimately produced a compromise, with the German notion of Kriegsräson gaining acceptance in the preamble, but Lieber's limitations on its use being imbedded in the text. For Root, Lieber was the "patron saint of international law"[15] whose work would show the way forward for generations to come.

So America's views were clear from 1863, were strongly reaffirmed in the 1890's, and were aggressively reasserted in 1905–07, and again in the lead up to the Second World War. After that war the new international human rights law system came into place. And then something very curious happened. We still don't know *exactly* what happened, and though much has come to the public eye in the last year, much also remains clouded in secrecy.

VI. What Happened in 2002?

Following a public spat between Secretary Powell and Secretary Rumsfeld over the application of the Geneva Conventions, President Bush resolved the matter against the Conventions, issuing an Order dated February 7, 2002, which provided "I hereby reaffirm the order previously issued by the secretary of defense to the United States Armed Forces requiring that the detainees be treated humanely and, to the extent appropriate and consistent with military necessity, in a manner consistent with the principles of Geneva." Many expressed relief when this order came. After all, "humane" treatment has been extensively defined in Common Article 3 of the Geneva Conventions. And, as I noted above, in American military doctrine and law, "military necessity" never had the meaning that Clausewitz gave to Kriegsräson. Moreover, the torture or mistreatment of prisoners of war were expressly excluded from military necessity by Articles 14, 15, and 16 of the General Order, which was consistently carried forward in all Army manuals and policy statements for over 140 years and then enacted into the Uniform Code of Military Justice.

---

[14] L. Friedman (ed.), *The Law Of War: A Documentary History* (1972), pp. 814–819.
[15] E. Root, *American Journal of International Law* 1913, p. 7.

However this relief was unwarranted. As used by George Bush, the word "humane" meant only that the detainees were given food, water, medical attention and a place to sleep; it provided no protection whatsoever against torture or physical abuse. Moreover, the views of Washington, Lincoln, Lieber, McKinley, Roosevelt, and Root were repudiated, and the views of Clausewitz, Bismarck stepped into their place; and I say with some concern that the views taken are remarkably like those of gentlemen who came to power in Germany some generations after Bismarck (Carl Schmitt would be the first name to mention). All of this occurred in secret with no public debate. For the most part it happened with the involvement of lawyers who demonstrated and still demonstrate an appalling ignorance of the operative principles of law, and a tendency to engage in political demagoguery rather than legal analysis. Let us turn now to consider what these lawyers wrought. As we will see, the ethically anchored, visionary approach of men like Francis Lieber and Elihu Root was betrayed. In its place has come a new breed of lawyers who might best be cast in minor roles in a staging of Bertolt Brecht's *Der aufhaltsame Aufstieg des Arturo Ui.*[16]

In July 2004, shortly after the first of the torture memoranda was published[17], a wide-ranging group of bar leaders, including eight presidents of the American Bar Association, scores of former judges, prosecutors, Department of Justice officials, law professors, and practitioners issued a statement saying that government attorneys had sought to justify actions that "violate the most basic rights of all human beings." The statement reviewed and repudiated the core conclusions of the administration's "torture" memoranda and the memoranda rationalizing the avoidance of Geneva Convention rights for detainees. It concluded "the lawyers who approved and signed these memoranda have not met their professional obligations."[18]

On August 5, 2004, in Atlanta, the House of Delegates of the ABA adopted a series of resolutions repudiating the torture memoranda and calling upon the United States to enforce the Anti-Torture Act, the Uniform Code of Military Justice, the Geneva Conventions and the Convention Against Torture in good faith and consistent with congressional intent.[19] The accompanying report concluded that the administration had embarked upon a course of wantonly lawless conduct, apparently violating the most fundamental norms of the Law of Armed Conflict. The ABA also called for the creation of a 9/11-style commission by act of Congress to investigate the key legal policy decisions that led to these memoranda, the

---

[16] B. Brecht, *Gesammelte Werke, Bd. 17* (1967), p. 1176 at p. 1179: "The great political criminals must be exposed, and principally by exposing their ridiculousness. They are above all not great political criminals, but rather the perpetrators of great political crimes, which is actually something quite different." (author's translation). Brecht composed this work in a freezing Finnish winter, awaiting papers to travel to New York, where he hoped to stage it as an explanation to the Americans of the essential criminality of the Nazi regime.

[17] "Memo Offered Justification for Use of Torture," *Washington Post*, June 8, 2004, at A1.

[18] Lawyers' Statement on Bush Administration Torture Memos, http://www.afj.org/spotlight/-0804statement.pdf.

[19] American Bar Association, House of Delegates, Resolutions, August 5, 2004.

process by which the memoranda were created, and to take appropriate remedial action. The ABA's resolution has been endorsed by dozens of newspapers around the United States, by local, municipal and state bar associations, and has gained the support of numerous civic groups. In the meantime we have seen a blizzard of DOD internal investigations stating conclusions crafted by politicians that cannot be reconciled with the substance of the investigative reports prepared by professional military investigators. These are the telltale signs of a cover-up.

The memoranda which have given rise to this outcry from the profession—and it is literally an outcry around the world—contain eight essential points, namely:

1. that Article II of the US Constitution gives the president unilateral power to suspend treaty obligations, including compliance with the Geneva Conventions;
2. that even if not suspended, deviations from treaty obligations can be justified on the basis of domestic law as a matter of national self-defense;
3. that customary international law is not federal law and therefore does not constrain the president or the actions of the military;
4. that the Third and Fourth Geneva Conventions do not apply to the conflict in Afghanistan—or that they apply in a manner that is totally incomprehensible; and that Taliban and al Qaeda are not entitled to prisoner of war protections under article 4 of the Third Geneva Convention;
5. that *torture* can be redefined to mean (i) intense physical pain or suffering (using medical triage precedents); or (ii) mental pain or suffering only if it results in psychological harm that lasts for months or even years;
6. that cruel, inhuman and degrading treatment is not proscribed because Congress failed to enact any special criminal legislation to implement that treaty requirement;
7. that under a pervasive notion of executive supremacy, any congressional act, or treaty that would constrain the president's commander-in-chief powers in dealing with detainees is presumptively unconstitutional; and
8. that the defenses of necessity and self-defense may be invoked by those using torture as a tool in dealing with terrorism suspects so as to preclude prosecution.

It is not my purpose here to dissect these contentions, but I allow myself the observation that some of these propositions rest on plausible but incorrect constructions of law, but most are radically false and unsupported in American legal doctrine and precedent. Still, note that the nation's well-entrenched military doctrine, which carefully addresses the issues of "torture" and "cruel, inhuman, and degrading treatment" is blithely ignored throughout these writings, as, for the most part are the congressional acts which transform this military doctrine into binding criminal law.

A discussion of the professional responsibility of the government lawyer needs to start with an understanding of the role that the government lawyer plays and the professional rules that govern his conduct. The bar has been grappling with this for a long time, and in many respects the results seem incomplete. For the most part, the rules governing government lawyers are the same as those governing lawyers in private life. But there are some major distinctions. For one, every government lawyer is required to swear an oath to "support and defend the Constitution of the United States."[20] This oath has a purpose, which is to stress that the

---

[20] 5 U.S.C. Sec. 3331.

government lawyer's client loyalty is subject to the Constitution. It is also to stress that the lawyer's fidelity to the law precedes his loyalty to his institutional client. These are principles which have characterized the profession since ancient times.

In my mind, the legal ethics considerations of paramount relevance to this case are Rule 1.2 and Rule 2.1.[21] The first addresses the question of client loyalty and the second, the lawyer's duty to render an independent professional judgment. There is a natural tension between these two rules, and there is also a clear indication of which obligation gives way first.

Over the last three decades there has been a lot of writing and discussion about the government lawyer's duty of client loyalty as distinguished from that of the private attorney. It has been suggested the government lawyer has a paramount loyalty to the public and that this trumps any duty to his immediate boss or to his agency head. Authority on this issue is still divided, but a discernible trend over the last twenty years suggests that the narrower view has broader support. A government lawyer owes a client duty to his immediate superiors and to his agency. As a special committee of the District of Columbia Bar has said, "A government lawyer will represent the legitimate interests the governmental client seeks to advance and not be influenced by some unique and personal vision of the 'public interest.'"[22] However, this rule is undercut by federal whistleblower protection legislation, which appears to authorize a betrayal of such a narrowly fashioned "client" definition in specific circumstances.[23]

For Department of Justice lawyers, a further issue exists concerning the particular role or function they play. Of special relevance here is the role of the Office of Legal Counsel (OLC) lawyer, who wields the Attorney General's special opinion-rendering function conferred by the Judiciary Act of 1789. This role has been characterized as "quasi judicial." Others, however, have said that the OLC lawyer is effectively "the president's lawyer," bound to defend and advance the interests of the executive. These conflicting characterizations raise particular problems that a number of scholars have addressed.

Rule 2.1 provides that "in representing a client, a lawyer shall exercise independent professional judgment and render candid advice." I believe that the core of the current dilemma lies in disrespect of this rule. Lawyers must reconcile their duty of loyalty to a client with their paramount duty to uphold, indeed, to champion the law. A lawyer is not a pipe fitter, who dispenses advice to suit a client's whim of the day. A lawyer must uphold the law. As Elihu Root said, "about half of the practice of a decent lawyer is telling would-be clients that they are damn

---

[21] American Bar Association, *Model Rules of Professional Conduct*, Rule 1.2; Rule 2.1.

[22] Report by the District of Columbia Bar Special Committee on Government Lawyers and the Model Rules of Professional Conduct, *Washington Lawyer* 1988, p. 53.

[23] A "whistleblower" under this act, 5 U.S.C. Sec. 2302 (b) (8), is shielded for lawfully disclosing information that he reasonably believes evidences illegality, gross waste, gross mismanagement, abuse of authority, or a substantial and specific danger to public health or safety. If disclosure is specifically prohibited by statute, or by Executive Order as classified on national security grounds, an employee is only protected if the disclosure is made to the agency chief or delegee, such as an agency Inspector General.

fools and should stop."[24] That remark may sound flip. It is not. It is very profound. If the torture memoranda writers had heeded Root's admonition, America and its armed forces would have been spared humiliation and grief.

Rule 2.1 mandates that a lawyer steer a client on a path consistent with the law. Indeed, this is mandated at all costs. Rule 1.2 (d) states that "a lawyer shall not counsel a client to engage, or assist a client, in conduct that the lawyer knows is criminal or fraudulent." Obviously the office of lawyer confers no immunity from criminal liability; to the contrary, due to their training and role in society, lawyers are justly prosecuted with vigor when they violate the law. Similarly, a lawyer who counsels a client to implement a criminal design may be subject to criminal enterprise or aiding-and-abetting liability.

Having now studied the torture memoranda for a year and having conducted extensive research into the circumstances that gave rise to them, I believe that legal ethics are the least of the concerns of the authors of these memoranda. Rather, these memoranda bear important hallmarks of a *criminal enterprise*. I hypothesize the following facts concerning the issuance of the torture memoranda. My hypothesis does not rest on conjecture. However, I stress that an appropriate investigation is necessary to fully develop these facts.

VII. Were Legal Opinions Crafted as a Tool to Coerce Recalcitrant Agencies into Acceptance of Torture?

Shortly following the commencement of War on Terror, a certain high official of the government, Dick Cheney, known for keeping to himself in a secure unidentified location, and known to hold the view that the time had come for the US intelligence services to "take the gloves off" and "use the dark arts" in order to improve human intelligence gathering, paid a number of calls on a government intelligence service. The principal goal of these visits was plainly to encourage the preparation of intelligence assessments which would support a military campaign targeting a certain oil-rich nation of the Middle East. However, the visits had an important secondary purpose. The senior official aggressively advocated a change in the service's authorized interrogation techniques to include "extreme" measures. He was told that in the opinion of the service, their current set of approved techniques went fully to the limit of what the law permitted.

Not satisfied with this response, Cheney involved his counsel and other White House lawyers, including one now at the helm of the Department of Justice, in a discussion over what steps could be taken to persuade the service to adopt these new techniques. For brevity's sake, I will define these new techniques as "torture." I do not know all of the techniques, but I know one of them is a procedure developed in the Dirty War in Argentina and then called *el submarino*, but today

---

[24] This legendary remark is quoted in *McCandless v. Great Atlantic & Pacific Tea Co.*, 697 F.2d 198, 202 (7th Cir. 1983).

more frequently called *waterboarding*. This technique plainly constitutes torture and is a violation of US criminal law.

At length, White House counsel involved justice, and in particular the OLC, in this issue. In the course of discussion with the service's counsel, it was offered that a series of memoranda would be prepared and issued under which OLC would opine that the particular torture and cruel, inhuman and degrading techniques used were consistent with law; moreover, as back-up, an opinion would state that even if not consistent, the president's commander-in-chief powers could authorize them and those using them would have the benefit of self-defense and necessity defenses.

These memoranda were offered and issued as inducement to secure a change in policy by the service—a change to policies that violated United States law as well as international treaty obligations. In fact, by several accounts, the service was told that it was bound by the opinions rendered and was thereby compelled to adopt the techniques that the certain senior official proposed. It was reasonably foreseeable from the outset that serious harm, including death, would result from the application of these new policies. In reliance on these OLC memoranda, the service changed its policies. Serious harm resulted to scores of detainees, including deaths in several cases. Justice, however, has declined prosecution with respect to one or more homicides produced by this policy change. This decision not to prosecute rests on the realization that any case would necessarily lead to the exposure of the facts I have just described.

A government opinion writer wields tremendous power, and with this power comes responsibility. There is no immunity for those who craft opinions, particularly for those who do so maliciously or with criminal intent.

VIII. Can Formulators of Legal Policy be Guilty of War Crimes?

An instructive case is *United States v. Altstötter*, before the Nuremberg Military Tribunal.[25] That case included the prosecution of two lawyers of the Ministry of Justice, one a deputy head of the criminal division, who participated in the preparation of legal rationalizations for and implementation of Field Marshal Keitel's "Nacht- und Nebelerlaß" of December 7, 1941. This decree provided a program with broad similarity to the current CIA- and Defense-run program of extraordinary renditions. To justify this program, the two justice lawyers identified technical rationalizations for the evasion of the Hague Convention of 1907 and the Geneva Prisoner of War Convention of 1929.

The United States charged that though the lawyers were merely involved in policy articulation, it was clearly foreseeable that injury and death would flow from their conduct, justifying a charge of homicidal intent. After trial, the two

---

[25] *United States v. Altstötter et al.*, in *Trials of War Criminals Before the Nuremberg Military Tribunals Under Control Council Law No. 10, Vol. III* (1949), p. 1086.

lawyers were sentenced to 10 years, less time served. The current case involving the OLC torture memoranda bears a number of remarkable similarities to the *Alt-stötter* case.

The memoranda that underlie this controversy bear a striking similarity to documents crafted in Berlin in 1939–44 between a very courageous group of German military lawyers and officials of the Nazi government. Anyone who has read these documents knows that the tactics used by the Bush administration to label opponents as "terrorists" and thus evade entirely application of the Geneva and Hague Conventions is nothing new. But looking at the debate that raged in Germany sixty years ago, I am moved more by the courage and conviction of a small group of German military lawyers than by revulsion at the Nazis and their thinking. One name in particular deserves to be remembered by us today: it is Helmuth von Moltke, a German military intelligence lawyer. Helmuth von Moltke is, by the way, the great grand nephew of the Field Marshal von Moltke who led the Prussian, then German armies to victory over Austria in 1866 and then France in 1870; and who read, and ordered the copying of Lieber's Code (edited, of course, to retain Clausewitz's view of military necessity). But of the two Helmuth von Moltkes, the judgment of future generations is likely to see in the younger idealistic lawyer more signs of lasting greatness than in the old Prussian soldier.

In America for the last three years uniformed lawyers have demonstrated courage and conviction. Their story has not yet been told. When it is, we will see that our armed forces also hold men and women who share the nobility of spirit of Moltke.

In the last months, Moltke's writings have been a companion for me as I have struggled to understand the horror, the depravity of the officially sanctioned torture unleashed by this administration. One statement in particular haunts me. It was written by Moltke shortly before his execution at the hands of Hitler's justice. Seeking the basis for a new, peaceful, and just society, Moltke envisioned a court to be convened at the war's end. He writes, "Any person who violates the essential principles of divine or natural law, of international law, or of customary international law in such a fashion as makes clear that he holds the binding nature of such law in contempt must be punished with special force."[26] Moltke's admonition, in a sense, is the legacy of Nuremberg and the new system that arose in its wake. It is the moral imperative of enforcement of the laws of war as the sole basis for a world worthy of humanity's aspirations rather than its fears. It is the vision of Kant, juxtaposed against the nightmare of Hobbes. That vision demands that those who violate the laws of armed conflict be punished, and that those who do so from positions of leadership, and whose conduct exhibits an attitude of contempt towards the law, be punished with special force.

Moltke wrote his wife Freya several letters in which he described meetings with cold and calculating officers of the Wehrmacht who spoke with derision and contempt of the Geneva and Hague Conventions. Field Marshal Keitel famously

---

[26] H. J. von Moltke, *Briefe an Freya 1939–1945* (1995), p. 46 (author's translation).

called the Geneva Conventions "obsolete"[27]—words which more recently tumbled from the mouth of Alberto Gonzales, now Bush's attorney general. Donald Rumsfeld has repeatedly denigrated and expressed contempt for the Geneva Conventions.[28] These acts, and the abuse and torture they have inspired, cannot go unpunished. If we permit this, we make willing accomplices of ourselves and our societies. Moltke's words, no less than Kant's, state a moral imperative.

---

[27] Keitel's comment was written in the margin of a memorandum from Admiral Canaris seeking a proper application of the Geneva Conventions. It was submitted into evidence at his trial in support of a request for the death penalty. His full remarks read: "Die Bedenken entsprechen den soldatischen Auffassungen vom ritterlichen Krieg! Hier handelt es sich um die Vernichtung einer Weltanschauung. Deshalb billige ich die Maßnahmen und decke sie. K., 23.9." (G. van Roon, *Helmuth James Graf von Moltke: Völkerrecht im Dienste der Menschen* (1986), pp. 258–259).

[28] See, e.g., "A Nation Challenged: The Prisoners," *New York Times*, January 12, 2002, p. A7 (quoting Rumsfeld: "These prisoners have no Geneva Convention rights"); "Geneva Conventions Apply to Taliban, Not Al Qaeda," *Defense-Link*, February 7, 2002 (quoting Rumsfeld on "irrelevance" of Geneva Conventions). Rumsfeld also directed the introduction of interrogation techniques that violated the Geneva Conventions into the theatre in Iraq.

The Prohibition of Torture: Absolute Means Absolute

*Nigel S. Rodley**

I. Introduction

Our values as a Nation, values that we share with many nations in the world, call for us to treat detainees humanely, including those who are not legally entitled to such treatment ... As a matter of policy, the United States Armed Forces shall continue to treat detainees humanely.[1]

These seemingly encouraging words, purporting to reaffirm the best humane traditions of the United States and other nations, are in fact a high-profile representation of a serious and sustained assault on basic legal values previously asserted by the United States and many other nations. For the words unmistakably assert a legal right *not* to treat at least *some* detainees humanely. If that is so for the United States, it is also the case for other nations, whether or not they share the United States' values as a nation.

The statement was made on the basis of legal opinions emanating from, and signed by, political appointees in the Department of Justice's Office of Legal Counsel (OLC), opinions at least partly contested by the Department of State's

---

* The article was previously published in the *Denver Journal of International Law and Policy* 2006, pp. 145 et seq. It is based on an address commissioned by the Urban Morgan Institute of Human Rights entitled *Torture in the 21st Century: The Practice and the Law*, with subsequent versions delivered at the University of Denver and the annual meeting of the American Society of International Law. See generally N. S. Rodley, *William J. Butler Lecture on International Law at the University of Cincinnati: Torture in the 21st Century – The Practice and the Law* (September 23, 2004); N. S. Rodley, *Myres S. McDougal Distinguished Lecture at the University of Denver: The Absolute Prohibition of Torture and Why It Should Stay That Way* (March 10, 2005); N. S. Rodley, *ASIL Proceedings* 2005, pp. 402 et seq.

[1] Memorandum from President Bush to Vice President Cheney et al. (February 7, 2002), reprinted in M. Danner, *Torture and Truth: America, Abu Ghraib, and the War on Terror* (2004), p. 106.

Legal Adviser's office.[2] Several subsequent opinions from the OLC continued the legal construct that was calculated to allow the military and/or the Central Intelligence Agency (CIA), or similar bodies, to take off the proverbial gloves.[3] The most notorious of these was an OLC memorandum of August 1, 2002, specifically dealing with interrogation practices (2002 Interrogation Memorandum).[4] They were supplemented by a 2003 Department of Defense (DoD) Working Group Report, also apparently finalized by politically appointed lawyers over the strenuous objections of the career lawyers, notably in the various Judge Advocate Generals' offices.[5] There was a partial attempt to undo the damage created by the 2002 Interrogation Memorandum; it was replaced by a December 30, 2004 memorandum (2004 Interrogation Memorandum).[6] It is not clear how valid the DoD Working Group Report remains now that its chief legal inspiration has been withdrawn.[7]

In this paper, I shall set out the legal arguments according to which humane treatment of all detainees is indisputably required by international law—both international humanitarian law applicable in armed conflicts and international human rights law.[8] In the process, I shall seek to refute what I take to be the key ar-

---

[2] See Memorandum from Alberto Gonzales to President Bush (January 25, 2002), reprinted in M. Danner, *supra* note 1, p. 83; Memorandum from William H. Taft IV to Alberto Gonzales (February 2, 2002), reprinted in M. Danner, *supra* note 1, p. 94; Memorandum from Jay S. Bybee to Alberto R. Gonzales (February 7, 2002), reprinted in M. Danner, *supra* note 1, p. 96. The Secretary of State and the Attorney General were themselves part of the correspondence: Memorandum from Colin Powell to Alberto Gonzales (January 26, 2002), reprinted in M. Danner, *supra* note 1, p. 88; Letter from John Ashcroft to President Bush (February 1, 2002), reprinted in M. Danner, *supra* note 1, p. 92. The memoranda in question are also reproduced in K. J. Greenberg and J. L. Dratel (eds.), *The Torture Papers: The Road to Abu Ghraib* (2005).

[3] M. Danner, *supra* note 1, p. 33, quotes an email from an unnamed captain in Military Intelligence: "The gloves are coming off gentlemen regarding these detainees, Col. Boltz has made it clear that we want these individuals broken."

[4] See generally Memorandum from Jay S. Bybee to Alberto Gonzales (August 1, 2002), reprinted in M. Danner, *supra* note 1, p. 115 (hereinafter 2002 Interrogation Memorandum).

[5] See Department of Defense, *Working Group Report on Detainee Interrogations in the Global War on Terrorism: Assessment of Legal, Historical, Policy, and Operational Considerations* (April 2, 2003), reprinted in K. J. Greenberg and J. L. Dratel, *supra* note 2, p. 286; 151 Cong. Rec. S8772, S8794-96 (daily ed. July 25, 2005) (statement of Sen. Lindsey Graham), available at http://www.humanrightsfirst.org/us_law/etn/pdf/jag-memos-072505.pdf (noting the OLC opinion does not incorporate concern for military service members).

[6] See Memorandum from Daniel Levin to James B. Comey (December 30, 2004), available at http://www.usdoj.gov/olc/18usc23402340a2.htm (hereinafter 2004 Interrogation Memorandum).

[7] It is reported that the Department of Defense is revising its Army Field Manual in respect of interrogation methods, see *New York Times*, April 28, 2005, at A4.

[8] See, e. g., M. E. O'Connell, *Ohio State Law Journal* 2005, pp. 1231, 1235; A. N. Guiora and E. M. Page, *The Unholy Trinity: Intelligence, Interrogation and Torture* (Case Western Reserve University Research Paper Series in Legal Studies Working Paper 05-13, July 2005), available at http://ssrn.com/abstract=758444.

guments raised by the US government's lawyers. These arguments will apparently follow a strategy, according to which, either the relevant treaty does not apply to these detainees, or the practices at issue do not constitute torture.

I must make two preambular points. Unlike some, I do not view the atrocities of September 11, 2001, as just another set of terrorist acts of the sort much of the world has had to endure in recent decades. The images and reality behind them will haunt us for decades, maybe centuries. They are the stuff of evil. The scale of the attacks, their enormity, places them on a substantially different plane from prior situations characterized by terrorism. Yes, other societies may have lost more people in facing ruthless terrorist enemies—internal or external—over a protracted period, but precisely the fact that the perpetrators of 9/11 could destroy in a single hour lives and property that other terrorist movements have taken years to destroy makes them an enemy requiring maximum resistance, provided that the resistance is within the law.

My second preambular point relates to the interrogation practices that have been the subject of national and international concern. It would not be appropriate for me, as a member of the Human Rights Committee established under the International Covenant on Civil and Political Rights, to address contested matters of fact. Nor is it necessary to my purpose, which is to elucidate the relevant legal norms. So I shall not comment on how aberrant or otherwise were the scandalous violations of Abu Ghraib, in respect of which some courts martial have taken place.[9] But a number of hitherto unauthorized techniques approved by the Secretary of Defense for possible use by interrogators would be capable of constituting torture and/or cruel or inhuman treatment, namely:

- Hooding
- Sleep adjustment (e.g., reversing sleep cycles from day to night. We are told this technique is *not* sleep deprivation)
- False flag (convincing the detainee that individuals from a country other than the United States are interrogating him)
- Threat of transfer (threatening to transfer the subject to a third country that subject is likely to fear would subject him to torture or death. The threat would not be acted upon, nor would the threat include any information beyond the naming of the receiving country)
- Isolation for up to 30 days

---

[9] Albeit only of those at the lowest level, caught on camera. The extent of the practices has been documented in three official reports: Major General A. M. Taguba, *Article 15-6 Investigation of the 800th Military Police Brigade* (2004), reprinted in M. Danner, *supra* note 1, pp. 290–296; Lieutenant General A. R. Jones, *AR 15-6 Investigation of the Abu Ghraib Detention Facility and 205th Military Intelligence Brigade 4-6* (2004), reprinted in M. Danner, *supra* note 1, pp. 412–414; Major General G. R. Fay, *AR 15-6 Investigation of the Abu Ghraib Detention Facility and 205th Military Intelligence Brigade 68-137* (2004), reprinted in M. Danner, *supra* note 1, pp. 504–573; *Final Report of the Independent Panel to Review Department of Defense Detention Operations* (2004), reprinted in M. Danner, *supra* note 1, pp. 363–373 (hereinafter Schlesinger Report).

- Forced grooming (consider the effect of forced shaving on a devout Muslim)
- Use of stress positions such as prolonged standing (up to 4/24 hours)
- Sleep deprivation
- Removal of clothing
- Increasing anxiety by the use of aversions, e.g., presence of dogs
- Deprivation of light/auditory stimuli, i.e., sensory deprivation techniques[10]

I refer to these as they must be presumed to be illustrative of the kinds of interrogation techniques that the authors of the legal memoranda were concerned should pass legal muster. Any combination of them, especially over a protracted period of time would certainly "amount to" torture. Many of these techniques have been used at Guantánamo. The sin apparently committed at Abu Ghraib is that they were used without the appropriate safeguards (and on camera). It was not done by the book, even if it was contemplated by the book. And it is a book approved by people with legal credentials. I am not aware of the case for the following not to constitute torture or cruel or inhuman treatment: seizing and transferring people to the other side of the world for months or years without end;[11] holding them isolated from the outside world, sometimes hidden from the ICRC ("ghost detainees"); "extraordinary renditions" to countries where the rendered person faces torture. That case would make for interesting reading.

II. International Humanitarian Law

To start with international humanitarian law, since that is where the Presidential Directive starts, it always seemed reasonably straightforward. As far as *international* armed conflict is concerned, several provisions of each of the Geneva Con-

---

[10] See *Schlesinger Report, supra* note 9, at app. E, pp. 393 et seq. (providing a list of approved interrogation techniques).

[11] One OLC memorandum argues that the United States "may, consistent with Article 49 [of the Fourth Geneva Convention], (1) remove 'protected persons' who are illegal aliens from Iraq pursuant to local immigration law; and (2) relocate 'protected persons' (whether illegal aliens or not) from Iraq to another country to facilitate interrogation, for a brief but not indefinite period, so long as adjudicative proceedings have not been initiated against them." (Memorandum from Jack I. Goldsmith III to Alberto Gonzales (March 19, 2004), reprinted in K. J. Greenberg and J. L. Dratel, *supra* note 2, pp. 367–368). Article 49, first paragraph, states that "individual or mass forcible transfers, as well as deportations of protected persons from occupied territory to the territory of the Occupying Power or to that of any other country, occupied or not, are prohibited, regardless of their motive." (Geneva Convention Relative to the Protection of Civilian Persons in Time of War Art. 49, August 12, 1949, 6 U.S.T. 3516, 75 U.N.T.S. 287, hereinafter Fourth Convention). The reader is invited to consult the memorandum to discover by what juridical alchemy its author can assert that even protected persons who are not illegal aliens may be removed, albeit "for a brief, but not indefinite period." (Memorandum from Jack I. Goldsmith III to Alberto Gonzales, see above).

ventions demand humane treatment. For example, the Third Geneva Convention on the Protection of Prisoners of War provides in Article 17:

> No physical or mental torture, nor any other form of coercion, may be inflicted on prisoners of war to secure from them information of any kind whatever. Prisoners of war who refuse to answer may not be threatened, insulted or exposed to any unpleasant or disadvantageous treatment of any kind.[12]

Similarly, the Fourth Geneva Convention on the Protection of Civilian Persons stipulates in Article 32:

> The High Contracting Parties specifically agree that each of them is prohibited from taking any measure of such a character as to cause the physical suffering or extermination of protected persons in their hands. This prohibition applies not only to murder, torture, corporal punishment, mutilation and medical or scientific experiments not necessitated by the medical treatment of a protected person, but also to any other measures of brutality whether applied by civilian or military agents.[13]

Indeed, all the Geneva Conventions consider as grave breaches "torture or inhuman treatment" and "willfully causing great suffering or serious injury to body or health."[14] Grave breaches are a species of war crime. They are subject to jurisdiction by any state party "regardless of their nationality."[15]

Meanwhile, Article 3 common to all the Geneva Conventions, which applies in *non-international* armed conflict, requires that "persons taking no active part in hostilities, including ... those placed *hors de combat* by ... detention ... shall in all circumstances be treated humanely."[16] Among certain acts "prohibited at any time and in any place whatsoever" are "violence to life and person, in particular murder of all kinds, mutilation, cruel treatment and torture" as well as "outrages on personal dignity, in particular humiliating and degrading treatment."[17] Violations of these provisions have been considered war crimes by the International Criminal Tribunal for the Former Yugoslavia.[18] They are so considered by Article

---

[12] Geneva Convention Relative to the Treatment of Prisoners of War Art. 17, August 12, 1949, 6 U.S.T. 3316, 75 U.N.T.S. 135 (hereinafter Third Convention).

[13] Fourth Convention, Art. 32. See also, Fourth Convention Arts. 27, 31, 37, 118, 119; Geneva Convention for the Amelioration of the Condition of the Wounded and Sick in Armed Forces in the Field Art. 12, August 12, 1949, 6 U.S.T. 3114, 75 U.N.T.S. 31 (hereinafter First Convention); Geneva Convention for the Amelioration of the Condition of Wounded, Sick and Shipwrecked Members of Armed Forces at Sea Art. 12, August 12, 1949, 6 U.S.T. 3217, 75 U.N.T.S. 85 (hereinafter Second Convention); Third Convention, Arts. 13, 14, 87, 89, 99.

[14] First Convention, Art. 50; Second Convention, Art. 51; Third Convention, Art. 130; Fourth Convention, Art. 147.

[15] First Convention, Art. 49; Second Convention, Art. 50; Third Convention, Art. 129; Fourth Convention, Art. 146.

[16] See, e.g., First Convention, Art. 3.

[17] Id.

[18] *Prosecutor v. Tadić*, ICTY Case No. IT-94-1-I, Decision on the Defence Motion for Interlocutory Appeal on Jurisdiction of October 2, 1995, para. 134.

8 of the Statute of the International Criminal Court (ICC).[19] It is worth noting that the only legislative definition in international humanitarian law of terms such as "torture" and "cruel or inhuman treatment" are to be found in the Elements of Crime agreed by signatories to the ICC, including the United States.[20] Thus both "inhuman" (international armed conflict) and "cruel" (non-international conflict) are defined as the infliction of "severe physical or mental pain or suffering."[21] There is no distinction between them. The only element that distinguishes each of these from torture is that torture has the additional element of purpose: the pain or suffering must be inflicted "for a purpose such as obtaining information or a confession, punishment, intimidation or coercion, or for any reason based on discrimination of any kind."[22]

What then could possibly be the basis for denying the legal obligation of humane treatment? The strategy is to argue that the treaties do not apply. The OLC has asserted that the war in Afghanistan (and presumably, by extension, the war against al Qaeda) was an international armed conflict.[23] So, according to the argument, first, the benefits of the guarantees were vouchsafed only to "protected persons."[24] The Taliban are not covered as protected persons because they are apparently "unlawful combatants" (a category unknown to the Conventions) and al Qaeda are not covered because they were unlawful combatants and they do not belong to a contracting party, i.e., a state, that is also a party to the conflict.[25] Second, the protection of common Article 3 which would cover *anyone* in the hands of any party to a non-international armed conflict, do not apply because it is an *international* armed conflict.[26]

This view that Professor Wedgwood and James Woolsey have described as "captious"[27] may come as a surprise to anyone brought up on the observation a-

---

[19] Rome Statute of the International Criminal Court Art. 8, July 17, 1998, 2187 U.N.T.S. 90.

[20] See Elements of Crimes, ICC Doc. ICC-ASP/1/3, p. 126 (September 9, 2002), available at http://www.un.org/law/icc/asp/1stsession/report/english/part_ii_b_e.pdf (hereinafter *Elements of Crimes*).

[21] Pursuant to Article 9 of the Rome Statute of the ICC, signatory states met to formulate the crimes contemplated by the Statute in precise terms in a document entitled "Elements of Crime" (see note 20). As a participant in the Rome Conference the United States participated in the Preparatory Commission that drafted the text that was adopted by the Assembly of States Parties. See id. at Arts. 8(2)(a)(ii)-2 (international armed conflict) and 8(2)(c)(i)-3 (non-international armed conflict).

[22] See id. at Art. 8(2)(c)(i)-4.

[23] See Memorandum from John Yoo to William J. Haynes II (January 9, 2002), pp. 1–2, 7, 10, available at http://www.gwu.edu/~nsarchiv/NSAEBB/NSAEBB127/02.01.09.pdf.

[24] See Fourth Convention, Art. 4.

[25] See Memorandum from Jay S. Bybee to Alberto Gonzales (January 22, 2002), pp. 9–11, available at http://www.washingtonpost.com/wp-srv/nation/documents/012202bybee.pdf. For the ICRC and many others, the Taliban, if not prisoners of war, must be protected civilians. There is no third category. Of course, persons in either category may be tried for criminal activity.

[26] Id., at p. 10.

[27] *Wall Street Journal*, June 28, 2004, at A10.

bout common Article 3 in the great commentary on the Geneva Conventions compiled by Jean Pictet: "Representing, as it does, the minimum which must be applied in the least determinate of conflicts, its terms must *a fortiori* be respected in the case of international conflicts proper, when all the provisions of the Convention are applicable."[28]

Nevertheless, let us allow, for the purposes of argument, that the guarantee articulated in common Article 3, although applicable to anyone in the hands of a party to a non-international conflict, does not apply to such a person in international armed conflict if they are not "protected persons." There is still the little matter of customary or general international law.

In a long-awaited, recently published study, the International Committee of the Red Cross includes the following rule of customary international humanitarian law: "Rule 90: Torture, cruel or inhuman treatment and outrages on personal dignity, in particular humiliation and degrading treatment, are prohibited."[29]

One of the sources cited for the proposition is Article 75 of Additional Protocol I (1977) to the Geneva Conventions.[30] That article closes the "gap," if there ever was one. It covers "persons who are in the power of a Party to the conflict and who do not benefit from more favourable treatment under the [Geneva] Conventions." Such persons are to be "treated humanely in all circumstances." The article goes on to prohibit "torture of all kinds, whether physical or mental, … outrages upon personal dignity, in particular humiliating and degrading treatment … and any form of indecent assault," as well as "threats to commit any of the foregoing acts." Since the United States is not a party to the Protocol, for reasons having nothing to do with Article 75, it is not bound by it as a matter of treaty obligation. However, like common Article 3, which the World Court has already considered as articulating "fundamental general principles of humanitarian law" and "a minimum yardstick" even for international conflicts,[31] Article 75 is generally considered as on par with common Article 3. Indeed, the United States Army Judge Advocate General's own Operational Law Handbook (2003) has taken the view that Article 75 is one of a large number of articles that are "either legally binding as customary international law or acceptable practice though not legally binding."[32] It

---

[28] J. Pictet, *Geneva Convention (III) relative to the Treatment of Prisoners of War, Commentary* (1960), p. 38, available at http://www.icrc.org/ihl.nsf/COM/375-590006?OpenDocument (emphasis added).

[29] J.-M. Henckaerts and L. Doswald-Beck, *Customary International Humanitarian Law, Vol. 1* (2005), p. 315.

[30] Protocol Additional to the Geneva Conventions of August 12, 1949, Art. 75, June 8, 1977, 1125 U.N.T.S. 3. The 1949 Geneva Conventions were supplemented by two Additional Protocols adopted in 1977 by Diplomatic Conference on the Reaffirmation and Development of International Humanitarian Law Applicable in Armed Conflict; Additional Protocol I applies to international armed conflict, while Additional Protocol II applies to non-international armed conflict.

[31] *Military and Paramilitary Activities in and Against Nicaragua (Nicaragua v. US), ICJ Reports* 1986, pp. 113-114.

[32] Col. T. Johnson, *Operational Law Handbook* (2003), p. 11, available at https://www.jagcnet.army.mil.

cites an article by the Department of State's Michael Matheson that includes Article 75 among a number of provisions that are already, or should be recognized as binding.[33]

The OLC memorandum has the following to say about the customary international law dimension:

> Some may take the view that even if the Geneva Conventions, by their terms, do not govern the treatment of al Qaeda and Taliban prisoners, the substance of these agreements has received such universal approval that it has risen to the status of customary international law. Customary international law, however, cannot bind the executive branch under the Constitution, because it is not federal law.[34]

There is nothing more. But there one can probably see, leaping out of the bag with a grin as wide as it is long, the cat. For the relevant federal law is the War Crimes Act, which incorporates, not customary international law, but the Geneva Conventions.[35] If the Geneva Conventions fail to protect the Taliban and al Qaeda detainees, then those who ill-treat them will not be committing offenses under the War Crimes Act. The fact that the victims are entitled to protection under customary international law is of no concern, any more than is the fact that the perpetrators may be committing war crimes under customary international law.[36] What a far cry this is from the humane vision of ICRC member Daniel Thürer, for whom international humanitarian law could be seen as the basis of a constitutional system of public international law.[37]

III. International Human Rights Law

Article 5 of the Universal Declaration of Human Rights states simply, "no one shall be subjected to torture or to cruel, inhuman or degrading treatment or punishment."[38] The prohibition is found in the International Covenant on Civil and

---

[33] M. J. Matheson, *American University International Law Review* 1987, pp. 419, 420; see also Department of Defense Memorandum from W. Hays Parks (Chief, Int'l Law Branch, DAJA-IA), Lt. Commander Michael F. Lohr (JAGC, USN), Lt. Col. Dennis Yodek (USAF-AF/JACI), and William Anderson (USMC/JAR) to John J. McNeill, Assistant General Counsel (International), OSD (May 8, 1986) (on file with author). This document states the joint view of the legal branches of the four armed services that certain provisions of Protocol I, including Article 75, "are already part of customary international law."

[34] Bybee Memorandum, *supra* note 25, p. 32.

[35] War Crimes Act, 18 U.S.C. Sec. 2441 (1996).

[36] *Prosecutor v. Tadić, supra* note 18, paras. 128–137.

[37] D. Thürer, in S. Baldini and G. Ravasi (eds.), *Humanitarian Action and State Sovereignty. International Congress on the Occasion of its XXXth Anniversary, San Remo 31 August–2 September 2000* (2003), pp. 46–58.

[38] Universal Declaration of Human Rights, Art. 5., G.A. Res. 217A (III), UN Doc A/810 at 71 (1948).

Political Rights,[39] the American Convention on Human Rights,[40] and the European Convention on Human Rights.[41] None of the pertinent provisions can be derogated from, even in time of war or other public emergency threatening the life of the nation.[42] It is also prohibited by Article 5 of the African Charter on Human and People's Rights, which has no derogation provision.[43] It is the practice of the bodies set up under the treaties (the Human Rights Committee under the ICCPR and the European and Inter-American Courts of Human Rights) to consider that states parties are obliged to investigate allegations of torture *and* the graver forms of other prohibited ill-treatment with a view to prosecuting the perpetrators.[44] All victims of a violation of the pertinent provision are expected to be compensated.[45] Moreover, where there are substantial grounds for believing that there is a real risk of any violation of the prohibition, no one should be sent to a country where they would be exposed to that risk.[46] The difficult problem with the treaties is that, like the Geneva Conventions, they do not offer a definition of torture or other forms of prohibited ill-treatment. I shall return to this point.

In addition, there are the United Nations (UN) Convention against Torture and Other Cruel, Inhuman or Degrading Treatment or Punishment (CAT) and the Inter-American Convention to Prevent and Punish Torture. Although the Inter-American Convention is generally more embracing in its protection, especially in its definition of torture, I shall focus on the UN Convention, which may, at present, be a better guide to the relevant general international law; and it has also been ratified by the United States.

The CAT, having defined torture (see below), makes it clear that "no exceptional circumstances whatsoever, whether a state of war or a threat of war, internal political instability or any other public emergency, may be invoked as a justification of torture."[47] It rules out the defense of obedience to superior orders.[48] It establishes criminal responsibility by requiring criminalization, not only of the in-

---

[39] International Covenant on Civil and Political Rights, Art. 7, G.A. Res. 2200A (XXI), UN Doc. A/6316 (1966), hereinafter ICCPR.

[40] American Convention on Human Rights Art. 5, November 22, 1969, 1144 U.N.T.S. 123.

[41] Convention for the Protection of Human Rights and Fundamental Freedoms, Art. 3, November 4, 1950, 213 U.N.T.S. 222 (note the word "cruel" is absent), hereinafter European Convention on Human Rights.

[42] General human rights treaties allow States Parties to suspend or derogate from some of their provisions, when confronted by a state of emergency such as internal or external conflict, but some of their provisions are insulated from being so suspended. See ICCPR, Art. 4; European Convention on Human Rights, Art. 15; American Convention on Human Rights, Art. 27.

[43] African Charter on Human and Peoples' Rights, Art. 5, June 27, 1981, 21 I.L.M. 58.

[44] See N. S. Rodley, *The Treatment of Prisoners under International Law*, 2nd ed. (1999), pp. 110–112.

[45] Id., pp. 114–115.

[46] Id., pp. 116–120.

[47] Convention against Torture and Other Cruel, Inhuman or Degrading Treatment or Punishment, G.A. Res. 39/46, Art. 2, para. 2, UN Doc A/39/51, 1465 U.N.T.S. 85 (June 26, 1987), hereinafter CAT.

[48] Id., at Art. 2, para. 3.

fliction of the torture, but also the instigation of, consenting to, or acquiescence in torture,[49] as well as complicity or participation in torture.[50] It requires submission of the case for prosecution, or extradition to another country having jurisdiction, of any person present in the territory against whom there is information that the person has committed torture, i.e., (quasi-)universal jurisdiction.[51] It requires redress and compensation for victims[52] and incorporates the common law idea of inadmissibility in legal proceedings of statements made under torture.[53] It prohibits the sending of a person to a country in which there are substantial grounds for believing that the person would be in danger of being subjected to torture.[54] It also requires states to prevent "other acts of cruel, inhuman or degrading treatment or punishment which do not amount to torture."[55] This, "in particular," means that certain provisions of the Convention apply both to torture and to cruel, inhuman, or degrading treatment or punishment. These do *not* include the provisions I have referred to. Those embraced are the obligation to train relevant personnel,[56] the obligation to keep interrogation practices under review "with a view to *preventing* any cases of torture*,"[57] and the obligation to investigate not only specific allegations of torture[58] but also ex officio whenever there is reasonable ground to believe that an act of torture has occurred.[59] However, the failure to include other provisions does not necessarily mean that the principles contained in the other provisions cannot apply to ill-treatment not amounting to torture, for the provisions of the Convention are expressly "without prejudice to the provisions of any other international instrument or national law which prohibits cruel, inhuman, or degrading treatment or punishment."[60]

How, then, does the OLC instruct us on these matters? It focuses on the CAT rather than the ICCPR, which was totally ignored in the withdrawn 2002 Interrogation Memorandum and has graduated to a "see also" reference in a footnote to the 2004 Interrogation Memorandum.[61] Having in the 2002 Interrogation Memorandum asserted a number of ways of avoiding responsibility for torture—the president's commander in chief powers and claim of necessity and self-defense—the 2004 Interrogation Memorandum refrains from addressing these on the grounds that they are "unnecessary" in the light of "the President's unequivocal directive that US personnel not engage in torture."[62]

---

[49] Id., Art. 1.

[50] Id., Art. 4.

[51] Id., Arts. 4–7.

[52] Id., Art. 14.

[53] Id., Art. 15.

[54] Id., Art. 3.

[55] Id., Art. 16, para. 1.

[56] Id., Art. 10.

[57] Id., Art. 11.

[58] Id., Art. 13.

[59] Id., Art. 12.

[60] Id., Art. 16, para. 2.

[61] 2004 Interrogation Memorandum, *supra* note 6, p. 1.

[62] Id., p. 2.

I have difficulty following how the president's policy makes understanding of the legal responsibility of US personnel involved in interrogations unnecessary. But, since this is the official position now, I shall refrain from dealing with these disturbing doctrines—doctrines that have not been retracted and were evidently approved, if not encouraged, by the present Attorney General of the US.[63] What is common to the OLC memoranda is the central reliance on a theory according to which torture is at the top end of a pyramid of pain or suffering. This theory is based on the practice of the organs of the European Convention on Human Rights.

The locus classicus is the case of *Ireland v. UK*, in which the European Court of Human Rights found five interrogation techniques used in 1972 by the British security forces against IRA suspects to be inhuman and degrading, but not torture.[64] The five techniques were: hooding, wall-standing, deprivation of food and drink, deprivation of sleep and subjection to loud noise, in combination, but for less than 24 hours.[65] According to the Court, these practices did not deserve the "special stigma" of torture.[66] It invoked the recently adopted 1975 UN Declaration against Torture, according to which torture constituted "an aggravated and deliberate form of cruel, inhuman, or degrading treatment or punishment."[67] Over the years the Court has maintained its insistence on the torture being at the top of a pyramid of suffering. However, it should be noted that it has manifestly adjusted downward the line between torture and inhuman treatment. It did this in *Selmouni v. France* (1999).[68] In that case, the applicant had been subjected to sustained beatings, leaving medically certified trauma on various parts of the body. In a series of similar cases, going back to the Northern Ireland case (which involved more than just the five interrogation techniques), the Court had considered such treatment as inhuman and degrading but as not deserving what it called the "special stigma" attaching to torture.[69] This time it announced that it was changing track. Invoking its doctrine of the Convention being a "living instrument," the Court said it

considers that certain acts which were classified in the past as "inhuman and degrading treatment" as opposed to "torture" could be classified differently in future. It takes the view that the increasingly high standard being required in the area of the protection of human rights and fundamental liberties correspondingly and inevitably requires greater firmness in assessing breaches of the fundamental values of democratic societies.[70]

It has generally been assumed that the Court's language of acknowledging change in what constitutes torture applies not just to physical brutality, but also to

---

[63] *New York Times*, January 5, 2005, at A1.

[64] *Ireland v. United Kingdom*, 25 Eur. Ct. H.R. (ser. A) at para. 246 (1978).

[65] Id., para. 96.

[66] Id., para. 167.

[67] Declaration on the Protection of All Persons from Being Subjected to Torture and Other Cruel, Inhuman or Degrading Treatment or Punishment, G.A. Res. 3452 (XXX), Art. 1, para. 2, UN Doc. A/10034 (December 9, 1975).

[68] See *Selmouni v. France*, 1999-V Eur. Ct. H.R. at 16.

[69] Id., at 29; *Ireland*, 25 Eur. Ct. H.R. at 59. See also *Tomasi v. France*, 241 Eur. Ct. H.R. (ser. A) at 22 (1992); *Ribitsch v. Austria*, 336 Eur. Ct. H.R. (ser. A) at 21 (1995).

[70] *Selmouni*, *supra* note 68, at 31.

the mixed physical and psychological pressures involved in the five interrogation techniques used in Northern Ireland. Why is this regional case law relevant to our concerns? Because the pyramid approach is being used to interpret the CAT. CAT Article 1 defines torture as follows:

> For the purposes of this Convention, the term "torture" means any act by which severe pain or suffering, whether physical or mental, is intentionally inflicted on a person for such purposes as obtaining from him or a third person information or a confession, punishing him for an act he or a third person has committed or is suspected of having committed, or intimidating or coercing him or a third person, or for any reason based on discrimination of any kind, when such pain or suffering is inflicted by or at the instigation of or with the consent or acquiescence of a public official or other person acting in an official capacity. It does not include pain or suffering arising only from, inherent in or incidental to lawful sanctions.[71]

Like the 2002 Interrogation Memorandum, the 2004 Interrogation Memorandum stresses the distinction the CAT makes between torture and other cruel, inhuman or degrading treatment or punishment.[72] It footnotes the definition contained in the CAT's predecessor, the UN Declaration against Torture, which defined torture as "an aggravated and deliberate form" of other ill-treatment.[73] Yet it does not ask *why* that language about aggravation is missing from the CAT. Apparently there was a desire to leave the matter less certain. This can be inferred from compromising language used in Article 16.[74] Article 16, it should be recalled, refers to acts of ill-treatment "not amounting to torture."[75] Those, led assiduously by the United Kingdom, who wanted to place torture at the top end of pain or suffering, pressed for the formula: "which are not sufficient to constitute torture." Others, wishing to avoid the pyramid approach, urged the formula: "which do not constitute torture." The result was a standoff, but a standoff in which the Declaration's reference to aggravation is missing. This is part of an argument I have developed elsewhere, proposing that, European Convention practice notwithstanding, the better approach is the one taken by the "Elements of Crime" for war crimes under the ICC Statute—that is, that the element of purpose be understood as the distinguishing factor.[76] None of this appears in the 2004 Interrogation Memorandum. Nor does it refer to the watershed *Selmouni* case.

What is clear is that the pyramid theory was present in documentation before the Senate when it was deliberating on its advice and consent to ratification of the CAT. So this point may be perceived as relevant to the interpretation of US legislation giving effect to the CAT. And, again, here we may have the nub of the matter. The issue is what action may the US courts be expected to take vis-à-vis US personnel involved in interrogation.

---

[71] CAT, Art. 1(1).

[72] 2004 Interrogation Memorandum, *supra* note 6, p. 6.

[73] Id., p. 6 n.14.

[74] CAT, Art. 16.

[75] Id.

[76] N. S. Rodley, in M. D. A. Freeman (ed.), *Current Legal Problems 2002* (2003), pp. 467, 470, 475; Elements of Crime, *supra* note 20, Art. 8(2)(c)(i)-4.

This leads to the question of what US courts would consider to be "cruel, inhuman, or degrading treatment or punishment." At the time of the deposit of the US instrument of ratification, the United States stipulated its understanding that the term would mean "the cruel, unusual, and inhumane treatment or punishment prohibited by the Fifth, Eighth, and/or Fourteenth Amendments to the Constitution of the United States."[77] This led the authors of the 2002 Interrogation Memorandum to assert that torture could not be found if the behavior did not rise to that level.[78] The DoD Working Group Report followed suit. The point is not made in the 2004 Interrogation Memorandum. I find it difficult to follow whether US judicial practice interpreting these constitutional provisions would be substantially at variance with the practice of international bodies.

It must be acknowledged that the tone of the December 2004 memorandum is altogether more consistent with mainstream legal discourse on the issue than its 2002 predecessor. Particularly welcome is its explicit rejection of the lurid threshold of severity for torture expressed by the earlier document, namely, that the pain would have to be "excruciating and agonizing" or "equivalent in intensity to the pain accompanying serious physical injury, such as organ failure, impairment of bodily function, or even death."[79] Also welcome is the reexamination of the notion of specific intent, especially the affirmation that "there is no exception under the statute permitting torture to be used for a 'good reason,'" such as with the motive of protecting national security.[80]

Nevertheless, we are left with the uncomfortable feeling that the Humpty Dumpty doctrine of verbal strategy remains operative: "'When *I* use a word,' Humpty Dumpty said in rather a scornful tone, 'it means just what I choose it to mean—neither more nor less.'"[81] It is, after all, worth noting the statement in the December 2004 OLC memorandum, according to which "we have reviewed this Office's prior opinions addressing issues involving treatment of detainees and do not believe that any of their conclusions would be different under the standards set forth in this memorandum."[82]

---

[77] U.S. Declarations and Reservations: Convention Against Torture and Other Cruel, Inhuman or Degrading Treatment or Punishment, Art. I, (1) 136 Cong. Rec. S17486-01 (daily ed. October 27, 1990).

[78] 2002 Interrogation Memorandum, *supra* note 4, pp. 12–13.

[79] 2004 Interrogation Memorandum, *supra* note 6, pp. 1–2 (quoting 2002 Interrogation Memorandum).

[80] Id., p. 17.

[81] L. Carroll, *Alice Through the Looking Glass* (1940), p. 125. As Professor Paust has it, "moderate coercion to extract information from unwilling human beings and to create a sense of hopelessness in the minds of detainees is as lawful as moderate rape." (J. J. Paust, *Wayne Law Review* 2004, pp. 81–82).

[82] 2004 Interrogation Memorandum, *supra* note 6, p. 2 n. 8. Even as he rescinded the list of approved techniques referred to in the text (accompanying note 10 *supra*), the secretary of defense reinstated some of them, including sleep adjustment, false flag, and isolation for up to 30 days or more and indicated that others could be authorized on an ad hoc basis: Memorandum from Department of Defense to Commander, US Southern Command, *Counter-Resistance Techniques in the War on Terrorism* (April 16, 2003), reprinted in M. Danner, *supra* note 1, pp. 199–204.

There can be no serious doubt that the prohibition of torture and cruel, inhuman, or degrading treatment or punishment is not only a rule based on treaties, but also a rule of general or customary international law. While this is not the place to give extensive justification for this assertion, a few specific elements may serve to elucidate the issue. First, the fact that all the human rights treaties make the prohibition non-derogable is telling, as is the fact that torture and cruel or inhuman treatment are war crimes under international humanitarian law. Second, the UN General Assembly resolution by which the CAT was adopted spoke of the desire for "a more effective implementation of *the existing prohibition under international and national law of the practice of torture and other cruel, inhuman or degrading treatment or punishment.*"[83] Third, states do not claim a right to engage in activity contemplated by the prohibition; rather, they deny the facts, or claim that the acts do not fall within the prohibition. Fourth, the relevant practices are usually unlawful under domestic law. Fifth, national and international courts have considered the prohibition one of general international law, if not *jus cogens*.[84] Sixth, the teaching of the most highly qualified publicists overwhelmingly concurs.[85]

As far as the prohibition of torture is concerned, it can now safely be said that the United States' position is unequivocally consistent with this understanding of the law. The 2004 Interrogation Memorandum, in its first paragraph, affirms that the prohibition is one of customary international law. Indeed, in a footnote, it cites cases from the United States and United Kingdom, as well as the Restatement (Third) of Foreign Relations Law of the United States, in support of the suggestion that the prohibition is one of jus cogens.[86]

The memorandum is silent as to whether the analysis applies also to other prohibited ill-treatment. Certainly, all the international authorities for the proposition that torture is prohibited by a rule of international law (possibly jus cogens) apply *pari passu* to other prohibited ill-treatment. It is hard to know how to interpret the silence, because the memorandum does not draw any conclusions from the acknowledgement of the customary law nature of the prohibition of torture.

The 2002 Interrogation Memorandum did not refer to customary international law. However, it will be recalled that the January 22, 2002, memorandum on the Geneva Conventions did acknowledge the possible customary international law status of the substance of the Geneva Conventions, but that "customary interna-

[83] G.A. Res. 39/46, UN Doc. A/RES/39/46 (December 10, 1984) (emphasis added).
[84] *Prosecutor v. Furundzija*, ICTY Case No. IT-95-17/1-T, judgment of December 10, 1998, paras. 144, 153–156; *Regina v. Bow Street Metropolitan Stipendiary Magistrate, ex parte Pinochet Ugarte* (No 3), [2000] 1 A.C. 137, 198; *Siderman de Blake v. Republic of Arg.*, 965 F.2d 699, 714 (9th Cir. 1992). A rule of jus cogens is a rule of general international law that is considered peremptory and incapable of being varied even by treaty.
[85] E.g., Restatement (Third) of Foreign Relations Law of the United States Sec. 702 (1987).
[86] 2004 Interrogation Memorandum, *supra* note 6, p. 1 n. 2. In December 2005, the Detainee Protection Act (the McCain Amendment), Section 1403, expressly prohibited all US personnel from engaging in cruel, inhuman or degrading treatment or punishment, as reflected in the US reservations, declarations and understandings to the CAT. However, it created no new crime or civil cause of action, but it did provide a new defense to any criminal charge or civil suit (Section 1404).

tional law ... cannot bind the executive branch under the Constitution because it is not federal law."[87] As far as I am aware, this memorandum has not been withdrawn, and it may reasonably be inferred that the philosophy behind the statement applies also to the prohibition of torture or other ill-treatment in international human rights law. Indeed, the April 2003 DoD Working Group Report, considering both international humanitarian law and international human rights law, quoted the January 2002 OLC memorandum for both this proposition and that "any presidential decision in the current conflict concerning the detention and trial of al-Qaida or Taliban militia prisoners ... would immediately and completely override any customary international law."[88]

IV. Conclusion

Concerning obligations under the Geneva Conventions requiring humane treatment of any detainee and, in particular, avoidance of torture and cruel, inhuman, or degrading treatment or punishment, the OLC memoranda have maintained that certain detainees are not protected by them. In so doing, they have induced the President of the United States to deny a legal obligation of humane treatment. Later memoranda, including the controversial August 2002 memorandum, subsequently withdrawn, and the replacement December 2004 memorandum, have not challenged the applicability of the CAT. Rather, the accent has been on torture as treatment at the apex of prohibited cruel, inhuman, or degrading treatment or punishment, in terms of the pain or suffering inflicted. The legislation giving effect to the CAT only criminalizes torture (committed abroad), not other prohibited ill-treatment. Customary international law seems to be dismissed as unenforceable (at least through the criminal law) in US courts.

The approach can be summarized by a modified version of the famous definition of law given by the great American jurist, Oliver Wendell Holmes, Jr.: a prediction of what the American courts will do in fact, and nothing more pretentious, is what we mean by international law.[89] Such an approach to international law does a disservice to the values of the United States and the world community, just as the practices at Abu Ghraib and elsewhere, as found in the Taguba, Fay, and Schlesinger reports, have done to their image.[90]

---

[87] Bybee Memorandum, *supra* note 25, p. 32.

[88] *Working Group Report, supra* note 5, p. 6.

[89] In *Harvard Law Review* 1897, p. 461 (reprinted in S. J. Burton (ed.), *The Path of the Law and Its Influence: The Legacy of Oliver Wendell Holmes, Jr.* (2000), p. 336), he states, "The prophecies of what the courts will do in fact, and nothing more pretentious, are what I mean by the law."

[90] See reports cited *supra* note 9. In the words of the *Schlesinger Report*, "The damage these incidents have done to U.S. policy, to the image of the U.S. among populations whose support we need in the Global War on Terror and to the morale of our armed forces, must not be repeated." (pp. 18–19).

As early as two months after the September 11, 2001, atrocity, in my capacity as UN Special Rapporteur on Torture, I made a valedictory statement to the UN General Assembly. I there said:

> However frustrating may be the search for those behind the abominable acts of terrorism and for evidence that would bring them to justice, I am convinced that any temptation to resort to torture or similar ill-treatment or to send suspects to countries where they would face such treatment must be firmly resisted. Not only would that be a violation of an absolute and peremptory rule of international law, it would be also responding to a crime against humanity with a further crime under international law. Moreover, it would be signaling to the terrorists that the values espoused by the international community are hollow and no more valid than the travesties of principle defended by the terrorists.[91]

That lawyers at the highest level of US officialdom were already about to provide opinions contemplating precisely what I was warning against is a challenge to the world community's most deeply held legal values. It can only be hoped that serious efforts will be made to try to put the genie back in the bottle. Measures the United States could take to help restore its traditional reputation for adherence to the legal principle that every person in the hands of a state or any party to an armed conflict is entitled to humane treatment and, in particular, not to be subjected to torture or cruel, inhuman, or degrading treatment or punishment, within the meaning of general international law would include: replacing the 2002 Presidential Directive with a new one that accepts the *legal* right of everyone not to be subjected to torture or cruel, inhuman, or degrading treatment or punishment; amending the law to ensure that all war crimes under international law involving torture or cruel, inhuman, or other inhuman treatment are war crimes under US law; ensuring that all agencies of the US government are subject to that law; ensuring that they obey it; and, producing any remaining "ghost detainees" to the ICRC, giving them substantial compensation and never again resorting to the practices that created them. In a landmark judgment the United States Supreme Court in *Hamdan v. Rumsfeld* has determined that common Article 3 of the Geneva Conventions applies after all to any armed conflict, including that said to exist with "Al Qaeda, its affiliates and supporters." As such and subject to possible legislative amendment, it is now part of United States law.

[91] The Special Rapporteur, *Statement by the Special Rapporteur, 14, delivered to the Third Committee of the General Assembly*, UN Doc. E/CN.4./2002/76 (November 8, 2000).

Litigating Guantánamo

Michael Ratner

It seems like a long time ago. On November 13, 2001, two months after the 9/11 attacks, President Bush issued Military Order Number One. The order stated that the president could direct the Secretary of Defense of the United States to detain any non-citizen from anywhere in the world. Once the president designated the person, the US could arrest, capture or kidnap the person without complying with extradition laws or worrying about a country's borders. The only criterion for the president's designation was that he, the president, deemed the person to be an alleged terrorist. There need be no charges, no trial and the detention could remain secret. Those detained could be held indefinitely. The order went on to say that if such detainees were tried, they would be tried in special courts called military commissions with special rules, rules that many critics, including military lawyers, believed did not guarantee fair trials that complied with the Geneva Conventions and due process. The order made clear that the detainees never had to be tried, but could be jailed forever without any trial. It was only a short time after the issuance of Military Order Number One that the president also asserted the authority to detain citizens as well.

The president claimed that he had the power to issue this order under his constitutional authority as commander-in-chief of the US armed forces and under the laws of war. Underlying this claim of authority was the claim by the administration that the fight against terrorism was a war, albeit a different kind of war than that of one country against another. The president claimed he had unlimited power to fight that "war" by any means he deemed appropriate and could ignore restraints placed on his conduct by international law and treaties.

US officials have stated that many of those held at Guantánamo will be held indefinitely.[1] According to Secretary of Defense Rumsfeld, this means until the war against terrorism is over, which could be many years; that is, until "we feel that there are not effective global terrorist networks functioning in the world."[2] Although military commissions may eventually try some of those at Guantánamo,

---

[1] See, e.g., "Airport Gun Battle Firefight Erupts as Prisoners Are Flown to Cuba," *New York Daily News*, January 11, 2002, p. 27.

[2] "Rumsfeld Backs Plan to Hold Captives Even if Acquitted," *New York Times*, March 29, 2002, p. A18.

Rumsfeld has said that even if such commissions acquit some detainees, they may still be detained on the base. In other words, the administration considers itself entitled to capture, arrest, and detain people from anywhere in the world, interrogate them, refuse them access to lawyers and family, not charge them or bring them before any courts, not release them even if tried and acquitted, and imprison them indefinitely, year after year.

At the Center for Constitutional Rights (CCR) in New York where I work, we were shocked and dismayed upon reading Military Order Number One. CCR is a civil rights and human rights litigation organization; a non-profit with progressive politics that has been deeply involved in civil rights struggles in the US as well as the creative use of litigation and international law to protect fundamental rights. Even prior to the issuance by the president of Military Order Number One we had been concerned by the dangers to liberties and rights that were unfolding in the wake of the attacks of 9/11. We were involved in representing scores of internal Muslim immigrants arrested in the wake of 9/11 and had vehemently opposed the Patriot Act, new legislation passed after 9/11 that was unleashing widespread government spying in the United States.

However, Military Order Number One, and the president's claim that he had unlimited and unchecked power to combat terrorism was by far the most serious threat to liberty and fundamental human rights in the post 9/11 world. It was of a different character than the granting of more powers to the CIA and FBI. The president, under the military order, was claiming that he had the authority to arrest and detain people forever. This claim to unlimited detention power undercut the key principle underlying democracy: the principle that authority (the president, prime minister or king) is under law. This principle goes back at least to the key founding document of the Anglo-American legal tradition, the Magna Carta of 1215. That document, which the King of England was forced to sign, guaranteed that no person was to be imprisoned without a trial and ultimately led to the most important legal protection of the individual freedom: the writ of habeas corpus. Almost every country now has a legal procedure similar to the writ of habeas corpus which gives every detained person the right to test their imprisonment in court. This right is contained in numerous treaties including the International Covenant on Civil and Political Rights (ICCPR).

I recall well November 14, 2001, the day after Military Order Number One was issued. We met at CCR and made the decision that we would represent the first person detained and or tried under this Military Order. We did not make the decision lightly. CCR, in more normal times, was more used to defending the rights of those we generally agreed with, those involved in making progressive social change such as civil rights workers in the South or opponents of the US contra war in Nicaragua in the 1980s. This was something new. We might well be involved in the representation of those involved in the planning of the 9/11 attacks. We had no idea who would be our first clients. While we understood that every defendant deserves and is entitled to vigorous defense, some of us were not sure those legal defenders should be us. In addition, this was shortly after 9/11 and the anger and hate in the country was running high. We would be setting ourselves up as targets. Despite these concerns we decided to go ahead. (At the time we made this decision and for almost two years after we began the Guantánamo litigation, we did not know that torture was routinely employed in interrogations at Guantánamo and elsewhere. We believed we were litigating a case challenging arbitrary detention.)

This short article is an overall description of our legal efforts, which employed international laws and treaties, now have engaged well over five hundred lawyers, and continue litigation in courts in the US and around the world. As this article is being written Guantánamo is still open and some five hundred detainees remain there although almost four hundred have been released, sometimes to freedom and sometimes to jails in their own countries. The US administration has stated that it is no longer sending detainees to Guantánamo. That is an important victory. However, shutting down Guantánamo, if and when that occurs, will not put an end to indefinite detentions and interrogations under torture. Stories about such detentions at Bagram prison in Afghanistan and secret CIA detentions facilities around the world confirm that we, other lawyers, and human rights activists will be working for many years to restore fundamental rights.

I. Early Efforts at CCR

When CCR first decided to challenge indefinite detentions, it faced three major obstacles. First, we needed allies both in terms of the amount of work involved as well as to give any lawsuit legal and political force. Unfortunately, no other US civil rights legal organization was willing to join us. They were frightened of the anger that legal challenges on behalf of alleged terrorists would arouse in the country and they also thought the litigation had no chance, legally and politically. A few death penalty lawyers were willing to join us; they were used to suffering the anger of the community for their representation of unpopular clients. So CCR and a few other lawyers had to go it alone. Second, legal precedents were arguably against us. Some earlier US cases could be read as saying that non-citizens detained during wartime, particularly if the detention was outside the United States, had no right to go into a US court and test the legality their detentions. In other words, it could be argued that US courts had no jurisdiction over detentions outside the US during war. The courts might not even consider a writ of habeas corpus. Moreover, even if courts did so, and found they had jurisdiction over writs of habeas corpus filed by detainees held outside the United States, the courts might find that such detainees had no legal rights. The Bush administration would argue that there were precedents indicating that the Geneva Conventions were not enforceable and that the Constitution did not apply to non-citizens held outside the US. Third, where would we find our clients? For all we knew they would be kidnapped or captured, detained, taken to some secret prison and never heard from again. So in the first weeks after Military Order Number One we tried to gather our legal team and research the law.

Our break in finding our first client came in January 2002. A newspaper article quoted an Australian lawyer stating that he represented the family of a man named David Hicks; Hicks had been flown to the US Naval Station at Guantánamo Bay,

Cuba. The US Naval Station at Guantánamo Bay is held by the United States under a perpetual lease extracted from Cuba in the early 1900s by the US as a condition of giving Cuba its independence in the wake of the Spanish-American War. I quickly called the lawyer in Australia. Over the next few weeks we at CCR agreed to represent the family and file a habeas corpus petition in the US federal court in Washington DC on behalf of David Hicks. We did so despite not being able to communicate with David Hicks. He was held incommunicado and we were denied any communication with him. Under US law we were permitted to represent David Hicks by representing his family in Australia although David had no knowledge that we were doing so and had no knowledge of the filing of the case.

The fact that David Hicks, along with others, had been taken to Guantánamo raised special legal problems for the litigation. The US government, despite its perpetual lease over the naval base, considered Guantánamo outside the US and it argued that no court had jurisdiction to hear a case of a non-citizen held outside the United States. CCR had had prior experience with Guantánamo under the first President Bush and under President Clinton.

II. Earlier Legal Challenges to Detentions at Guantánamo: Haitians & Others

Prior to the 9/11 detentions Guantánamo Bay was used as a detention camp for Haitians and Cubans seeking refuge in the United States, including the world's first camp for HIV-positive refugees. These detentions set the precedent for the Guantánamo detentions and demonstrate that using the base as a zone outside the law was not the brainchild of the Bush II administration.

In 1990, during the administration of Bush I, President Aristide was overthrown in Haiti and the ensuing bloodbath caused thousands to flee. The United States did not want these Haitian refugees coming to the United States and decided to hold them at Guantánamo.

Apart from its physical location near Haiti in the Caribbean, Guantánamo provided many advantages to the United States. It is remote, off-limits to reporters and relatives of servicemen, and can only be visited with the permission of the United States government. However, it is still close enough to the US for soldiers and officials to shuttle back and forth to the mainland with ease. Most importantly, it has been treated by the US as a law-free zone. That is to say, the Bush I administration, the Clinton administration, and the Bush II administration have all operated as if no court in the world could hear a case brought on behalf of a Guantánamo detainee. In effect, this meant that the US government could treat detainees however it wished; it could beat them, punish them, send them back to their oppressors in Haiti, and there was nothing any court or anyone could do about it.

This claim was soon tested by lawyers from CCR and elsewhere who brought suit in US courts on behalf of refugees in danger of being sent back to Haiti and on behalf of HIV refugees seeking release from the camp. The cases were bitterly contested by the government and they ultimately resulted in conflicting court decisions on whether or not judges could hear claims by people held at Guantánamo. To the extent those courts concluded that the naval base at Guantánamo was akin to United States sovereign territory, they permitted judicial review and determined that the refugees had some constitutional protection.[3] To these courts Guantánamo is effectively American territory, much like Puerto Rico or the Canal Zone.

Other courts, however found Guantánamo more akin to a foreign country, and used this theory to deny detainees any right to judicial review or constitutional protection.[4] The Supreme Court itself never addressed the status of Guantánamo prior to the current Guantánamo cases.

III. Legal Challenges: International Legal Challenges & Early Victories

CCR decided to act quickly to challenge the post 9/11 Guantánamo detentions. We did not file our first case in a US court, but at the Inter-American Human Rights Commission of the Organization of American States (IAHRC). Our plans were to take the case into every tribunal we could and put maximum pressure on the US to comply with fundamental human rights law and humanitarian law including the Geneva Conventions. We were aware that US courts were the least likely to give us a sympathetic hearing; favorable rulings from other courts might well influence US courts. Our claims at the IAHRC were asserted under international law and treaties. We filed a month after the detentions at Guantánamo began and were successful. While the IAHRC is not a court, its mission is to enforce the principal regional human rights treaty, the American Declaration of the Rights and Duties of Man, the provisions of which protect the right to life, fair trial, due process, and freedom from arbitrary detention. In its decision of March 13, 2002, the IAHRC urged the United States to "take the urgent measures necessary to have the legal status of the detainees at Guantánamo Bay determined by a competent tribunal."[5] The IAHRC explained that everyone who is captured by a state must have a legal status, and that it is for a tribunal, not the executive, to determine that status. In strong language the IAHRC found that

the detainees remain entirely at the unfettered discretion of the United States government. Absent clarification of the legal status of the detainees, the Commission considers that the rights and protections to which they might be entitled under international or domestic law cannot be said to be the subject of effective legal protection by the state.[6]

Although the IAHRC had previously ruled that member states of the Organization of American States are under an "international legal obligation" to comply

---

[3] *Haitian Ctr. Council v. McNary*, 969 F.2d 1326 (2nd Cir. 1992).

[4] *Haitian Refugee Ctr. v. Baker*, 953 F.2d 1498 (11th Cir. 1992).

[5] Ibid.

[6] Decision of the Inter-American Commission on Human Rights of the Organization of American States, *Detainees in Guantánamo Bay, Cuba*, March 13, 2002.

with its decisions, the United States has refused to do so. The Commission reiterated its order mandating hearings to determine status in July 2002 and held a session on the failure of the United States to implement this ruling. The United States has still not complied, and there is no power in the IAHRC to compel compliance.

Another challenge to the detentions was filed in the courts of the United Kingdom on behalf of one of the detainees, Ali Abbasi, a British citizen. Although the British Court could not order a remedy for the detentions because the Untied States government was not a party to the lawsuit, it described the detention situation in stark terms: "In apparent contravention of fundamental principles recognized in both jurisdictions [US and UK] and by international law, Mr. Abbasi is at present arbitrarily detained in a 'legal black hole.'"[7] The Court was especially critical of the US government's claim that there was no court in the United States that could review the indefinite detentions in a territory over which the United States has exclusive control. It hoped that the appellate courts in the United States would find otherwise.

IV. Legal Challenges: The Supreme Court Victory in June 2004

The primary challenge in the US to the Guantánamo detentions was brought by the Center for Constitutional Rights and cooperating attorneys. As explained earlier, CCR represented its first Guantánamo detainee, David Hicks, in January 2002. Within a few weeks we were representing additional detainees whose families had contacted us. The writ of habeas corpus was filed in Washington DC in February 2002. We argued that the courts could hear the case both because the US had complete jurisdiction and control over Guantánamo and also that any person detained by the US anywhere in the world had the right to test the legality of his or her detention in court. In other words, we argued the court had jurisdiction over the case. Our underlying claim in the case was made under both international law and the constitution. We argued that treaties, customary international law, and the Constitution prohibited arbitrary detention, required some form of trial and that any trial had to comply with due process. Even if somehow the constitution did not apply to the detainees at Guantánamo, international law including the Geneva Convention and the ICCPR did.

Initially, our filings and the few lawyers helping us received little public support. In fact, CCR received hundreds of pieces of hate mail, accusing us of supporting terrorism. As the case continued, support particularly in the legal community increased. Lawyers seemed to understand what was at stake: the writ of habeas corpus and its fundamental guarantee that the state or the executive could not arbitrarily take one's freedom. Many compared the case to the shameful and illegal detentions of the Japanese in the US during World War II. The most well-

---

[7]   The Queen on the application of *Abbasi & Anor. v. Secretary of State for Foreign and Commonwealth Affairs*, (2002) EWCA Civ. 1598.

known of those Japanese detained during that period, Fred Korematsu, supported the case with a legal brief written on his behalf. By the time we the case went to the Supreme Court, more then two years after it began, a lot more people saw the danger of granting the president unreviewable detention powers.

The case was decided by the Supreme Court on June 28, 2004. The Supreme Court combined the CCR case on behalf of English and Australian citizens detained in Guantánamo with a later case brought on behalf of Kuwaiti nationals.[8] The two lower courts had found in favor of the government, and held that US courts had no jurisdiction to hear the challenges and thus could not rule on the legality of the detentions. These courts found that US courts could not hear cases brought on behalf of aliens held by the Untied States outside the territory of the United States. They determined that despite the US government's "complete jurisdiction and control" of Guantánamo Bay, the naval base was outside the US courts' authority.

These lower court rulings are quite remarkable. Despite the fact that the US has imprisoned the detainees in a prison camp it totally controls, those prisoners cannot avail themselves of any court in the United States. This would leave their jailers free to hold them for any length of time and under any conditions it chooses, without recourse. There is no check on the government; it can act above the law.

The question the Supreme Court answered on June 28, 2004, is not whether the detentions are legal, but only the preliminary question of whether any court in the United States can hear these cases. In a 6-3 decision, the Supreme Court found that courts in the United States have jurisdiction to consider the legality of the detentions of non-citizens detained at Guantánamo. In non-legal language this decision means that the detainees can argue in US courts that they are being unlawfully detained.

The *New York Times*, quoting legal scholars, called the decision "the most important civil rights case in half a century." It was indeed a great victory. Until this decision, the Bush administration had argued that no court in the world could consider the legality of the Guantánamo detentions. In terms of US law, it was the first time that the Supreme Court had clearly stated that non-citizens detained by the United States, outside the United States, could use the courts even during a period the administration labels *wartime*.

The decision was also a major political blow to the Bush administration and its claim that it could carry on the so-called war on terror free from judicial oversight and beyond any constitutional or international constraints. It was seen in the US as an important setback to the manner in which the administration is carrying out its war on terror. The six-judge opinion was written by Justice Stevens and relied on early precedents from England. He invoked the Magna Carta, and quoted approvingly an earlier dissenting opinion, in an analogous executive detention case from 1953:

---

[8] Two cases were filed in federal court in Washington DC and consolidated for the arguments and the decisions: *Rasul v. Bush* and *Al Odah v. United States*, 215 F. Supp. 2d 55 (D.D.C. 2002), aff'd, 321 F.3d 1134 (D.C. Cir 2003), reversed and remanded, 542 U.S. 466 (2004).

Executive imprisonment has been considered oppressive and lawless since John at Runnymede pledged that no free man should be imprisoned, dispossessed, outlawed, or exiled save by the judgment of his peers or the law of the land.[9]

Despite the importance of the decision, it does not spell freedom for the Guantánamo detainees; it only means that the courthouse door is now open. It is now up to the lower courts to determine whether each individual detention is lawful. We cannot predict how this will develop. The detainees' lawyers, of whom this author is one, take the position that the next proceedings ought to take place in the federal courts; that the government must come forward and justify each detention; and that each detainee has the right to an attorney and the right to contest the government's claims. To that end, on July 13, 2004, CCR, assisted by other major law firms, filed scores of new cases on behalf of the detainees in the District Court, asking for immediate access to the detainees by attorneys.

The Bush administration did not expect such an adverse ruling and initially seemed in disarray. However, on July 8, 2004, it announced plans to set up "combatant status review tribunals" at Guantánamo. This is an obvious attempt to forestall federal court review of the cases. The tribunals are supposed to determine whether individual detainees are "enemy combatants." The hearings will take place at Guantánamo before three handpicked military officers whose decisions be forwarded to other Pentagon officials for a final ruling. Detainees will not have the right to an attorney, but will instead be "assisted" by a personal representative who is a military officer, and has no duty of confidentiality. The evidence used against the detainee can include hearsay, including any statements he may have made after two and one-half years of detention and coercive interrogation.

This is hardly a fair system for determining whether someone should be indefinitely detained incommunicado at Guantánamo. Without detailing all of the tribunals' deficiencies here, it seems obvious that detainees should have attorneys; that any statements made during their detention must be considered coerced, unreliable, and should be suppressed; and that panels of military officers are not neutral fact finders. In addition, the definition of enemy combatant for these new tribunals is meaninglessly vague, and does not comply with the recent decision of the Supreme Court in the case of Yaser Hamdi. In that case, the court adopted a narrow definition of the term limited to those fighting against the US in the war in Afghanistan. The Center's hope is that the detainees at Guantánamo will get a real review of their status and not the sham hearings that have been suggested. In many ways, the Guantánamo litigation is only at its beginning.

Another interesting aspect of the Supreme Court's ruling was its decision that the detainees can sue not only to test the legality of their detentions, but can also sue regarding the conditions under which they were detained. As we now know, coercive interrogation techniques, amounting to torture were employed by the United States. The ruling in the Guantánamo cases opens the door to lawsuits by

---

[9] Justice Stevens for the court in *Rasul v. Bush* No. 03-334 (June 28, 2004) quoting Justice Jackson's dissent in *Shaughnessy v. United States ex rel. Mezei,* (http://caselaw.lp.find-law.com/cgi-bin/getcase.pl?navby=case&court=US&vol=345&invol=206&pageno=218) 345 U. S. 206, 218-219 (1953).

detainees to stop the use of such techniques and to try to recover money damages for their ill treatment.

The 2004 victory in the Supreme Court dealt a major blow to the administration's grab for untrammeled power. The decision, while not detailing the rights a Guantánamo detainee will have, does permit writs of habeas corpus to be filed; this means the detainees will have lawyers and will have their day in court. As I write this, the lower courts are in the midst of enforcing this right and deciding its scope. Unfortunately, as is detailed below, the US Congress became involved and substantially restricted the rights guaranteed by the Supreme Court. As of this writing, litigation to enforce rights for Guantánamo detainees has continued in the federal courts in Washington DC. That litigation and efforts in Congress to stop it are described below.

V. Developments After June 2004 Supreme Court Victory

There have been a number of significant developments since the victory in the Supreme Court in June 2004. The remainder of this article will briefly survey these developments. As is well known, documents, memos, and photographs have emerged demonstrating that the Bush administration has routinely employed torture in interrogating detainees captured in the "war on terror." Such torture has occurred at Guantánamo, Bagram in Afghanistan, in detention facilities in Iraq and secret CIA detention facilities around the world. While torture in its grossest form may have stopped at Guantánamo—only because attorneys have, since the Supreme Court victory, visited the base—torture continues to be employed at other US detention centers. Many lawsuits have been filed in efforts to stop the use of torture, numerous governmental investigations have examined the issue, and some lower level military personnel have been tried and convicted. But impunity for those up the chain of command, in the Pentagon and in the Bush administration continues and so does the torture of detainees. This is a terrible and awful truth that explains the necessity for prosecutions in courts outside the United States under laws granting such courts universal jurisdiction.

A positive result of the litigation has been the response of the legal community in the US and other countries. As of this writing some five hundred attorneys have joined the efforts to represent Guantánamo detainees. They come from major law firms and small law firms; they are Republican and Democrat; and they are Christians, Jews and Muslims. Obtaining rights for the Guantánamo detainees is recognized as crucial not just for the detainees but for the rule of law in the US as well as the world. In some ways, this joining together of an amazing group of attorneys should give us all hope for a world ruled by law and not executive fiat.

These five hundred attorneys, coordinated by CCR, now represent almost every Guantánamo detainee. The most critical aspect of this representation has been these lawyers' visits to Guantánamo and the time spent with their clients. While the court cases continue, these visits have at least prevented much of the worst torture and allowed challenges to the manner in which some aspects of the camp are

conducted. It is sill not a rosy picture at Guantánamo. Hundreds are still indefinitely detained without trial, suicide attempts are frequent and a hunger strike was
essentially stopped by torturing the detainees by inserting thick feeding tubes into
their stomachs through their noses while they were strapped into specially made
detention chairs.

In June 2006 the US government announced that three of the Guantánamo prisoners had committed suicide by hanging themselves in their cells. The three men,
two from Saudi Arabia and one from Yemen are: Yasser Talal Al Zahrani, Mana
Shaman Allabardi Al Otaibi, and Ahmed Abdullah. The families as well as some
former Guantánamo prisoners have not accepted the government's claims of suicide. The reaction of officials within the government was shocking and demonstrates they have no conception of the desperation they have caused to the prisoners. Colleen Graffy, a senior State Department described the suicides as "a good
PR move to draw attention" and "a tactic to further the jihadi cause." Guantánamo's commander, Navy Rear Admiral Harry Harris, said they "have no regard
for human life, neither ours nor their own. They are smart, they are creative, they
are committed. I believe this was not an act of desperation, but an act of asym-
metric warfare against us." The CCR, in addition to its call to close Guantánamo
and end indefinite detentions, has demanded an independent investigation into the
deaths. Considering the government's reaction to such demands in the past, this is
unlikely to happen. The deaths make clear the absolute necessity of closing Guantánamo and other unlawful interrogation camps.

The question of legal rights for Guantánamo detainees is still in the courts. The
issues concern whether the Constitution applies at Guantánamo and whether the
Geneva Conventions, the ICCPR, and customary international law can be enforced
in US courts. So far, the lower courts have split on these questions, although some
answers may be forthcoming from the Supreme Court in the summer of 2006.
Amazingly, Congress—Democrats and Republicans—passed legislation that
could undermine the 2004 Supreme Court victory and prevent the Guantánamo
cases from continuing in the courts. The legislation, called the Detainee Treatment
Act, would allow the use of evidence obtained from torture to be used at the hearings which determine whether or not detainees can continue to be held at Guantánamo.

These issues are currently being litigated. At the same time, some detainees are
being sent out of Guantánamo, although this is a slow process. Some are sent to
their home countries and either released, imprisoned or tried. Others are sent to
third countries where they can obtain asylum. This is because their countries of citizenship could very well torture the returned detainees; CCR lawyers and others
have won orders preventing the return of detainees to countries where it is more
likely then not that they will be tortured.

The Bush administration has said that no new detainees have been sent to
Guantánamo since September 2004, a few months after the Supreme Court victory. This is a good thing. But there is also a dark side. Detainees are taken to Bagram or to CIA secret detention facilities. Lawyers do not have access to any of
these detention centers nor are the names of the detainees known. These detainees

languish in the black hole that Guantánamo was, without rights, access to courts, nor guarantee of safe treatment, which surely includes torture.

There are many lessons to be learned from the Guantánamo litigation. First, human rights lawyers must not shy away from difficult or very unpopular cases. Our societies depend on the rule of law and principles of justice and due process. These cases may not always win, but if we do not stand up for those most persecuted by the state, then who will? Second, difficult cases can be won even in frightening times. To do so requires work with lawyers and others around the world. CCR was ultimately joined in its efforts not only by US lawyers, but by lawyers from numerous countries all of whom understood the fundamental threat to liberty that Guantánamo represented. Third, it is critical to use every legal, political and organizing niche we can find. This includes UN bodies, the OAS, and national courts. It includes medical organizations such as Physicians for Human Rights and religious organizations of all denominations. Closing down an abomination like Guantánamo can only happen with organizing, demonstrations, protest and people speaking out. Finally, this struggle continues. Guantánamo has yet to close and other torture centers continue in operation. We must close everyone of those. We must hold accountable those officials in the US and elsewhere who authorized and engaged in the indefinite detention, torture, and disappearance of thousands of human beings. Accountability and prosecution of the perpetrators of these atrotious human rights violations is a necessity: a necessity if we are ever to have a world free from torture.

Universality, Complementarity, and the Duty to Prosecute Crimes Under International Law in Germany

*Florian Jessberger**

I. Abu Ghraib and the Complaint Against Rumsfeld and Others in Germany

On February 12, 2005, US Defense Secretary Donald Rumsfeld arrived in Munich to take part in the prestigious Munich Security Conference, along with Kofi Annan and numerous heads of government. In a Pentagon press release a week earlier, it was still unclear whether Rumsfeld would accept the organizer's invitation to the conference this year. The reason for this indecision was a criminal complaint filed by a US civil rights group, the Center for Constitutional Rights, and four Iraqi citizens before the Federal Prosecutor in Karlsruhe responsible for prosecuting crimes under international law.[1]

The complaint was brought against Defense Secretary Rumsfeld, as well as other high-ranking members of the US military and secret services. The incidents in the Iraqi prison Abu Ghraib in 2003 and 2004 were the subject of and reason for the suit. Bizarrely enough, these incidents were documented in a large number of photos taken by the US guards involved. Piles of human beings, naked prisoners in humiliating poses, prisoners facing baying dogs—the world was horrified as its eyes were opened to these unbelievable events.

The petitioners based their complaint on the findings of official US investigative commissions.[2] They particularly analyzed the reports of generals George Fay and Anthony Jones. They list and describe the abuse and humiliation of prisoners in detail, based upon numerous witness statements. The 180-page complaint ex-

---

* The text is based on a talk presented by the author at the conference *Global Constitution versus Realpolitik* held in Berlin on June 11, 2005. It has been left in the form of a talk.

[1] An English translation of the complaint is available at http://www.ccr-ny.org. For a discussion of the complaint, see also A. Fischer-Lescano, *German Law Journal* 2005, pp. 689 et seq., and the contribution of W. Kaleck in this volume.

[2] See the compilation of official documents by K. J. Greenberg and J. L. Dratel (eds.), *The Torture Papers* (2005).

plains exhaustively why the acts described in the reports constitute war crimes, especially the war crime of torture, under relevant provisions of international law and German criminal law. Internal guidelines and memos were used to prove that, while none of the high-ranking persons named were personally involved in the abuse, the acts of their subordinates could be imputed to them.

On February 10, 2005, two days before the start of the above-mentioned Munich conference, the Federal Prosecutor announced that he would not prosecute the charges made in the complaint.[3] Since then, the Stuttgart Court of Appeals (*Oberlandesgericht*) rejected the complainants' petition for a judicial decision, which would have forced the initiation of an investigation.[4] Thus, for now, there will be no criminal trials in Germany connected with the events at Abu Ghraib.

Before I come to the reasons given for the Federal Prosecutor's decision, I would like to discuss a preliminary question. How could a complaint be filed in Germany against a secretary and other high-ranking representatives of a powerful and allied foreign state, for a crime committed abroad in faraway Iraq?—a complaint, in addition, that even critical observers were unwilling to dismiss as the abstruse effort of misguided grousers. Let me mention three reasons. First, some of the suspects have spent time in Germany as members of the US military and were present on German territory. Second, no criminal investigations had been initiated either in Iraq or the United States—that is, neither on the site of the crime nor in the suspected perpetrator's home country—against the persons named in the complaint. Of the few trials that did occur, none involved the people named in the complaint. Only lower-ranking members of the guard units were prosecuted and in some cases convicted, the most prominent examples being Lyndie England and Charles Graner. And third, the jurisdiction of German courts is unusually broad when it comes to prosecuting crimes under international law. German criminal law allows the prosecution of war crimes, crimes against humanity, and genocide under the so-called principle of universal jurisdiction—that is, even if they are committed abroad, among foreigners, and the crime has no direct link to Germany. The legal basis for this is found in the German Code of Crimes Against International Law.

II. Universal Jurisdiction and the German Code of Crimes Against International Law (VStGB)

The Code of Crimes Against International Law (*Völkerstrafgesetzbuch*, or VStGB),[5] which went into effect in 2002, adapts German substantive criminal law

---

[3] An English translation of the prosecutor's decision is available at http://www.ccr-ny.org.

[4] Oberlandesgericht Stuttgart, decision of September 13, 2005, *Zeitschrift für internationale Strafrechtsdogmatik* 2006, pp. 143 et seq., available at http://www.zis-online.com.

[5] Art. 1 Gesetz zur Einführung des Völkerstrafgesetzbuches, *Bundesgesetzblatt* 2002 I, pp. 2254 et seq. For details see G. Werle and F. Jessberger, *Criminal Law Forum* 2002, pp. 191 et seq.

to the provisions of the Rome Statute of the International Criminal Court and regulates the conditions for prosecution of genocide, crimes against humanity, and war crimes by German courts. It should be noted that the Rome Statute not only created the International Criminal Court, but also, serving as a "code of universal criminal law," defines certain crimes and regulates in detail the requirements for individual criminal responsibility under international law. The German legislature undertook this adaptation primarily by creating new provisions for crimes against humanity and war crimes, and also by transferring the crime of genocide from the Criminal Code.

For our purposes, Sec. 1 of the VStGB is especially relevant: "This law applies … to the crimes it describes even if the crime was committed abroad and has no domestic linkage." This means that, regardless of where, by whom, or against whom a genocide, crime against humanity, or war crime is committed, the perpetrator may be punished under German criminal law. Under Sec. 1, the definitions of crimes in the VStGB claim universal applicability even in the absence of any specific link to Germany. With these plain words, the legislature unmistakably rejected the law as heretofore applied by the Federal Supreme Court (*Bundesgerichtshof*). That Court had found that a genocidal act committed abroad by foreigners could only be subject to German jurisdiction if an additional, "legitimizing link" connected the act with criminal prosecution in Germany, such as the suspect's residence in Germany.[6]

In contrast, Sec. 1 of the VStGB embodies the principle of universal jurisdiction in its purest, least restrictive form. This broad notion of universal jurisdiction finds support in customary international law that, while not uncontroversial, is sustainable.[7] Universal jurisdiction derives its legitimacy from the fact that crimes under international law are directly antithetical to the fundamental interests of the community of nations, in particular to world peace and international security. Crimes under international law are of interest to everyone, not just the state of commission or the perpetrator's home country. The nature and severity of the crimes themselves form a sufficient linkage to allow the application of national criminal law. The point of view of national sovereignty, which in its interpretation as a principle of non-intervention sets limits to the state's power to regulate extraterritorial matters, has no traction here.

By so broadly expanding the scope of criminal law, Germany has taken perhaps a courageous, but also a lonely path in comparison with other countries.[8] However, the German legislature also recognized that the unlimited universal applicability of German criminal law to all crimes under international law committed anywhere in the world could create great difficulties for the criminal justice system—difficulties of an evidentiary, economic, and, not least, of a foreign policy nature. For this reason, too, it provided this broad universal jurisdiction with ac-

---

[6]   See, most recently, Bundesgerichtshof, judgment of April 30, 1999, *BGHSt 45*, p. 65.

[7]   See, e.g., I. Brownlie, *Principles of Public International Law* (2003), pp. 303 et seq.; G. Werle, *Principles of International Criminal Law* (2005), pp. 58 et seq.; for a critical view see C. Tomuschat, in G. Werle (ed.), *Justice in Transition* (2006), pp. 231 et seq.

[8]   See the comparative analysis by L. Reydams, *Universal Jurisdiction* (2003).

companying procedural law that not only aims to prevent perpetrators of crimes under international law from going unpunished, but also ensures that prosecutors and courts are not burdened with cases in which prosecution in Germany would have little chance of success from the start.[9]

Section 153f of the Code of Criminal Procedure, added upon adoption of the VStGB, regulates the prosecutor's option to refuse to prosecute a crime under international law committed abroad.[10] It is also seen as a procedural safeguard to cushion the broad applicability of substantive law. Its main characteristics can be summarized as follows: If there is *a domestic connection* to the crime, there is a duty to investigate and prosecute on the part of the prosecutor, even if the crime was committed abroad. Under the law, such a domestic connection exists, e.g., if the suspect is a German national; if he or she is a foreigner, but present in Germany, even if only temporarily; or if he or she can be expected to enter the country.

However, if there is *no domestic connection* to the crime, investigation and prosecution are discretionary. As a rule, the prosecutor should give precedence to the responsible foreign or international courts rather than making use of his or her own right to prosecute. In such cases, the law grants priority to the state in which the crime was committed, the suspect's home country, and to the state the victim is a national of, because of their special interest in prosecution and their closer proximity, in most cases, to the evidence. According to the law, an international court prepared to take jurisdiction over the case should also be granted priority.

---

[9] On the legislature's motives, see *Bundestags-Drucksache* 14/8524, pp. 11 et seq.; see also T. Weigend, in O. Triffterer (ed.), *Gedächtnisschrift für Theo Vogler* (2004), p. 197 at pp. 206 et seq.

[10] Section 153f reads as follows:

(1) ... the public prosecution office may dispense with prosecuting an offence punishable pursuant to Sections 6 to 14 of the Code of Crimes against International Law, if the accused is not present in Germany and such presence is not to be anticipated. If ... the accused is a German, this shall however apply only where the offence is being prosecuted before an international court or by a State on whose territory the offence was committed or whose national was harmed by the offence.

(2) ... the public prosecution office may dispense with prosecuting an offence punishable pursuant to Sections 6 to 14 of the Code of Crimes against International Law, in particular if

1. there is no suspicion of a German having committed such offence,
2. such offence was not committed against a German,
3. no suspect in respect of such offence is residing in Germany and such residence is not to be anticipated and
4. the offence is being prosecuted before an international court or by a State on whose territory the offence was committed, whose national is suspected of its commission or whose national was harmed by the offence.

The same shall apply if a foreigner accused of an offence committed abroad is residing in Germany but the requirements pursuant to the first sentence, numbers 2 and 4, have been fulfilled and transfer to an international court or extradition to the prosecuting state is permissible and is intended.

(3) ...

However, even where a domestic connection to the crime is lacking, it remains possible to try the case in Germany, for example, if prosecution is hindered in the state where the crime was committed or important witnesses are located in Germany. In short: discretionary prosecution does not equal non-prosecution.

III. From Universal to Complementary Jurisdiction: The Prosecutor's Decision

Let us return to the complaint against Donald Rumsfeld et al. In this case, the prosecutor found the requirements of Sec. 153f to be present and exercised his discretion by refusing to prosecute the crimes in the complaint. In this way, he could leave open the question whether the facts in the complaint were sufficient to justify suspicion of a crime under the VStGB.

His arguments may be summarized as follows: The purpose of Sec. 153f is to ensure that crimes committed abroad with no connection to Germany can only be prosecuted by German authorities if a jurisdiction with precedence either cannot or will not ensure prosecution of the crime. The prosecutor derived from the Rome Statute the idea that exercise of criminal jurisdiction on the basis of universal jurisdiction is only permissible as a backup mechanism, where the primary jurisdiction is unable or unwilling.

Against that background, a key issue with the prosecutor's decision can be found in Sec. 153f (2) sentence 1 no. 4. The prosecutor referred to this provision for those suspects for whom non-prosecution on the basis of Sec. 153f (1) sentence 1 was out of question because they were unquestionably located on German territory or, such as Donald Rumsfeld, they could be expected to come to Germany. Under Sec. 153f (2) sentence 1 no. 4, one of the conditions under which prosecution can be refused in particular is if "the offense" is being "prosecuted" either before an international criminal court, by the state in which the crime was committed, or by the perpetrator's or victim's home state. Applied to the instant case, the prosecutor correctly found that those states primarily responsible are Iraq and the United States. Remarkably however, the prosecutor concluded, that "no indications are apparent that US courts have refused to take action based on the circumstances described in the complaint."

The problem that, indisputably, no investigations have been launched of the persons named concretely in the complaint, like Donald Rumsfeld himself, either in the United States or anywhere else is resolved by the prosecutor through further reference to the Rome Statute. In his view, the crucial factor under Sec. 153f (2) sentence 1 no. 4 is not whether a jurisdiction with priority has taken action against the individual suspect. Instead, the prosecutor claimed that the distribution of authority regulated by Sec. 153f is based on a concept of "offense," as yet unknown in German criminal procedure,[11] which refers not to a certain individual or a cer-

---

[11] On the general concept of the "offence" (*die Tat*), see L. Meyer-Goßner, *Strafprozessordnung*, 47th ed. (2004), § 264, paras. 1 et seq.

tain act, but to the entire complex of (allegedly) criminal acts (*Gesamtkomplex*)—in this case, the events in Abu Ghraib in general. To justify this new concept of "offense," the prosecutor invokes Article 14 of the Rome Statute,[12] under which a state party may refer "a situation" to the International Criminal Court in which one or more crimes within the jurisdiction of the ICC appear to have been committed.[13]

Strictly applied, the prosecutor's interpretation would have far-reaching consequences: As soon as a jurisdiction with priority, such as the territorial state, takes criminal measures regarding conduct of one or a few individuals that can be attributed to such a situation (e.g., "Abu Ghraib," "Srebrenica"), Germany's subsidiary jurisdiction as a third state would be blocked in regard to any act and any individual allegedly criminally involved in the situation.

IV. On the Statute-Oriented Interpretation of Domestic Implementing Legislation

It cannot be denied that the decision possesses the charm of criminal-policy realism, for who would seriously maintain that the incumbent US Secretary of Defense could in fact be tried and convicted by a German criminal court? At the same time, perhaps unfairly, it leaves the bland aftertaste of a decision supported more by foreign policy opportunism than by a striving for unbiased implementation of the law. Anyway, the grounds for the decision also provide points of criticism from a purely legal standpoint.

The prosecutor's arguments are legally interesting, first of all, because in interpreting a provision of German criminal procedure, Sec. 153f, he refers explicitly and frequently to the provisions of an international treaty, the Rome Statute. A key starting point of the decision is that—as the prosecutor explicitly states—the Rome Statute provides the guidelines for the interpretation and application of Sec. 153f. This approach may be tempting; I would submit, however, that it is not convincing. Let me sketch three objections, one more general, which refers to the method as such, and two others, which refer more directly to the way the prosecutor implemented his methodological approach of (Rome) Statute-oriented interpretation.

First, the "reading in" of supposedly parallel provisions from the Rome Statute to a provision of German criminal law may seem to make sense against the background of the genesis and purpose of the VStGB; e.g., without a doubt, the provi-

---

[12] Article 14 (1) reads as follows: "A State Party may refer to the Prosecutor a situation in which one or more crimes within the jurisdiction of the Court appear to have been committed requesting the Prosecutor to investigate the situation for the purpose of determining whether one or more specific persons should be charged with the commission of such crimes."

[13] On the background of the concept "situation," see P. Kirsch and D. Robinson, in A. Cassese, P. Gaeta, and J. R. Jones (eds.), *The Rome Statute of the International Criminal Court, Vol. I* (2002), pp. 620 et seq.

sion on crimes against humanity as regulated in Sec. 7 of the VStGB is to be interpreted and applied in light of the definition of crimes against humanity in Article 7 of the Rome Statute.[14] Whether, however, as the prosecutor claims, the principle of Statute-oriented interpretation is valid as such, even beyond the definitions of crimes transferred into national legal systems, seems to me to require particular justification—a justification which neither the prosecutor's decision nor the materials on Sec. 153f provide.

Secondly, when the Federal Prosecutor attempts to define the concept of "offense" in Sec. 153f of the Code of Criminal Procedure through recourse to the concept of "situation" in Article 14 of the Rome Statute, I would challenge this particular Statute-oriented interpretation for a very simple reason: I am of the view that the prosecutor picked the wrong provision. Article 14 regulates a so-called trigger mechanism, specifically, referral by State Parties. Reference to "situations" in Article 14—and not to cases or individuals, for example, as provided for in Article 25 of the International Law Commission's 1994 draft—may primarily be attributed to concern that making complaints too specific could lead to unnecessary and counterproductive "politicization" of the work of the International Criminal Court as early as the pretrial phase.[15]

But in my view, the question addressed by the prosecutor in the Rumsfeld case had nothing to do with the matter regulated in Article 14, namely, whether *the complaint* must refer to a "situation" only or, in contrast, to a specific person or crime. Instead the question, which was answered by the prosecutor through recourse to the Statute, was whether and when the prosecutor can decide not to prosecute because a jurisdiction with precedence has already taken action. Therefore, the issue of interest is not covered in Article 14, but in Article 53, especially Article 53 (2) (b) in conjunction with Article 17 of the Rome Statute. Here, however, the Statute does not use the concept "situation," but rather the term "case": A trial before the International Criminal Court is inadmissible not if "the situation" is being investigated or prosecuted by a state, but if "a case" is investigated or prosecuted by a state. Unlike a "situation," a "case" refers to a specific person and a specific act or crime. If the Federal Prosecutor would have applied this standard in his interpretation of what is an "offense" within the meaning of Sec. 153f, it would have been very difficult, if not impossible, to argue like he did, namely, that there are no indications "the offenses" allegedly committed by the persons named in the complaint are not being prosecuted.

A third and final objection to the prosecutor's Statute-oriented interpretation of Sec. 153f of the German Code of Criminal Procedure may be based on the very simple fact that the Rome Statute does not provide for universal jurisdiction.[16] Instead, the jurisdiction of the International Criminal Court is—with the notable ex-

---

[14] On the necessity for interpretation of domestic implementing legislation in conformity with the Rome Statute, see generally G. Werle and F. Jessberger, *supra* note 5.

[15] See P. Kirsch and D. Robinson, *supra* note 13, p. 621.

[16] For details see S. A. Williams, in O. Triffterer (ed.), *Commentary on the Rome Statute of the International Criminal Court* (1999), paras. 15 et seq.; also see at paras. 6 and 7 the German proposal to provide the International Criminal Court with universal jurisdiction.

ception of UN Security Council referrals[17]—much more limited, since as a rule under Art. 12 (2) of the Rome Statute, a link to the territory or a national of a state party must be present. Against this background it is not at all self-evident that a set of legal norms regulating the exercise of jurisdiction by an international court on the basis of territoriality and nationality, should be guiding the interpretation and application of legislation providing for "pure" universal jurisdiction of domestic courts and its procedural supplements. I would think that the method of Statute-oriented interpretation, as rightly applied, e.g., on the definitions of crimes, should not be adopted here.

V. Conflicts of Jurisdiction Between States: Lessons to Be Learned from the Rome Statute

It is, however, another question, whether, as a matter of criminal policy and not as a binding guideline for interpretation, the system of complementary administration of justice anchored in the Rome Statute can serve as a model to deal with competing national jurisdictions. The hypothesis could be that the Statute establishes a mode of distribution of authority between national jurisdictions, on the one hand, and the jurisdiction of the International Criminal Court, on the other, which may also be applied to the relationship among other actors within the broader framework of international criminal justice—especially the relationship among various *national* criminal justice systems.

The Rome Statute views the International Criminal Court as an emergency court, prepared to intervene only when, but whenever the state primarily responsible for prosecution is not able or willing to genuinely investigate and prosecute. This idea is expressed in the so-called complementarity principle, given form in Article 17. Transposed to the relationship between competing national jurisdictions, this would mean the following: Within a graduated system of prioritized jurisdiction, courts would only become active as backup courts, on the basis of universal jurisdiction, if those of other countries fail. Such a concept of universal justice would take account of the fact that jurisdiction exercised on the basis of the universality principle, far from the scene of the crime and the evidence, is per se a rather bad form of criminal jurisdiction. To this extent, I am prepared to follow the prosecutor's conclusion that the exercise of criminal jurisdiction over crimes with no domestic linkage should be permissible only as a fallback mechanism.

Yet, if one rests this basic idea on the Rome Statute, the following must be considered: the Statute does not stop with this basic rule of distribution of authority, but contains clear provisions on the way in which this typically delicate question—whether a state has taken serious action or not—is to be resolved. The Statute does this for good reason. Crimes under international law are typically state sponsored crimes, and thus the state of commission or the home country of the perpetrators and victims is, as a rule, itself involved in the crime, or at least not

---

[17] See Art. 12 (2), 13 (b) of the Rome Statute.

willing or able to punish those responsible. Against this backdrop, under the mechanism provided for in the Rome Statute, the question whether a state is genuinely taking serious action is not simply an offhand decision; it is examined in a formal procedure. The salient features of this procedure are contained in Article 18 and include limitations, reporting requirements for the state with primary jurisdiction, and monitoring.[18] Coming back to the decision of the Federal Prosecutor in the Rumsfeld case, it appears that the prosecutor broke off individual elements from the Rome Statute's model of complementary jurisdiction, while failing to keep in focus its carefully structured overall system of regulation.

VI. Future Perspectives: On the Fates of the Complaint Against Rumsfeld and of the German Code of Crimes Against International Law (VStGB)

I would like to stop with this sketch of possible deficiencies in the Federal Prosecutor's legal arguments and finish with a few words on two questions regarding future perspectives: The question of the fate of the criminal complaint against Rumsfeld and others and the question of the future of the German VStGB, one of the prestigious projects of the recently defeated Social Democrat-Green governing coalition.

Regarding the first question, we observe that the criminal trials in the United States on the events at Abu Ghraib are largely completed. The possibility arises of once again filing the complaint in the same or in expanded form. The reference to prosecution efforts by a jurisdiction with precedence—as we have seen in one of the key arguments—would then be more difficult to sustain. Thus, there is a chance that the Federal Prosecutor will have to face a second complaint on the same matter, following the completion of the trials in the United States.

As far as the fate of the VStGB is concerned: experience gained in the initial years since the law went into force, with much advance praise, may have sobered many of its protagonists. Of the approximately twenty-five criminal complaints lodged with the Federal Prosecutor's office, not a single one has led to the initiation of a formal investigation. The Rumsfeld case fits into this trend.

The flood of criminal complaints many had feared did not materialize. From the point of view of the "fight against impunity," many may regret this, but in most cases there were good—or at least some—reasons for this practice. Where the complaints were directed against heads of state or government, for example, in connection with the Iraq War or the Middle East conflict, sovereign immunity posed an insurmountable obstacle to trial. When the subjects of the complaints were crimes committed before the VStGB went into force, the prohibition on retroactivity prevented application of the Code. Finally, we can assume that when in some cases—as, in the Federal Prosecutor's opinion, the Abu Ghraib case—no

---

[18] For details, see J. T. Holmes, in A. Cassese, P. Gaeta, and J. R. Jones (eds.), *The Rome Statute of the International Criminal Court, Vol. II* (2002), pp. 667, 681 et seq.

domestic link existed under the relevant provision of the Code of Criminal Procedure, the prosecutor could refuse to carry out a criminal investigation.

Given the daily reports of mass murder, torture, and abuse in many parts of the world, there is still no evidence that the German legal system can live up to the lofty aims of the VStGB. "German international criminal law," like international criminal law in general, still faces the task of overcoming the split between established legal positions, on the one hand, and the still-flawed, practical implementation and enforcement, on the other. This is perhaps the greatest challenge for the coming years; how it is met will determine whether international criminal law will survive, or whether it will once again disappear into bureaucrats' filing cabinets.

Contributors

Kai Ambos, Dr. jur.; Professor of Criminal Law, Criminal Procedure, Comparative Law and International Criminal Law, Georg-August-Universität Göttingen; chair, Department for Foreign and International Criminal Law, Institute for Criminal Law and Criminal Justice, Georg-August-Universität Göttingen; http://lehrstuhl.jura.uni-goettingen.de/kambos.

Jörg Arnold, Dr. jur.; Research Group Leader, Max Planck Institute for Foreign and International Criminal Law; honorary professor, Westphalen Wilhelms Universität, Münster; lawyer in Freiburg; member, expanded board of directors, Republican Lawyers Association (Republikanischer Anwältinnen- und Anwälteverein, or RAV).

Carla Ferstman, LLM; director, REDRESS; informal coordinator, NGO Coalition for an International Criminal Court's Victims Rights Working Group; member, British Foreign and Commonwealth Office's Expert Panel on Torture; called to the Bar in British Columbia, Canada in 1994; appointed executive legal advisor, Bosnia and Herzegovina's Commission for Real Property Claims of Displaced Persons and Refugees (CRPC) in 1999.

Andreas Fischer-Lescano, Dr. jur., LLM; Department of Law, J. W. Goethe Universität, Frankfurt a. M.; researcher, Peace Research Institute, Frankfurt a. M.

Christopher Keith Hall; Senior Legal Adviser, International Justice Project, Amnesty International.

Scott Horton, JD; partner, Patterson, Belknap, Webb & Tyler, LLP; chair, Committee on International Law, Association of the Bar of the City of New York; adjunct professor, Columbia University Law School.

Florian Jessberger, Dr. jur.; senior research fellow, Department of Law, Humboldt Universität zu Berlin.

Wolfgang Kaleck; chairman, Republican Lawyers Association (Republikanischer Anwältinnen- und Anwälteverein, or RAV); speaker, Koalition gegen die Straflosigkeit; filed in the name of victims the lawsuit against the military junta in Argentina and the lawsuit against Donald Rumsfeld and others.

Dieter Magsam; criminal defense lawyer; laureate, Price for Democracy and Human Rights of the Werner Holtfort Foundation, 2003; project director and judiciary, "Democracy and Reconciliation" in Rwanda, June 2003 to March 2005; adviser, Transitional Justice and Democratization in Sub-Saharan Africa.

Lorna McGregor, LLM; ICC Programme Lawyer, International Bar Association; former coordinator, State Immunity Project, REDRESS.

Michael Ratner, JD; president, Center for Constitutional Rights; his many honors include: 100 Most Influential Lawyers in the United States; Trial Lawyer of the Year from the Trial lawyers for Public Justice; Honorary Fellow, University of Pennsylvania Law School; Outstanding Alumnus, Columbia Law School; The Columbia Law School Public Interest Law Foundation Award; the North Star Community Frederick Douglass Award.

Nigel S. Rodley; professor of law, University of Essex; former UN Special Rapporteur on Torture.

Naomi Roht-Arriaza, JD, MPP; professor of law, University of California, Hastings College of the Law, San Francisco; member, Legal Advisory Council, Center for Justice and Accountability; member, Advisory Council, Human Rights Advocates.

Tobias Singelnstein; research associate, Department of Law, Freie Universität Berlin.

Peer Stolle; until 2005 research associate, Department of Law, Technische Universität Dresden; junior barrister in Berlin.

Jeanne Sulzer; lawyer, Paris Bar; coordinator, Legal Action Group of the International Federation for Human Rights (FIDH), a network of lawyers from around the world whose mandate is to assist victims of international crimes in bringing criminal cases before courts; until 2005 International Justice Director FIDH.

Michael Verhaeghe; lawyer, Bar of Brussels; represented victims in various cases under the Belgian UJ Statute; lecturer, K.U. Leuven University.

Peter Weiss, JD; president, Lawyers Committee on Nuclear Policy; vice president, Center for Constitutional Rights; vice president, International Federation for Human Rights (FIDH); vice president, International Association of Lawyers Against Nuclear Arms.